The Open Ear: Writer & Editor

KIM ECHLIN

A RAVEN CAWS. WRITER AND editor bend together over words. Between them, small bursts of laughter, questions, explanations, as each searches for the clear idea, the common word, or the formal word. I prefer to think of an editor as Joyce's ideal, insomniac reader given a chance to talk to the writer. What do you mean here? Is this the best word here? These are the only two questions the editor ever really asks.

In Sumerian, the word for "ear" and for "wisdom" is the same. When the goddess Inanna embarks on her quest, the poet sings, "From the Great Above she opened her ear to the Great Below." Sound coils down through the ear. Imperceptible waves transform into perceptible meaning. Words felt as a physical presence mean the writer is getting somewhere. Sometimes this happens when the writer suddenly hears a cadence or understands an idea in a fresh way. Sometimes this happens when an editor urges the writer to retrieve what is not yet written but already there. The writer shifts perspectives, finds the beginning in the end, possesses what was once not possessed. The writer discovers a new voice, discards the way once thought essential for the way as yet untaken. The writer must dive under the waters and fetch back a bit of dirt from which to create a new world. The writer risks the way of paradox. The editor waits on the surface. The best moment between a writer and an editor is when words and ideas resonate as a single whole, time stops, even the cawing of the raven is stilled. The periphrastic study gives way to the original. In this moment, language takes us into our own eternity and we arrive where we are.

To my mind, the strongest element of the Cultural Journalism program at The Banff Centre for the Arts is that writers are encouraged to experiment with language and form as a means to deepening their ideas. Under the energetic direction of Michael Ignatieff, Alberto Ruy-Sánchez, and Alberto Manguel, the writers in this book were urged toward intellectual honesty and strong attention to language. I had the great good fortune to work with Barbara Moon as my editor when I was a participant and with Don Obe as a fellow faculty member. They each have a huge talent for spotting the unteased thread of a story and a passion for the English language. They give generously of their critical skills and professional experience. Their teaching has been invaluable to me, and their editing has enriched writers during nearly a decade at Banff. I honour them here.

Many of the essays in this book take chances both stylistically and intellectually. For some writers, what seemed risky in an early draft becomes the only way possible by the end. The writer begins working out of the tradition of the essay and discovers through individual talent something fresh and new. With time at Banff to explore ideas and craft, with editors and fellow writers who open their ears, each writer has a chance for the extraordinary experience of feeling words as a physical presence. We are pleased to present in this book the work of twelve Banff essayists who have dedicated themselves to creating the best prose they can and to expanding the form of the essay. They have followed hunches and instincts, discarded pages of work, spent hours and days seeking a single word. Between will and humility, they have embraced the aporia that leads to a freshness of thought and style.

To Arrive

Literary

WHERE YOU ARE

Journalism

from

The Banff Centre

WITHDRAWN the Arts

EDITED BY KIM ECHLIN, BARBARA MOON, AND DON OBE

THE BANFF CENTRE

CANADIAN CATALOGUING IN PUBLICATION DATA

Main entry under title:
To arrive where you are

ISBN 0-920159-71-0
    1. Canadian essays (English)—20th century.* I. Echlin, Kim A., 1955– II. Moon, Barbara. III. Obe, Don. IV. Banff Centre for the Arts.
PS8373.T6 2000 C814'.608   C00-910404-6
PR9197.7.T6 2000

Edited by Kim Echlin, Barbara Moon, and Don Obe, with editorial
    assistance provided by Alice Van Wart
Cover and book design by Warren Clark
Cover photograph from EyeWire, Inc.
Printed and bound in Canada by Houghton Boston

The phrase "To arrive where you are" is taken from "East Coker, Four Quartets" from *Collected Poems 1909–1962* by T. S. Eliot. Reproduced by permission of Faber and Faber Limited.

The Banff Centre Press gratefully
acknowledges the support of the
Canada Council for the Arts for its
support of our publishing program.

The Canada Council | Le Conseil des Arts
for the Arts | du Canada

Banff Centre Press
The Banff Centre for the Arts
Box 1020-17
Banff, Alberta Canada T0L 0C0
www.banffcentre.ab.ca/Writing/Press

THE BANFF CENTRE
FOR THE ARTS

Contents

Non-fiction
Is a Form of Fiction

ALBERTO RUY-SÁNCHEZ

WRITING CAN BE A UNIQUE adventure. But not for everyone who writes. Perhaps even for very few. Some go through life complacently believing that writing is simply an act of reproducing reality that involves no fundamental challenges apart from being faithful to the facts. This belief is characteristic of our journalistic culture and of our era. But it has not always been this way. In other latitudes, other times, our most unremarkable normality might seem outlandish and extravagant.

For one of Mexico's most ancient cultures, writing was an initiatory adventure. Those who practised the trade of drawing symbols braved forces that overpowered them at the outset, but that they eventually dominated through the use of appropriate rituals. The course of that "voyage fraught with danger" was set in writing, revealing its tracks to the eyes of those with little experience in reading them. Reading was another ritual, another adventure. Those tracks, those symbols revealed humankind's connection to the world surrounding it, including the world of the dead (an underworld) and the world of the gods (an overworld). Writers—like warriors and priests—attended a kind of school where they were initiated into not only the techniques but also the transcendent significance of their activity.

Those who practised this trade in yet another ancient Meso-American culture were little more than accountants, keeping records on production, taxes and tributes paid to dominant tribes, reigning dynasties, boundaries of conquered territories, and important events in political history—wars, alliances, and more wars. They were scribes more than writers. They made inventories; they never told stories. To use writing that strayed far from an accounting of reality was not viewed very highly. There was no point in it. We do not know whether the prohibition was explicit or implicit.

In ancient Peru, writing was achieved not through signs drawn on paper or carved in stone, but by means of knots tied at different points in woven ropes (*khipus*). This was a sophisticated form of writing that began as simple record-keeping and evolved to tell mythic tales through a complex code involving the kinds of knots, the colours, the materials used for the cords, and the position of the knots. No other form of writing existed. Here, too, it is unknown whether there was any explicit ban on its use.

Among certain peoples of Chiapas, the ancient writers were primarily female weavers. The task of relating myths fell essentially to the women: writing was telling a story by means of symbols woven into a garment. When the weaver placed that garment upon the priestess's body, thus placing her work on view before her community, a sacred aura was formed around that publicly legible body. This woven writing was the sacred space that united all people with their origins and their destiny at once. To write was to help the community understand and embrace the profound significance of past and future life. But it was not the mere reproduction or revelation of meaning—rather, it was the making of meaning through the ritual that echoed it.

The first Christian missionaries in New Spain organized groups of indigenous scribes, leading to the establishment of yet another conception of writing: the viceregal codex. Combining traditional indigenous images with alphabetic Spanish writing, the missionaries' intention was to compile the knowledge of those ancient peoples, the builders of a strange civilization replete with wonders—"things never before seen nor even dreamed of," as the soldier

Bernal Díaz del Castillo wrote. In many cases, the codex resembled a compendium of the things of the ancient Mexicans, placing a heavy emphasis on the lore about their gods, which were considered demons by the missionaries. Writing meant learning about these gods so as to later exorcise them and convert the Mexican people to the Christian faith—the new reigning religion in those lands. To transpose them from their "Diabolical Fiction" to the new "Non-Fiction" contained in the truth attributed to the words revealed in the Bible.

For contemporary archaeologists and anthropologists, the deciphering of writing from different cultures has also been a great adventure. The story of how Champollion broke the code to the Rosetta Stone, so that Egyptian writing could at long last be read, constitutes the prototype of the modern-day adventure in knowledge. Each new step taken toward the deciphering of Mayan glyphs has radically altered our vision of the civilization that vanished mysteriously so many centuries ago. But it has not been many years since the complex meaning of Mayan human sacrifices and their connection to writing were understood (or were thought to be understood).

From the Egyptologist Jean-François Champollion in the nineteenth century to the Mayan scholar Linda Schele at the close of the twentieth century, the first step in reading an ancient code is to decipher the significance of writing and writers for those distant societies, and then to venture into the meaning of each sign and into the grammar. Faced with the diversity of cultural conceptions of the act of writing, no contemporary reader or writer can help but think about how strange the things we write today—and how and why we write them—would seem to a hypothetical archaeologist of the future, far removed from us in time and space, who could one day write something along these lines:

The ancient inhabitants of the American Continent during the twenty-first century—"A.D.," according to their mythic reckoning of time—held blindly to the belief that words could be so transparent as to glimpse reality just as it is through them. As demanded by their Puritan belief in the possibility (and the necessity) of a pure form of writing unsullied by what they called "subjectivity" (which was considered to be a perverse element that distorted the truth), they invented the extremely primitive concepts of "fiction" and "non-fiction" in order to classify all the written objects that were either available for sale in specialized shops called bookstores or placed in circulation through unbound sheets known as newspapers. In these pages, they established strict rules and regulations regarding the formulas that were acceptable as Non-Fiction and, as such, that were the bearers of truth. It seems the prestige of these sheets would have been toppled by the acceptance of the logical limits of the concept of Non-Fiction that are so clear to our eyes: the mark left on those writings by the bodies that created them.

They rarely gave themselves the time or distance necessary to see how everything they considered to be Fiction could be utilized—as we do now—as a document allowing the elaboration of a history of how they thought, desired, and felt during different centuries. Because their novels implicitly display the characteristics of each era, we see in them not anecdotes but passions marked by time. Likewise, the documents they classified as Non-Fiction are, in our view, equally fictitious. They serve a different purpose for our studies of these cultures, not so much as a demonstration of the truth but as evidence of what those primitive beings wanted to believe was the truth: their secular myths as sanctioned by something we may call—to use their own term—a collective subjectivity. A myth is not a lie but a narrative considered real by a social group, imbuing some of that group's activities with meaning. For many individuals of the time, writing meant the origination of a true echo of reality. Or the complete opposite: turning one's back on reality. To write was to tell the truth, or to distance oneself from it. Either being socially correct by concerning oneself with reality, or being an egoist concerned only with oneself. In that civilization, the writing of Non-Fiction was a severe moral statement, an act of faith, either giving testimony or refusing to do so.

We must try to ensure that this same archaeologist of the distant future has access to the necessary information to be able to write the following: "The Banff Centre for the Arts originated an exceptional ritual that encouraged certain ancient writers of the late twentieth and twenty-first centuries to become more creative in their writing, to undertake an artistic exploration of its possibilities, and to gain a broader view of their craft and of their era. Through such rituals, they recovered the sense of writing as an adventure." This book of essays will serve as proof of this hypothetical observation.

The authors included in this anthology have shared a unique experience. Each was selected from among many others for the heterodox strength of his or her writing project—already developed at the rough draft stage—and was convened along with seven other authors each year to meet in a privileged space, a spectacular retreat in the Rocky Mountains: The Banff Centre for the Arts. Each was provided time (one month) and space (a studio in the forest) in order to realize a more finished version (fit for publication) of his or her project, discussing it in a group along with the other writers and in private with professional editors. All the authors published in this book faced a range of problems, from writing techniques to the significance of the act of writing, for which they had to reach personal solutions. To ensure their concentration was focused on these subjects alone, a generous and qualified team saw to all other obligations of daily life.

Given that The Banff Centre for the Arts offers similar programs in dance, music, the visual arts, and new technologies throughout the year and especially in the summer, the authors of this book also came into contact with creators in other disciplines during their month of creative devotion. One of the texts here, by Eliot Weinberger, came from the weekly lectures linked to this program.

As the acting head of this ritual, I had a privileged viewpoint of what occurred during the summer of 1999. And though this book includes texts from different groups over a number of years, they likely underwent very similar experiences. Each author came to the program carrying an entire world in his or her baggage and allowed it to flow out at the discussion table, at meals, during walks in the woods.

Each writer had had some fundamental experience that he or she had begun to convert into a rough version of a text. That quest, that yearning for textuality, was the primary factor uniting the authors. But it was not only a technical and productive quest. Their initial motivation became the desire to tread common ground— that of the text that would touch others with its force. So, along with the institutional commitment to fulfill the requirements of the program, there was the added commitment implied by the presence of the other writers. A first opportunity to make public to a select group the project they had undertaken. A first opportunity to receive feedback from readers they held in esteem.

That summer, several of the authors were lucid travellers: visions from China, Sri Lanka, Burma, Indonesia, and Africa, among others, converged in our ears. Each one established the drama of being a stranger in another culture at a crucial moment in his or her own personal history or in History on a larger scale. Or of being radically different in his or her own culture or even community, due to a wide variety of mental or physical or cultural challenges. Each one established his or her inner alienation, and by doing so through written creativity, also established what each alienation might have in common with everyone present. There was a convergence of beings full of life and of alert intelligence manifested in the highly differentiated act of writing. An act also shared, thanks to the program, by the first readers of each work.

An irreplaceable affective and reflective space was created during that month in the mountains, a space where each author was a positive and wise presence for the others. The two professional editors, Don Obe and Kim Echlin, offered the same kind of presence but with the added element of their direct and detailed intervention in every text until they considered it publishable. Some writers read other works of their creation to the group in special sessions. An imaginary architecture was constructed with bodies and words, with affections and written compositions that were interwoven to the rhythm of the days. Sometimes even to the rhythm of music. During the group discussions, there were no precepts imposed—concerns were expressed and shared regarding the meaning and the cultural problems implied by each individual writing adventure.

Writing in the context of the Creative Non-Fiction and Cultural Journalism Program at The Banff Centre for the Arts every summer involves much more than simply participating in a cutting-edge professional training session. It is a challenge to creativity and reflection. It is a radical adventure.

At the root of this program lies the notion of setting up a situation of journalistic creativity that escapes the conditions currently dictated by the media. The idea is to offer writers the possibility of going beyond what is normally permitted by the commercial mass media's standards, getting past the stereotypes and progressing creatively in the craft of writing "non-fiction." The nature of the project—and the institution sponsoring it—motivates it to take the adventure even further, implicitly questioning the very concept of what is considered non-fiction. The adjective "Creative" is added, and a parallel distinction is made with the phrase "and Cultural Journalism." "Cultural" begins by designating events on the artistic scene, the subjects included in newspapers, cultural sections, but in the end it takes on a broader, more ethnographic sense: our conception of the world as defined by our times, our social group, our space is questioned, observed, and assessed through the act of writing. The need to open the doors to creativity and reflection on this vocation obliges us to consider and recognize to what degree our cultural conceptions are in fact only relative.

This program of The Banff Centre for the Arts helps us establish enough distance to be able to see ourselves and to recognize the passionate and also rigorous connection the writer maintains with reality and with his or her profession: the two sides of the writer's inner adventure.

Translated by Michelle Suderman

What She Carried

KAREN CONNELLY

You cannot carry this.
No, not that way, alone.
It is wrong to believe
you have the strength.
You do not.
You, too, are only a child.
You cannot carry this.

Yet you can hold it
for a few hours at a time.
For a day.
For two or three days
when you have eaten joy.
You wash the crushed face.
The veil of flies rises.
With practice, you learn
to say *human*.

Now you will carry
part of it
forever.

I sought out the stories of Burmese political exiles in order to continue working on a book I had started to write in Burma. After my second visit there, the military regime blacklisted my name and denied me a third visa, so I went to the Thai side of the Thai-Burmese border and continued learning about Burma through the many Burmese and Burmese ethnic people who live there.

Some of the people who spoke with me became friends, men and women who took me in, explained things far subtler than my questions, corrected me when I was wrong, fed me when there was not a lot of food, worried about me, too, and took care of me in a place where taking care is perhaps the greatest human act. Every single person—rebel soldier in jungle camp, woman nurse, woman medic, woman doctor, diplomatically inclined dissident in town or city, prostitute, migrant worker, journalist-with-two-names, thousands upon thousands of ethnic refugees whose histories of oppression are written plainly on their faces—every single person was a miracle. Each of them had survived.

With the passage of months, I came to know certain individuals better; in all their particular quirkiness and humour, their specific talents for laughter, or cooking, or music, or dancing. I also began to understand just how difficult their survival was, how precarious their illegal-immigrant, active-dissident/revolutionary lives in Thailand were at every moment. I learned how past violence inhabited their bodies and minds with the same intensity as the violence of the present.

The Burmese people became more familiar to me and more miraculous at the same time.

I asked the questions carefully.

And sat with my hands open, as though words could be caught and held. These people were giving me their histories, all they had. Each person told how they became politically involved, through friends at the university, through their parents or co-workers, before the protests and strikes of 1988, or during, or after. In 1988, after months of unrest and isolated incidents of violence, the military regime finally responded to the countrywide strikes and protests calling for political reform. Battalions of soldiers rolled into the streets of towns and cities across Burma, where they shot and bayonetted five to ten thousand citizens to death. Many of them were university and high school students. Thousands more were sent to prison.

The mass murders terrified some people, silenced them utterly. But the violence impelled the further involvement of the living. Aye Aye, a student activist from her first year in university, said, "I could not look away. Where to look? The crimes were all around us. I had to work against them."

I met Aye Aye in an ABSDF camp. Under a different name, the All Burma Students' Democratic Front had once been a student union. By the time I got to know various members of the group in 1996 and 1997, ABSDF had passed through many phases of evolution, from band of passionate, politically active university students to active guerrilla soldiers and strategists to factionally wrought, splintered organization to major dissident voice for Burma in the world of international diplomacy. I had come to know and to move among dissidents who worked in Bangkok, Chiangmai, and a number of small towns in Thailand, but I had never been to their jungle encampments, which served as bases for a small, active military force and radio operations, and as home to a few hundred men, women, and children.

The populations of the jungle camps are fluid; individuals move from one camp to another, from camp to town or city, from city back to camp, bringing books, mail, supplies, job assignments, and news. Dissidents have their work cut out for them; the supply of tasks and disasters is never-ending. They organize information exchange between various dissident and ethnic groups, compile human-rights abuse data, and write and publish reports, books, and press releases on current political events inside Burma and on the border. They also train and keep track of undercover agents who go back into Burma to collect information from the increasingly hard-pressed underground movements. Many of them have to learn the basic language and computer skills to accomplish this work.

Refugees have struggle forced upon them, repeatedly and violently, year after year; the great majority of them are peasants and merchants from very small villages and towns in the most undeveloped areas of Burma. The last camp I'd visited had just been attacked and burned down by a paramilitary group controlled by the Burmese army; though the camp was on Thai soil, the Thai military refused to protect it. Over ten thousand people who already owned almost nothing lost even their simple dwellings and their few clothes. The despair had been palpable there, among the burned-out timbers of huts and the hard stares of dust-painted, traumatized children. I had never seen so many ashes and so many haggard women in my life.

Though I had spent time in a number of large refugee camps on the border, I did not know what to expect in a small jungle camp run by revolutionaries and dissidents. I already understood that their dedication to struggle sustained them; the cause occupied the centre of their lives.

I left the Thai town of Mae Sarieng one hot April morning, travelling in the back of a pickup with ten Burmese people and a load of supplies. It was like leaving on a very important school trip: we were both serious and giddy with excitement when we started out, chattering to one another in loud voices over the labouring engine. It was a hired vehicle, driven by a burly Thai man with one eye. We never travelled on a paved road, but drove straight into the countryside on a trail used for water buffalo and motorcycles, through fields of vegetables and fallow rice paddies. Twisting and turning through the dry, hot air, we entered a wilder land without houses, where the few village hunters walked barefoot on the dust track, smoked wooden pipes, and carried ancient rifles with very thin, long barrels. When we approached these Thai hill people, we always stopped to see if they wanted a ride. They always did. So they rode with us for a ways, too, their tough, dark hands resting on the rice sacks and boxes of soy meal and duffle bags, and they stared very hard at me, sometimes with grave concern, as though they thought I was being kidnapped by the Burmese. I reassured them, in Thai, that I was just going out for a drive with my friends. This comment either turned their heads away from me in silence or split a huge grin out of their betel-stained mouths.

The land became increasingly uncultivated and hilly, and my Burmese companions started to nod off in the intense heat. This gift for sleeping has been bestowed on many Southeast Asian people, but no amount of cultural immersion had changed my general insomniac state. Instead, I lost myself to the entanglement of green and dust-washed plants by the road and far beyond it. This empty-minded observance was as perfect a release from thinking as sleep was. For months I had been deeply sad, lost in the tragic histories I was absorbing from people I had come to love. I recognized the land more easily than I recognized human beings anymore. As we drove farther and farther away, into the beginning of the jungle, I gave myself over to the living strength of the colour green.

Far beyond Mae Sarieng, a wide stream runs through the hills and empties into the great Salween River that divides Thailand from Burma. Along a particular stretch of this stream where the banks widen into a stony beach and the roots of an enormous banyan tree hang in the air like oil-soaked sailing lines, the earth rises up and buckles into a high hill. The camp I visited was built on the top of this hill and on the hillside that rose above it. The bamboo huts were invisible from the stream, though the switchbacking steps kicked into the reddish earth of the incline were a clear sign of human habitation. The steps were wet, slippery from the splash of water hauled up twice, sometimes three times, a day.

People came down the steep hillside to meet us, slipping and laughing, and we jumped out of the truck and crossed the stream, getting soaked to the thighs. It was a curious moment of home-coming. I knew a handful of people in the camp, having met them in other places along the border; I felt curiously moved by this greeting on the rocky beach. I realized in that moment how the jungle camps—isolated, harsh, and sometimes quite dangerous because of their proximity to Burma—were more a home to some of the dissidents than any Thai town or city ever would be. Burmese dissidents in Thailand are vulnerable to arrest and incarceration by the immigration police; they move quietly when outdoors and do not speak too loudly. But the welcoming by the stream, in the rich sunlight of late afternoon, was full of loud, loose-limbed joy, and became an immediate occasion for insider jokes and witty repartee.

I was not allowed, as a guest, to cross back through the stream and help unload supplies from the truck. Instead, a young man led me up the steep hill and delivered me to the thatch hut Aye Aye shared with three, sometimes four, other women and her daughter, September. This was the single women's hut, the proper place for a female visitor to sleep.

Aye Aye was brushing September's shoulder-length black hair when I was brought in. After exchanging pleasantries, we went about the business of comparing notes on the people we knew in common along the border, moving through a list of names of ABSDF members, non-governmental organization (NGO) work-ers, English teachers, and certain Burmese and ethnic Karen doctors and medics. Aye Aye's little girl stared at me while her hair was tugged smooth, parted, and put into two pigtails. Then she smiled shyly and went to play.

I was curious about her name. In Burmese it sounds more like "sep-taam-baa," with a rising tone on the last syllable. I asked, "Why did you call your girl September?"

Aye Aye looked at me with vague surprise, as though I had somehow missed a very obvious point. I raised my eyebrows. She said, "Because September is a beautiful word." Then she laughed.

Directness, appreciation for whatever was beautiful, and laughter: in the days that followed, I came to understand this as Aye Aye's formula for surviving a hellish life with grace. But I still do not know how she managed to keep that formula intact.

"I have to check the noodles first, then we'll prepare your sleeping place." She went out to the little attached shelter, where a large aluminum pot sat on burning cords of wood. With quick, sure movements, she poked and stirred, rearranged the coals around the pot, and rushed back inside to clear a place for me to sleep on the bamboo slats.

Set high off the dirt floor to avoid bugs, snakes, cold, and rain, the beds are built into the walls of the structure and double as shelves. Striped nylon bags (so common in Thailand at the local markets) contain the women's clothes, books, and personal effects; these objects have been collected, given, exchanged since 1988, when a flood of political activists poured out of Burma. Aye Aye showed me her small pile of books with quiet pride. Several novels, collections of Burmese poetry, and a few recent literary journals made up the treasure. As I looked at one of the novels, my throat tightened slightly; certain experiences in Rangoon came rushing back to me. "I met this writer when I was inside."

"Really?"

"Yes, we had dinner together a few times."

"You are so lucky!"

I handed her the book and she held it between her palms as if it were a square of antique silk. Knowing how lucky I was, I mentioned a number of other writers I knew in Rangoon and Mandalay. I was smiling, but it was the saddest name-dropping of my life. Though the border was so close, just a trek away, Burma was the farthest country. The dictators had even changed the name to Myanmar.

Aye Aye knew the work of every writer I mentioned and wanted to hear the details of our meetings. This was the very least I could do, having failed to bring her any new books. The thread I found in

Burma, in those sitting rooms and tea shops, stretched back, back over the border, to this woman who held a tattered novel in her hands.

"Oh, a library!" she said. "I used to love going to the library." We talked for a moment about the library at Rangoon University. Though it was officially closed to foreigners when I was in Burma, a friend had managed to get me in for a very brief look. But the rooms I described and the rooms Aye Aye remembered were not the same places.

She sat with her head crooked to the side. "So many things are different now. When I go back to my country, I will not recognize it." There was a moment of silence. She shook a handkerchief out of one of the bags, opened it, and vigorously rubbed her face. Then, from another bag, she pulled out an extra mosquito net. "Oh no! I forgot the noodles!" She leapt up, hooked the mosquito net to either side of the hut, over the place I was to sleep.

"Aye Aye, I can do it myself," I said, trying to take the strings of the net out of her hands, but she refused to hear me. Despite the boiled-to-mush noodles, she hung the net herself, happy to have me as a guest; Burmese hospitality thrives even in the jungle camps on the border. "And use the net tonight," she said as she hopped down, "even though it is very hot." Then she rushed out to the fire and its scalded pot.

I asked the questions carefully.

And held my breath.

It was like peeling the gauze off an infected wound.

Each man and woman told how he or she was tortured, the methods, how long, where, if they ever knew, which prison they were sent to after, Thayet or Insein or a work camp in the north, how long they stayed, how filthy it was, and what they lost forever.

Aye Aye spoke in a subdued and undramatic voice. Unlike some others, she did not make jokes, but the worst parts of her stories were punctuated by nervous laughter. She was interrogated by four different groups of men over a period of two weeks. She was a delicate-boned, attractive young woman of nineteen; she weighed about one hundred pounds. She had been a strike organizer at the university and, principally, the military agents wanted to know all the banned student union names she knew.

Elaine Scarry points out in her book *The Body in Pain: The Making and Unmaking of the World* that the real aim of interrogation and torture is rarely the acquisition of information. Confession plays a vital role in the *drama* of torture. The theatre is directed by the interrogators. Nothing the individual says or does can change the balance of power and its brutal manifestations. Even when the victim "tells everything," the torture may continue, because the interrogator is after the elusive, still-hidden shred of information, which exists not in the victim's mind, but in the interrogator's.

"They hit me over and over again, on the very top of the head, for hours. Very softly for a long time, like water torture, and then harder and harder, until I was about to fall down. But I was not allowed to fall down." Eventually, Aye Aye fell. Her long black hair had come undone and was matted with sweat and blood.

The real aim of torture and interrogation is to affirm the ruling regime's absolute power over an entire society by destroying individuals. The body's exterior is beaten, cut, electrocuted, prodded, forced, forced against itself. Inside, all meaning and all language are broken apart. Before exhaustion and agony bring silence, the victim cries and whimpers, pushed into the abyss beyond language.

Sometimes the people who go back to Burma to work with the remaining dissidents are discovered and arrested by the extensive military intelligence network. These individuals suffer particularly long torture throughout their interrogations. Their bodies represent the entire resistance movement, particularly the uncontrollable, living voices from the border. A civil war is taking place in Burma; in the interrogation cells, the war is waged against those voices, those bodies, and, in the theatre of the interrogator, the war is always won. Though there are many different methods, the most common torture takes the simple, devastatingly intimate form of beatings.

Beatings with the fists, with boots, with sticks, with leather belts. Beatings standing up, beatings squatting down half naked or naked with hands clasped behind the head. Beatings tied or hand-cuffed to a chair. Beatings until the individual's face and body are bruised and swollen beyond recognition. Beatings until certain internal organs are irreparably damaged; beatings that cause perma-nent paralysis. Beatings with a black hood over the head.

As though the victim in the interrogation cell, through her actions and her voice, has become her own executioner.

When Western newspapers state, "Every kind of political dissent is crushed," they mean that Aye Aye, nineteen-year-old student of literature and biology, collapses on the floor and is beaten unconscious.

She was twenty-eight years old when I met her. The day after I arrived at the camp, we washed clothes together. Squatting at the edge of the wide stream at the bottom of the hill, she told me about her time in Insein Prison. We fed the fabric through the funnel of our closed hands, then our tightened fists pounded the fabric against the long flat stones of the stream bed. We doused every soon-to-be-pounded length of fabric in the water. It was early morning, but the sun was already too hot; we splashed water on our faces and heads as we washed our clothes. The stream's light jumped into and out of our squinting eyes. Water squelched from T-shirts and the brilliantly wet *longyis,* Burmese sarongs. The stream ran shallow at the edges, as streams will, and deeper in the centre, where we bathed in the evenings. My clothes by that time had already taken on the history of places: it was strange to wash my familiar ochre and black *longyi* from a popular Rangoon market with a woman exiled from Rangoon ten years before. As soon as she saw the plumed design of peacock-like birds, Aye Aye knew the *longyi* was from Burma.

She touched the material, examining its unprinted side. She sighed, then brushed her face with her hand, brushing off the sigh as an indulgence. "We all need new clothes. We get clothes from the charities. Sometimes very nice. Sometimes …," she let her voice trail off delicately.

"Sometimes," I said, "unbelievably ugly! So ugly no one wants to wear them, I bet."

She covered her mouth with her wet hand but laughed very loudly anyway.

Aye Aye's own lime green *longyi* slapped against the wet black slate as she murmured, "Very, very bad. Two years. I got very thin, covered in scabies. So many bugs! Much worse in prison than in the jungle. And I was always afraid of what they could do. You know, a young Burmese girl. They could do anything they wanted. When I got out, I knew I couldn't stay in Burma. I was too angry."

Sometimes, her eyes became lit with the high, black glisten of despair, but the Burmese are not given to expressing grave emotion in public. Beside their great love of social engagement, their gifts for storytelling and dancing, their impeccable sense of hospitality, they are also very private. I spoke with many people about "very bad" things, the crimes committed against them. Most of them described these crimes with quiet intensity, and a number of men even spoke with a determined, triumphant matter-of-factness. Every gesture of their hands, every flicker and gleam of their eyes declared how they had already won the war against the oppressors of Burma with their own flesh. These men, who were also the most vengeful, made me very sad.

What they had lost, how they had been injured, showed on their faces like a scar, like a cross-hatching of tiny layered scars, shifting as their lips and eyes moved. Knowledge of their vulnerability manifested itself in a kind of raw nervousness. Aye Aye often glanced around herself or, on hearing a noise, went still as a deer and lifted her head to stare into the trees. She did not seem fearful but very careful. She did not burn herself, lifting the cooking pots off the fire or rearranging the scarlet embers with a blackened fork, her fingertips surprisingly close to the heat.

In the quiet of morning, after she had finished boiling the day's drinking water (which she had just hauled from the stream where we washed our clothes and bathed), she sometimes stared into the intense glow of the coals, just for two beats, three, four, before turning away to begin her other work. Now almost thirty years old, with a daughter, and her husband disappeared, Aye Aye was living in a rebel military camp in the jungle near the Salween River.

After her release from prison, she had joined a group of other student activists and walked through the jungle, out of the country where she was born. She had learned that unimaginable things can happen there; unimaginable, terrible things happen there all the time. These events are not random, like floods and earthquakes. The violence is organized and executed by men, with great purposefulness and great individual passion.

"What they do is unbelievable," she told me. "But then, you have to believe it, don't you?"

Active political dissidents in Burma face one of two risks that, statistically, are likely to become realities. They will go to prison for their work or they will escape prison by escaping the prison of their country. Often, as in Aye Aye's case, they will experience both losses by going to prison first, then, on release, leaving Burma to join hundreds of other political exiles on the Thai-Burmese border, women and men working against the Burmese regime from the outside in.

In 1988, when the students and other activists left their towns and cities, they believed that a number of the ethnic armies on the border would be able to give them shelter and military training. Many left Burma with the express idea of taking up arms against the Burmese regime.

The Karen, Mon, Karenni, Shan, Kachin, and Naga people have been engaged in a civil conflict with successive Burmese governments; some of these groups have been fighting a guerrilla war for over fifty years. Grandfathers have passed arms to fathers, and fathers to sons, and the mothers and daughters and sisters have nursed them and often fought beside them in armed combat. These long, bloody battles with the powers-that-be in Rangoon have been further complicated by a war within a war, for control of—or for various sizable chunks of revenue from—the opium trade. After Afghanistan, Burma is the world's largest opium producer, a narco-dictatorship; most of the country's undisclosed revenue comes from the sale of that drug.

The ethnic peoples want a measure of political autonomy, with guaranteed language, land, and religious rights. During the past few years, one ethnic army after another has signed precarious ceasefire agreements with the Burmese regime, often predicated on access to safe passage for opium shipments. Only the Karen National Union (KNU) continues to refuse any deal arbitrated solely by the military government. Traditionally, the Karen people have not trafficked opium; the KNU enforces the death penalty for traffickers. The Karen believe that to capitulate by signing a ceasefire agreement would ensure the death of their culture.

In 1988 and 1989, troop after troop of city-bred, angry, and idealistic university students found their hazardous way to various places along the border, where they made contact with seasoned jungle guerrillas. The students wanted to join an army and fight against the dictators of Burma. The civil war on Burma's borders had, in a different form, penetrated the heart of the country. The students had seen their classmates shot dead in the streets around the university and near Sule Pagoda in downtown Rangoon. They were witnesses to the death-by-bayonet of marching line after line of junior high schoolgirls. Their siblings were in jail, or their parents were, or their professors, or their friends, or their favourite writers. Through violent political upheaval, they lost what most of us take for granted when we wake up every morning: a future.

They had reason to be angry.

Before the military's retaliation, these young people, and some of the older dissidents who later joined them, had also witnessed their country explode into a chaotic freedom: the organized strikes, the protests, the street performers, the sudden appearance of dozens of free photocopied and carbon-copied newspapers full of independently described current events. Millions of people—from housewives groups to sections of the military—went on strike and marched through their own streets, demanding political reform. Twenty-six years of dictatorship seemed to come to an end simply because the people finally said no.

Aye Aye shook her head. We were in the hut, smoking a cheroot together. Two yellow candles standing upright in their melted wax gave us enough light to see each other's face. Aye Aye spoke very seriously but smiled, because that was the form her face had learned to take. September was asleep behind us, under the mosquito net. Aye Aye whispered, "We thought Burma was free. We thought it was over. We did not know the struggle was just beginning. What did we know? We were children, really. We were too young!"

This last sentence she said in a chiding, loud voice, as though she were speaking back to her former self, hoping it would hear the admonition. In answer, September whimpered and flung the sheet away from her sleeping body. Aye Aye and I swivelled around to look at her, a girl of three. She was a small, exquisite ghost under the mosquito net. Her face bore a serious furrowed brow, with full purple-dark lips parted slightly, ready to argue. But her arms and legs splayed out loosely on either side of her body, like a child (I thought, knowing the metaphor was from the wrong world) about to make an angel in the snow.

When the political activists reached the border in 1988 and 1989, the ethnic armies were not able to help them as much as they needed. "They didn't have any weapons for us. We thought America was helping them, or some foreign country was giving them money, so we could join their struggle, because it was our struggle, too. The Karen wanted to help us, but there were too many of us. We started getting sick."

Snake bites. Malnutrition. The rebel armies gave the students rice, but that was all they could spare. The young people started to eat anything they could catch: frogs, snakes, fish, lizards, small rodents. Dysentery became a problem. They lived in ragtag jungle camps and knew nothing about surviving without running water and electricity. They were, after all, university students. Eye and skin infections were common.

"But malaria was the worst."

Ah, malaria. On the Thai-Burmese border, malaria is a rite of passage, an all-encompassing metaphor for both the malaise and challenge of the border life. Malaria is almost an unwritten prerequisite to revolutionary action. Malaria, among the white NGOs and teachers and doctors, is a badge of honour.

Malaria, I thought, shuddering in the candlelight, is a weeder-out of sensitive souls. I flapped my hand agitatedly at a mosquito, but it was too small, too quick. I knew that mosquitoes are malarial vectors. Aye Aye giggled a deep, low giggle, hand over mouth. "There are too many to kill," she said in a cheerful tone of voice, and continued, "I was so sick I was sure I was going to die. And there was no money, no money anywhere in the camp for quinine. We just had no money!" Now she sat staring past me, large eyes larger with incredulity, her hands open on the knees of her crossed legs.

Almost a decade later, the camps are different. Their inhabitants are used to living in the jungle, used to malaria. A small number of aid projects, medics, and Burmese doctors keep the population relatively healthy. Though they receive some food supplies from non-governmental organizations, they also plant gardens and raise rabbits and fish. Aye Aye's incredulity comes from the past, when young Burmese students died of dysentery and malarial fever simply because there was no way to get them drugs. "Something happens to the brain—or, if it's the other kind of malaria, the—this part, how do you say—the kidneys! The kidneys stop working. I thought, You too, Aye Aye. Bye bye!" She shrugged and shook her head again, still unwilling to believe her own brush with death.

I brushed away another mosquito, feeling slightly nauseous, knowing that nausea was one of the early symptoms of malaria.

Aye Aye's eyes shone black in the flickering light. Her hair was swept up into a ponytail but cut in curly bangs around her forehead. Even when she whispered, her voice and face moved with energetic vitality. She raised her eyebrows, rolled her eyes upward. "I just went back to sleep. My head was so sore I thought being dead would be more comfortable."

Unable to stand it any longer, I hopped off the high bed where she and September slept, crossed the hut to my own bed platform, where a Thai jungle version of Off was hidden, somewhere, in my canvas bag. Pure DEET, it offered a difficult choice between malaria or cancer, but I forged ahead and lathered the reeking stuff on my arms as Aye Aye continued to tell her story.

"But you see, here I am, still. Somebody traded a watch or a pair or glasses or something—I don't know—maybe it was a mother's jewellery, and the Karen brought us some quinine, and we got better. But it took a long time. The malaria stays in your blood, your body needs to get used to it, so you get sick again for a while."

"You get recurring attacks?"

"For the first year."

"You get sick with malaria for a whole year?"

"Every month, for a week or so. Very annoying!"

"You get sick for a week every month for a year." I needed clarification because I had no idea that the recurrences lasted so long.

"Sometimes longer, if you're not eating well. And if you get sick with something else, then you are weak again and the malaria comes back. If I get a bad cold and don't take care, then the malaria will come back again."

"That's so depressing!"

"Depressing?"

Depressing was a word she didn't know until she met me. "You know, very sad, it makes you feel very … unhappy in a deep way."

She smiled. "Ah, yes. But everybody has it. We're used to it. Sometimes it's comforting. You get to rest!" Here she laughed. "Vacation for the sick."

I took another swipe at a flying insect.

"Karen!" Aye Aye said in a schoolteacher's voice. "That's just a butterfly."

In silence, we watched the moth approach the candle flame and begin to circle wildly, the shadows of its wings flapping large against the thatch walls. Aye Aye blew out both candles before it dove into the guttering flame. We got ready for bed by the light of the moon streaming into the windowless windows and doorless doors of the hut.

Soon after Aye Aye reached the border in 1989, the students, who came from all over Burma, began to organize themselves into groups loosely corresponding to the unions or political organizations they had already belonged to in their towns and cities. Many had held positions of relative authority among their peers, but on the border, amid thousands of students, not every one could be a leader, or even a second-in-command. Personality conflicts between the young men and arguments about dedication to the cause added to the physical hardship of jungle life. Not only were they neophyte guerrillas, the young people also had no experience in the laborious exigencies of compromise. Some of the groups splintered. The politics of factionalism, so well documented in every revolutionary and underground movement, began to carve deep rifts among the students.

By then, the Karen National Union Army and the Mon State Army had started to give them military training. Like the men, the women donned fatigues and submitted themselves to an intensive physical-training program. In their rubber flip-flops, they practised with wooden replicas of weapons because real ones were in short supply.

"And then, when we went on patrol carrying real guns, we were shocked! The guns were so big, so heavy, and we had to be ready to shoot them. We did push-ups to make our arms stronger. We wanted to be able to do what the men could do. It was very hard, because we were still getting sick with malaria, and we didn't have very good food.

"It's the hardest work, to be a soldier. And there are fewer and fewer of them now. Some of the students still are guerrillas attached to Karen battalions, but the Burmese military is too big. It gets bigger and stronger every year." A nation without foreign territorial enemies, Burma uses (or stockpiles for use) rocket launchers, bomber planes, helicopters, grenades, land mines, machine guns against its own people. The country is also one of the UN's designated "most underdeveloped countries in the world," where the state of (once-universal) education, health care, and social infrastructure deteriorates further every year under the regime's policies. After the democracy uprisings of 1988, the military closed down the universities in an attempt to control the politically rebellious students. Though certain institutions have opened sporadically over the last decade, quality secondary education is non-existent.

Aye Aye's generation was really the last to embark on a normal university career. "And we ended up in the jungle, the most difficult university! But I am glad. I made the right choice. If I were still in Burma, maybe I would be in prison. I would not be able to do very much for my country. I would not have this experience. My life would be different."

"But don't you think, if you had stayed in Burma, that it might be better?"

"You mean more easy?"

I thought for a moment, then nodded.

"But inside Burma, the people are less free. If you want to do political work, you will go to prison, you are a prisoner. The country is still closed, even though tourists can visit now. Next month I go to Bangkok to work for an NGO. I will learn the computer, practise my English. And all the work is for Burma. We have a very strange life, but I don't think about what is easy, what is more difficult. I made my choice when I left my country.

"And life was more difficult before." Her smile was a half-grimace. "I mean, during military training!" She clearly relished remembering it. "Patrols in the rain were the worst. In the pouring rain, the most difficult. Ha! When it's time to eat, you just stand there for lunch or dinner, all soaked, and even your cold rice gets wet as you put it in your mouth."

I looked in awe at this long-necked, slender woman of graceful bearing and tried to imagine her with a semi-automatic rifle over her shoulder, tramping through the monsoon jungle. As if to aid my vision, she piped up, "And we never had more than slippers to wear on our feet." I looked at her orange flip-flops, thinking how little things had changed.

My own feet blistered no matter what I wore on them. On a trek to a camp farther up the Salween, my expensive sports sandals proved completely useless because we kept trudging through streams and shallow pools of water. They were too awkward to take off and put on for the water crossings, but the wet straps rubbed against my ankles and toes. Blisters. One of the guides was thrilled to give me his flip-flops in exchange for my sandals, but the flip-flops just gave me different blisters, on the top of my feet instead of on the sides of the toes and ankles.

I wanted to go barefoot, but my male companions refused to allow it on the pretext of danger (as if a pair of slippery, too-big flip-flops was going to protect me from anything), but I knew it was the lack of civility that rankled. As one of the men said to me, quite gravely, "We may be in the jungle, but we do wear shoes."

How amazing that tiny pieces of irritated skin can cause such suffering. Though I mentioned this as little as possible, I'm sure I must have thought about it constantly. I had just spent over a week with Aye Aye and the other women of the camp, whose lives were difficult on a daily basis. We hauled water from the stream (Aye Aye refused to allow me to do this, but I did it anyway). In the oven-like heat of April, we boiled water, which never really cooled down. Drinking warm water in 42°C made me dream, literally, of ice cubes. The women cooked on open fires, a messy, time-consuming, physically draining task, like washing clothes by hand. Those clothes, I discovered, also included the rags women used during their menstrual periods; the store-bought kind were a luxury that only sick women used, if and when they were available. The latrine situation was very primitive, and the bamboo slats we all slept on were hard but not as cold as paving stones. The most physically pleasing thing we did was to bathe, twice a day, in the stream, sitting down and lathering up through our bathing sarongs. This tiny pleasure became immense to me and was always a time of camaraderie and laughter with the other women.

But by my tenth or eleventh day in the camp, my hips were bruised and my back was aching from the bamboo. Despite the cancerous DEET, mosquito bites dotted my ankles and back. I was constipated and had no appetite. My increasingly frequent, increasingly uncomfortable trips into the bamboo grove indicated, beyond a doubt, that I was also coming down with a urinary tract infection.

And my feet were blistered, top, bottom, and sides.

Supposedly, if I had lived there as long as Aye Aye and the other women, who even gave birth in their huts if their labour came on early, I too might have toughened up. But in my heart, I doubted it then, and I still doubt it now. A far more likely scenario is that I would have run away, in abject, unforgivable disgrace, with the one-eyed Thai driver of the pickup truck who brought us to the jungle. He knew his way out of that place.

Absolute necessity had forced the camp inhabitants to a point of a high endurance that had already lasted almost ten years. I was in awe of everyone around me, particularly the women, who had less power and political clout than the men, but who were in full possession of themselves and knew it.

The days were filled with moments of the women's strength and resolute grace, but one occasion in particular remains vivid in my mind. It was the afternoon of carrying stones.

To lessen some of the intensive daily labour of the camp, intensive labour had to be done. Already gathered near the centre of the collection of huts, several men were tearing open bags of cement and walking around the impressive-looking water pump. They were preparing to lay a cement foundation for the pump and the generator that would power it. The women's contribution to the project was already designated: carrying stones up from the stream bed at the base of the hill. I commented, in a joking tone, about this interesting division of labour. No one laughed.

At the edge of the small worksite, I picked up a tin bucket with surreptitious possessiveness. Aye Aye and I walked together to the edge of the steep hillside and looked down on the women in their red and yellow and green *longyis,* their milling rainbow of blouses and T-shirts. They had already started to work. The bucket knocked hollow against my knee. I had no intention of standing around to watch communal work take place among people who had been feeding me. As she started down the hill, Aye Aye glanced over her shoulder and said, "We do not want you to help." I laughed. We reached the bottom of the hill. Another woman came and gently took the bucket out of my hands. "*Sayama* doesn't do this work." *Sayama* is a respectful term for a woman teacher or intellectual.

"Aye Aye is also a *sayama,* also a writer, and she can do this work." Aye Aye wrote poetry occasionally, in the evening, and talked about a time in the future when life would be different, and she would have time to write a book about her experiences in the jungle.

"Yes, but you are our visitor, you are a guest."

I smiled sweetly, first at Aye Aye, then at the younger woman holding my bucket. Pushing at the boundaries of cultural decorum can be the wrong way to go, but this time it wasn't. My shoulders, I pointed out, were bigger than the other women's (and a lot of the men's). I said, "How will I understand how you live here if you don't let me understand?"

Aye Aye gave a vigorous horse-shake of her head. "Karen, you are very naughty." Then she handed me another bucket and we went to the water's edge.

By late afternoon, the stream bed became a haven of coolness and green shadow, tunnelled on both sides by trees and boulders, bushes and red clay banks. Beneath the enormous banyan tree, we kneeled or squatted at the edge of the stream, very close to where I had arrived by truck that first day. Jostled by the current, the stones in the stream were easier to collect than the ones packed tight on the wide beach. Rippling larger and weightless under the water, the stones rose up small, gleaming, and surprisingly heavy in our cupped hands. We scooped load after load into the buckets.

The stones were beautiful greys and blacks, with an occasional flash of dark red tumbling down. From the size of pebbles to the heft of duck eggs, they rolled and growled against one another, then clattered and thumped into the tins with a tremendous racket. While the stream rushed singing over brown hands and wrists, over a leopard-spray of stones, the voices of women rose against gravity up the hill.

Aye Aye showed me how to wrap a rag around my hand and place the flat knot of it on the top of my head. The first time, she helped me hoist the filled bucket onto that small round pad. It was a shock. Did a large bucketful of stones weigh twenty or thirty or forty pounds? I thought I was stronger than I was. Wobbling slightly, I started to walk. At the beginning of the work, we lifted one another's buckets, but within twenty minutes we were transformed into a carrying factory, and to pause in our own work broke the rhythm of the machine. Unless another woman clearly needed help or lost her balance, we worked on our own, together, scooping, loading, carrying, dropping the load into a pile. The twisted pad of cloth on the head was a crucial aid, but it was an exercise of good posture and balance for me to keep it there. Cloth on skull, I had to lower my body far enough to get hold of the heavy bucket, then heave it up without letting the cloth slide off.

Try that at home. For three hours.

The ascent of the hill was no laughing matter, though the women filing up and down sometimes laughed. Water from the buckets dripped through our hair onto our faces and necks. Within four trips of dumping loads into the growing batter of cement, our shirts and *longyis* were wet. Every return trip to the edge of the stream brought with it an irresistible animal desire: I wanted to lower my mouth and drink—for the first time in two weeks—*cool* water. But of course the water here was too unclean to drink.

Physical labour makes the body forget the mind, forget itself. That is the only reason people can tolerate it for hours on end, year after year. The labouring body that has hit its stride becomes its own purpose, capable of forging through aches, pains, exhaustion. As I worked beside the women of the camp, George Orwell's assertion echoed repeatedly in my mind, "All people who work with their hands are partly invisible, and the more important the work they do, the less visible they are … It is only because of this that the starved countries of Asia and Africa are accepted as tourist resorts." I remembered the women and children water-carriers of Pagan, Burma, balancing their loads by hanging them from shoulder-poles, and I remembered the Europeans who took photo after photo of their difficult ascent up the banks of the Irrawaddy. With the rise of "adventure travel," the tourist with a camera has learned to see the brown labouring body as a thing of grace and beauty, a rightful addition to an exotic landscape. "Thing" is the operative word. Taking their picture is a peculiar way of rendering human beings invisible, but it works as well as ignoring their actual presence.

The women worked, and worked, and worked. The steps kicked in the reddish earth grew wet and slippery, until they were nothing but bumps for sliding downward, grappling upward. Someone got a hoe and dug them out again, one at a time, as each woman passed with her burden balanced on her head and her eyes moving carefully up the steep path before her feet.

Though I had been wearing a *longyi* every day, I sorely regretted wearing it for this particular task. A *longyi* is a tube of cloth worn like a long skirt, wrapped around the body and tucked in at the waist. At an awkward moment, three-quarters of the way up the hill, mine started to loosen. I needed only one hand to steady the bucket on my head, but properly tightening and tucking in the sarong required two hands. I couldn't stop on the busy path, with women in front of and behind me. Stepping off the path itself, onto the sheer incline, was too risky. So I just left the *longyi* for a moment, hoping the material would stay up until I reached the top of the hill.

Ridiculously, I was also counting on the women to be too absorbed in the task at hand to notice my *longyi* struggle. However, the very second the elastic band of my underwear slipped into shocking view, the women filing down started to shriek with a mixture of real horror and absolute delight. Having not yet reached a safe place to stop, I could do nothing as the report leapt like flame on oil all the way down to the stream and up across the camp to the men's worksite. "The *sayama's longyi* has fallen down!"

They were exaggerating—it didn't fall down that much—but I was deeply embarrassed. Laughing despite myself, I put down my stones, refolded and retucked my sarong, then hoisted the bucket back up on my wet head. By that time, my body no longer ached, but my arms were trembling visibly. The contraction of muscles from my jaws through my neck and shoulders down my spine and into my stomach was like a live wire snapping through me: not pain, but great energy. Aye Aye caught up to me at the worksite and whispered, in a gallant attempt to make me feel better, "The same thing happens to September when she tries to wear a *longyi*." September, of course, was three years old.

The foundation was laid now, and the rest of the stones in the pile would be used for another project. One of the men gave us a bottle of a warm neon pink liquid, its carbonation gone. We passed this bottle around, gulping down the flat sweetness and smiling at one another. Yes, we were all smiling, at the large square of wet cement, at the water pump, still unassembled, beyond it, at the cluster of camp children who had come to watch. The shadows of the trees fell long now, across the camp huts and across our faces.

Aye Aye smoothed back her damp hair and said, "Let's go. It's time to take a bath." The thought of submerging my body in cool water made me weak with happiness.

That night, after we bathed and ate dinner, Aye Aye turned on the little short-wave radio to listen to Voice of America's Burmese programming. It was something everyone in the camp did. Those without radios went to their neighbours' to listen. After news of Burma—the generals' latest development projects, the newly arrested members of parliament, Aung San Suu Kyi's smuggled-out address by video to the UN—came the English lessons. It was already dark in the jungle; my attention wandered from the English lessons to the great orchestra of crickets around us. September was in bed, not sleeping but humming quietly to a tune no one else could hear. In front of a mirror the size of my palm, Aye Aye brushed her own freshly washed hair by candlelight.

I stepped outside, saying I was going to look at the stars. Instead I walked toward the centre of the camp and turned around, in a slow circle, to survey the huts, each lit by yellow candle-glow and dotted here and there with the red coals of men's cheroots.

There in the dark, I realized the women's voices were sharpest, the most determined and the least embarrassed to respond to the radio as though it were a living teacher. Besides the frontline soldiers, they were also the ones who rarely travelled into the world outside the jungle, where English was a crucial skill.

Some radios buzzed with the static; others pronounced with a disconcerting, British-colonial sharpness, "Would you like to go the library tomorrow?"

"Yes," responded voices high and low, lighthearted or solemn, "I would like to go to the library tomorrow." Plates clattered from the other side of the camp; a baby began to whimper. I made out the slightly singsong pitch of Aye Aye's voice among the others. As I walked back toward the hut, crickets fell silent around my feet, and her voice grew distinct in the darkness.

The radio asked, "Would you like to go to the university tomorrow?"

"Yes, I *would* like to go to the university tomorrow," she answered, the irony deepening her tone. Eclipsing the next question, she broke into the clear, irreverent laughter of a rebellious student.

> You are able to pronounce
> some word you heard once
> from your mother,
> from one of the mothers
> who cook on these fires,
> these women who taught you
> how to carry stones on your head, uphill,
> these women who wash their children
> in the dirty stream where you, too,
> will gather the parasites
> in the open net of your flesh.
> These you will carry far, in ignorance.
> They come as readily as the fireflies,
> they glow in you secretly.
>
> Later, when you become ill
> and stumble half blind to the hospital
> you will consider, correctly,
> *how lucky I am, this hospital.*
> You will think, with an unforgivable

measure of self-pity, I cannot
carry this, I am too weak
for this sickness, perhaps
I will die here.
But you will be forgiven.

Even when you throw open
your hands, crying,
Take this
I can't carry it,
it's covered in blood
I'm afraid
you will be forgiven.
You will rest.
Shh, the nurse will say, shhh.

Aye Aye arrives.
Her hair swings with the rhythm
of her long red skirt.
She lived for years in the jungle.
Don't worry, she says.
She laughs.
She is still very thin,
her thinness will never leave her.
She carried a machine gun.
It was too heavy, half her height.
Now she carries to me
flowers from Naing Aung.

Aye Aye is humming.
The song is her own.
Her very slender fingers
through the fever
snap off every thorn.
The tiles reverberate
each sharp crack, the click
and hush of green leaves.

Suddenly, filling
my white hands, roses.

1999

My Violent Art

PATRICIA PEARSON

*Ah! How solid we would be within ourselves if we
could live without nostalgia and in complete ardor, in our
primitive world.*

Gaston Bachelard

*A story about murder, whether real or fictional, is also,
obliquely, a story about the existence or absence of God.*

Wendy Lesser

A GIRL HOLDS A GUN TO THE HEAD
of a man, perhaps for a flash, maybe for minutes. She doesn't say
later. You fill in the blanks. The gun would be heavy, because her
hand is small—she's thirteen years old, and even in my thirties I was
awkward with my grip on a Smith & Wesson. I'd guess that it bobs
and slips against the man's skull in spite of her adamant straining.
He's still driving his cab, bouncing over potholes, when he first feels
the metal butt. I don't know what he does then: winces, swears,
turns electric with terror.

She probably growls at him, this girl, with a scabrous anger born
of her own fear. Snarling about the money, or saying, "Yo, fucker,
freeze," or "Stick 'em up," or some other refrain she's picked up
somewhere, thrown out now in a rudimentary attempt at ritual.

Then she kills him. And the sound of it deafens her. And the
reverb throws her arm back into the gloom of the cab. And the
power and shock of murder make her rush like nothing else, no
drug she's done.

She offers this up to the guy she's fucking, and he brags to someone else, and the gossip crackles outward from there: it's so easy for cops to trace the talk, they could do it in their sleep. And then she's arrested.

And somebody calls me on the phone.

"This sounds like a story," they say.

I know it does.

I can guess where their curiosity's going as they lean back in their chair, swivelling lightly, doodling with an editor's red pencil. Because the shooter is a girl, because cabbies are so vulnerable, because there may be a gang link, or a gun-control hook, or a battered child defence.

They call me because I'm a crime writer. Or I was. It's important. To say, No. Stop bringing these stories to me as if I'm a disinterested connoisseur of murdered children. Stop handing me the rotten heart of human nature, saying, Make this diverting.

It seems far too indignant, the way I take umbrage at these offered assignments—the way I actually bristle with insult. The editors don't see the ground they're on, and I realize that I need to explain. I need to run down my resumé for them and mark the points at which I lost control of violence and it, instead, took hold of me.

My curiosity took a morbid turn in college, when the first wave of serial killers washed across the bookstore shelves. I was an instant convert to the spare, plodding paperbacks then being published about Ted Bundy, Kenneth Bianchi, John Wayne Gacy Jr. Serial killers interested me the way wild weather does, as a magnificent force of chaos. I remember curling into my hand-me-down armchair, one hand supporting my tilted head, reading a report on Gacy, how he'd crammed dead, discarded boys into a crawl space in his cellar and covered them with lime, until there were so many that the house began to choke.

That a man could surround himself with ghosts of his own making, that intrigued me. That he could give himself over to senseless, relentless predation—that posed an extraordinary imaginative challenge for a girl raised in a tranquil valley in a peaceable nation, by a family whose notion of conflict was the smiled remark behind one's back. "His courage bowls you over. His brutality makes you shudder," Diderot once wrote, setting the murderer apart from the crooked politician or humdrum thief.

I never cared for the ingenuity of crime: the great bank robbery, the perfect heist. I had no interest in detective fiction. I wasn't a social activist given to freeing people from prison. I was, perhaps, a psychologist *manqué,* wanting to solve the puzzle of vicious minds from the vantage point of my armchair.

When the murderer made his literary debut in the nineteenth century, via Poe, Dostoevsky, and Stendhal, he was a secular adaptation of Satan, whose hold on the Romantic imagination was falling away. "The figure of the criminal," writes the cultural historian Joel Black, "is all that remains in the modern age of the sacred and demonic characters of the age of myth."

Nothing else had mythic power for me then. I was coming of age without respect for danger in the flat, relativized landscape of the late 1970s. Madonna trilled vapidly on the radio. Politics were platitudes. Sex meant dissolute recreation on a Saturday night and no claim made on Sunday morning. Moral purpose had evaporated ritual was scarce. One night, I dreamt of dismembering my boyfriend, of whom I'd grown bored. I carted his head and shoulders about in a state of embarrassed bafflement, searching for a place to put him, worried that his family would discover this inexplicable thing I had done. It seems to me, now, that the dream was an apt summary of my generation's peculiar malaise. We were being haplessly destructive in the aftermath of a social revolution—dumping our lovers, wincing at pregnancy scares, avoiding commitments, getting too drunk too often, staggering a little under the weightlessness of things. When the baby boomers tore up the fabric of meaning, leaving no instructions as to what to weave next, the unequivocal meaning of murder remained. My shelves began filling with true crime.

In 1987, I headed for the University of Chicago—Fort Brain, Kingdom of Abstract Thought, the most relentlessly intellectual campus in America—to study cultural history, except that I could not. I was too compelled by the way the place was surrounded on three sides by bullet-shattered ghetto. I read the weekly "Campus Crime Map"—most recent rape here, last mugging there—with a quickening interest, imagining Bloom and Bellow as they puttered from seminar to library, lost in Aristotle, hopelessly vulnerable to a shakedown with a box cutter, if they were lucky, or a .457 if they were not. I learned that assault rifles were being run through to Libya by gangs in the burned-out projects of Cabrini Green, a few blocks from my dorm. The violence around me was everywhere implied, and everywhere highly arousing.

I was drawn to the sense that life was actually at stake, here on the South Side. I skipped my readings on Foucault and explored the surrounding projects with my camera, taking quick swings through in a car, hopping out, hopping back in, getting the hell out of there. I began to hang out at the Checker Board, a tiny South Side blues club where whites are scarce but not unwelcome, where I danced for hours, chasing my beer with Jack Daniel's. Junior Wells played there a lot, sometimes commenting on my moves—"You doin' good, girl"—offering an easy grin beneath his excellent brown velour fedora. My pleasure was different than his, more ruinous and hungry, but there was an intersection there, and I got hooked.

I transferred to Columbia and enrolled in journalism school. I wanted to study danger.

The autumn that I arrived in New York, Ted Bundy was approaching his date with retribution in Florida, and that was the talk of my criminal-justice reporting class. Bartering for time, Bundy was offering to confess to more savagery. He also wanted to talk about pornography, how and why it was to blame for the way he had bludgeoned thirty-three women in secret, while otherwise studying law. More than once before his execution, I dreamt that I was Bundy's lover, the one he wouldn't murder, wouldn't dare to. I chided my subconscious for turning me into a girl on a joyride with a psycho, for recklessly copping the thrill.

In New York, there were thousands of lives to live vicariously, thousands of stories to tell, and each morning my instructors sent me into the city to find them. As I grew comfortable moving through burned-out, garbage-strewn neighbourhoods in Harlem, Brooklyn, and the Bronx, I began to walk with a tougher stride, rolling my hips more, loping. "You walk like a hooker!" a cop later told me. That was good, I thought. To fit in, in New York, you had to adopt a touch of criminality yourself: a little swagger, some egocentricity, a stirring of greed.

At Columbia, high on Manhattan's Upper West Side, we worked out how much a reporter should trust in a criminal tale, for this was also the autumn of Tawana Brawley, the Yonkers teen who became a race flashpoint after claiming to have been covered in shit by white supremacists, when, in truth, she had been afraid to get in trouble with her mother for coming home late.

"This city is full of liars," my instructor told me. "Your job is to cut through the bull." We learned to listen for people's confessions, to move with the rhythm of their egos and insecurities, to let them take us to places they felt were important and to hear what they didn't say.

On certain afternoons, celebrated journalists appeared in the august rotunda to address us solemnly about our obligations. Ted Koppel, John Gregory Dunne, Anthony Lewis, Roger Rosenblatt— we gathered before them like humble apostles. Objectivity was the great creed of these American media stars. One of them announced that he did not vote, for that would declare his bias. But in crime reporting, objectivity was irrelevant. Janet Malcolm sparked argument in the J-School that fall when she charged, in the *New Yorker*, that a journalist who didn't understand himself to be a con man was "either a liar, or a fool." It was empathy that mattered, and a certain kind of cunning. Thieves did not hold press conferences. You could not raise your hand as they stood before a podium and demand clarification on their ethics. You had to con them, and in the process, you had to take their view of things.

Crime was an ingredient in New York City's glamour. The city was proud to be irascible and tough, home to hard-boiled journalists, clever cops, cool criminals. It was incorrigibly macho; it still is, its danger has become a cliché. But the energy and style with which it corrupted were thrilling.

The big event in the winter of 1992 was the racketeering trial of John Gotti, boss of the Gambino crime family. I covered it with huge excitement, as if I'd been given tickets to the Super Bowl or an invitation to the Oscars. On the first day in the fourth-floor courtroom, two rows of men on the left stood up respectfully when the "Dapper Don" ambled in. This caused the spectators to stand up, too, which generated confusion, because the lawyers rose only when Federal District Judge I. Leo Glasser entered the room. Eventually, it was sorted out that the one to stand up for was the one you wanted to win.

Gotti's associates were easy to spot because nobody else in the room looked like gangsters. The associates swaggered in and out with the *New York Post* jammed into the crook of their arms, mouthing off about that day's coverage to anyone with a pen, scanning the room for celebrities, and monopolizing the pay phones. A reporter from *New York Newsday* gained close access to them by running a column called "Today's Gotti Garb," which featured the best gangster outfit in court on a given day. On the morning that Gotti's defence attorney, Anthony Cardinale, described the proceedings as "the most important criminal trial in American today," Gotti Garb featured an exotic fuchsia-and-mandarin tie.

Excitement multiplied a thousandfold when Sammy "the Bull" Gravano took the stand. This was because Gotti's former underboss could confirm the FBI's speculations. He could say, in effect, Yeah, we're mobsters. We are not zipper salesmen. We bully companies into giving us tons of money, after which they go bankrupt, and then we hijack trucks. Gotti's defence attorneys seemed to be experiencing a constant impulse to jump up, rush over, and stuff socks in Gravano's mouth.

The media had the opposite reaction. They never, never wanted Gravano to shut up again in his whole life. He made the *Godfather* movies come to life, and that, I presume, is where the writers were culling their narrative cues, because the more Gravano talked, the more the newspapers denounced him for being a traitor—not to the city, which he had turned upside down and shaken until all the change fell out, but to his friend. "Betrayal," one famous columnist penned solemnly in his notebook, underlining the word three times. The next day, I read the columnist's account of how the Dapper Don was "stoic" and "graceful" in the presence of the best friend who'd "shamelessly" turned on him. That is not what I recall. I have a distinct memory of Gotti entertaining himself by plucking his attorney's handkerchief out of his pocket, wrapping it around his head, and pretending he was a bandit.

Gotti was stupid, brutal, and childish, but that wasn't a narrative of choice for New Yorkers. The actor Anthony Quinn even showed up at the court one day to express his sympathy for the Don's predicament. "I grew up in a tough neighbourhood, too," he said to the TV reporters amassed on the courthouse steps. "I know the importance of friendship."

"The criminal appropriates the sacred by violating society's most sacred taboos," notes the critic Joel Black. Horror becomes sublime.

There were always a few curmudgeons who begged to differ. I found them in the New York City Police Department, headquartered in a fifteen-storey building in lower Manhattan, amid a cluster of power centres that include the marble-halled courts, the US Attorney's office, and the tumultuous corridors of City Hall. The elevator at the NYPD was slow and crowded. The offices were as small as cupboards, coffee-stained and overstocked with metal filing cabinets. The cops who cock-strutted through the security check in the lobby were bitter, humourful, and beleaguered. They hated the sleekly spun theories of the experts and FBI agents whose stars were ascending in the culture of criminal celebrity. They figured no one had the right to open their mouths until they'd slogged through a garbage dump looking for body parts and then broken the news to a parent. Their prejudices were refreshingly overt.

"I have no trouble with schizophrenia," one detective gruffly told me when I went to see him about a case involving an insanity defence. "I understand that people get sick. I got no problem with that. I just wanna know one thing. How come the voices in their heads always say 'Kill your moo-th-err … kill them aaalll …'? How come they never say 'Get a joobbb'?"

But I was fascinated by madness. It seemed to me that the boundaries were untraceable, no matter what the legal plea, that no act could be deemed strictly insane or strictly sane. What was sane about Bundy bursting into a sorority house in Jacksonville, Florida, with a wooden board in one hand, manically darting from room to room and clubbing every woman he found, as if on a seal hunt? What unfamiliar guise of sanity had the Florida courts insisted upon for that?

My first full-length piece of crime reporting was a novice philosopher's walk around madness. My subject was a cop. His name was Sergeant Rudy Hays, thirty years plus with the City's Finest, a refined Gary Cooperesque man who'd worked his beat in Queens. I found him from a brief mention in the *New York Post*. Hays had been charged with the shooting death of a young psychiatric nurse, whom he never knew and claimed not to remember. Evidence proved, the *Post* said, that the bullet in Sharon Walker's back had been fired from a Smith & Wesson Model 36, the pistol that the off-duty sergeant yanked from his ankle holster on a December night in 1984. Experts for the defence had argued that he'd sustained a disorienting concussion after he and Walker collided in a minor traffic accident. Car doors flew open, voices shouted, the pair got into a sidewalk fight. Because of the concussion, coupled with an automatic "self-defence" reaction integral to long police training, Rudy Hays could not be found criminally responsible for shooting the unarmed Walker as she fled from him.

I got to know a lot about Rudy Hays as I wrestled with his murderous act. I read the transcript of his trials. I spent hours with his highly theatrical lawyer. I interviewed half a dozen New York psychiatrists about the insanity defence, some in well-appointed Park Avenue offices, others in the hell of public hospitals. I learned that madness was a construct of convenience to the law, and I still remember how I found this revelation shocking, standing in the wood-panelled office of Hays's lawyer, a bald ex-boxer with beefy arms. "Insanity is just a hook for juries to hang their hat on," he boomed at me, small neophyte that I was with my notebook, all ears. "Hand them a concussion, and if they like your client, they'll hand you an acquittal."

Not that people didn't go mad, he went on to say. But sometimes it was the world around them that was maddening. Sometimes that was more to the point. Violence spooks cops, everybody knows that from TV. They take their revenge in different ways. Some lash out and get brought down. Some develop conspiracy theories, scouring the landscape for mutilated cattle and charging after Satanists. Others chase homosexual child-porn rings in neat concentric circles. The big guns hunt celebrity, trying to trump the murderer's power with their own shamanistic power to decipher him. Strolling through the true crime section at Dalton's on Sixth Avenue in the early nineties, I began to notice the autobiographies of cops alongside those of criminals: *Mind Hunter, Whoever Fights Monsters, Serpico,* the celebrated tomes.

Hays had become uncommonly passive in prison. Didn't care much about his case, dropped the master's thesis he'd been working on, went quiet. I needed to talk to him. But I was afraid to meet my killer. I wanted to read him like a paperback, or write him like a novel. I did not wish to *know* him, you see. I did not want him to witness me knowing him. I didn't think he'd regard his life as any of my business. A friend sent me taunting postcards: "Patricia, call your killer." You can be a voyeur for only so long. At some point, you must enter the story.

This, from the story I filed:

> On January 11, 1989, courtroom J2 in Queens Criminal Court was filled with sunlight and silence. A handful of people—vagrants in rumpled coats, court officers, a Legal Aid lawyer—wandered in and out without words. Rudolph Hays, elegant in a tailored, three-piece suit, sat upright with his 86-year-old mother, Marjorie. The rich cadences of Hays's deep voice rose and fell as he fashioned idle comments. His long fingers, which tapered to manicured nails, tapped together gently. Mother and son gazed calmly ahead, at the vacant altar of justice.

And behind them sat me, brightly curious twenty-four-year-old Canadian in a Hudson's Bay sweater, paralyzed with embarrassment. For twenty minutes I stared at the back of his neck, at the flesh of him, and finally I raised my hand—it weighed about five pounds—and crane-lifted it through the six inches of immovable air between us and tapped him on the shoulder.

"Sergeant? I'm the journalism student. I wrote you that letter?" Yes indeed I wrote him a letter. It was so self-effacing and apologetic I might as well have sent him a blank sheet of paper and signed it "Love, Patsi."

He smiled very graciously. "Oh, yeah, yeah I got that. I'm sorry, I really don't want to talk about this case anymore."

"Okay," I singsonged, idiotically solicitous.

I was a student. It didn't matter yet. It would.

One winter after journalism school, in my customary flux between freelance gigs, I met a man at an East Village party who looked like

Paul Simon with beadier eyes. The man had tired of his family cosmetics business and wanted to become a producer. Impulsively, he
offered me a job on a series he aimed to create called *Confessions
of Crime*. The show, he explained, would feature videotaped statements made by killers, gathered from boxes of trial evidence stashed
away in American courthouses. The practice of videotaping sus-
pects' statements was new then. He had hit upon a gimmick that
could get him into the crowded theatre of infotainment. I seemed
to know stuff about criminal psychology. That could help him,
he figured.

A month later, he hired two ill-tempered, cut-throat producers
from *Hard Copy* to package the video into half-hour stories. I was
the field producer, the one who would find the cases, talk to the
people whose worlds had ended, and persuade them that it was
somehow in their interest to have private loss and sorrow moulded
into quick jolts of entertainment on TV.

In long, tender telephone conversations with murderers, I let
them know I understood, and I did begin to understand a little.
How the son reared up and destroyed the hectoring, demeaning
father; how the mother finally just needed to punish, punish, punish the child who'd been indifferent to her—had "conduct disorder"—had been out of control for so long; how the wife could no
longer bear the apprehension of attack. How the slow accumulation
of insults erodes one's composure 'til there's nothing left but the
grabbed-up knife and the "Fuck you, FUCK YOU!" in a vibrant
black rage.

Some wanted their fifteen minutes; now we had come calling
to offer it. Others did not. But, I'd tell them, perhaps there would
be healing through service to others, if they offered testimonial, if
they gave warning.

"If we could just let other parents know the dangers of keeping guns in the house ..."

"People need to understand child abuse, what it does ..."

Behind me, in our renovated loft office on lower Broadway, I'd hear the *Hard Copy* producers slamming down the phone after their own calls, yelping "Got 'em! Yeah!" like they were shooting skeet.

The show's executive producer was a bored expatriate Oxford Brit who drank too much. One night, he took me out for Chardonnay and lamented the banality of his show. "You cannot say 'Hard Copy' and 'Bosnia' in the same sentence without experiencing a mid-life crisis," he muttered, swiping my last cigarette. "It's an impossibility."

The premise was transparent. I think that's what made crime so alluring a sale at that time. Clarity fled from politics with the exit of Reagan and the demise of the Cold War. Everything else—foreign wars, social policies, the technological revolution—had grown too complex to discuss. But "Bang, bang, you're dead," well, the import was obvious. Then everyone could play. Vote for or against O. J. Simpson, Lorena Bobbitt, Rodney King. We were using violence to construct something else, a collective understanding. We were building a public discourse from the dead. And what did I build? A beat, a reputation, a career.

We did not illuminate violence on *Confessions of Crime.* Our phone conversations were bait, a lure to the camera. Once the killers were up on the screen, the script denounced them as "monstrous" and "evil," which maybe would have meant something, if we'd meant it, but we didn't know what violence meant at all.

In the end I came upon death casually, in an inappropriately short dress I'd pulled on frantically after waking late one morning to find the impatient, sighing producers waiting outside my SoHo walk-up in their limo. I was in the business of making violence visual, yet violence had never been visible to me. Now I needed to see it for a dramatic re-enactment on our show.

In the Nassau County police department, the good-humoured, polyester-suited detectives greeted us with vending machine coffee and jokes. They had time to kill, I suppose. Either that, or TV was a god to whom they could not resist being supplicant. We were there about a boy who'd shot his parents with a high-powered rifle when they opposed his choice of girlfriend. It was my episode, my story to tell, and I had it smoothly plotted.

I sat down with my coffee at a cluttered desk and began to sift through the crime-scene snaps. I found the boy's mother in her immaculate kitchen, flat on her back on the floor. Her striped cotton skirt had flown above her plump waist to reveal her fully—her baggy blue panties, her clammy white thighs. This was none of my business. Her head, which had taken the bullet and exploded, lay cradled on a loaf of bloody Wonderbread. The gunshot had blown her tongue clear out of her mouth. I found it in another picture in the pile, sitting atop her white microwave oven. What this was, I thought, was ignominy. Abandonment. Erasure. The detectives began chuckling. "This is what's real, Miss Glamorous, this is what it comes down to."

I left New York after *Confessions of Crime,* but I did not leave danger behind. I kept tunnelling into the minds of vile men, gazing at the faces of strangled boys and mutilated women, sitting for hours in a car in the pouring rain while the father of a dead child sobbed, taking notes. I'd like to say I was taunting myself on purpose, testing my courage, but it wasn't like that. It was an act of empathy that I was getting very good at, that was bringing my writing to life, that was paying my wages. After Tim Cahill wrote his book about John Wayne Gacy, he locked his office door and walked away, intending to return that afternoon. He could not walk back through it for a year. I do remember reading that somewhere and finding it interesting and missing the point.

One Christmas, I went to visit my elder sister in her lovely small Ontario town. Her husband was ferrying me past the town square in his minivan, having fetched me from the bus, and a crowd had gathered there, milling around a platform. "Are they organizing a search for a missing child?" I asked. My brother-in-law gave me a long, slow look of amusement. "No," he said. Just: no. You are a crazy girl. "They're singing Christmas carols, Patricia."

Looking back over my letters and journals, I can trace the growth of deformity in my perception. A tendency to witness the behaviour of lovers and friends as pathological, as menacing. A dark imagining of desire as predation, my seducers as psychopaths. Or myself as the one who was dangerous.

I dreamt that I was a poisoner's accomplice, working furtively and senselessly, the perspiration pricking my neck.

In a letter to a friend, sparked by reading a riff by the serial killer Dennis Nilsen on his fellow murderer Jeffrey Dahmer in *Vanity Fair*, I wrote, "Lately I have discovered in myself a rage of distrust not dissimilar to the emotion attributed to these killers."

For the first time, my doctor began taking a look at my mental health. How much coffee, any intravenous drugs? Family history of anxiety? Symptoms, past symptoms, did any doctors treat me? I got her involved inadvertently, through seeking out a prescription for Xanax to quell my fear of flying. I didn't see that fear as connected to anything else, such as fear of loving, fear of working, fear of dark, fear of wind, a pervading sense of doom.

I went to see a psychic to ask when this would end, when love would come, and she told me I was allergic to cheese.

Out of this hall of mirrors, in the summer of 1995, came two people who collapsed the detachment of every crime reporter in the country—every reporter, that is, who got the coveted press pass to Ontario District Courtroom 641 in downtown Toronto. The murderers on trial were Paul Bernardo and Karla Homolka. I hate even saying their names. Good-looking kids from good families, good marks in college, good manners, watched *The Simpsons,* loved thrillers, infatuated with themselves, went down the river and hooked up with Kurtz. They went on a spree of rape, abduction, and murder, all eagerly recorded on their camcorder alongside Disneyland and Hawaii and their Ken & Barbie wedding.

We are used to this now, this incessant self-recording, every life a pitch for brief celebrity, for a prize on *America's Funniest*

Home Videos, for a clip of catastrophe to sell to TV. We were destined, sooner or later, to encounter the cruelty of psychopaths narcissistically recorded the same way. But we were wholly unprepared.

Days and days of intolerable videos in the courtroom as the heat hits 100°F on the sidewalk outside. We heard young women raped over and over, as if we were there, listening behind a locked door. Sixty people hunched over with their eyes on the floor. "Pleeeeeeeeese," the victim wails, so loud, it's so loud, winding upward into a sustained shriek as she is anally raped. One summer evening discussing her new boyfriend with grade nine pals, a guy she savoured holding hands with, maybe even kissing, and by dawn, abducted from her parents' front lawn, turned into a sex slave, about to be dismembered. She's blindfolded. She never saw her captors, but they saw her, and recorded her, and watched her again, and now lawyers were watching, and jurors, and court buffs, and reporters like me.

After that wail, I walked out of the courtroom directionless, yelling bitterly at a fellow reporter without cause, striding fast toward the doors. I hit the street and zigzagged aimlessly. I could not think and I finally gave up, sinking to my knees on a patch of grass in a traffic circle. The traffic rumbled around me, the light began to slant, and after a while, after a few absently smoked cigarettes, I remembered where I belonged, what my geography was, where I was meant to be in the world. I hailed a cab to a friend's.

In the early twilight I sat with my friend's child, Natalie, in the garden, watching her twirl about with her love-worn security blanket, tossing it up into the lilac tree, then shaking it free, so that it fluttered down to cover her, smiling. I thought how Leslie Mahaffy's mother must once have watched her tiny child, spinning and wheeling, and suddenly Natalie's blanket became the T-shirt tied around the victim's eyes. All evening, objects of delight transformed themselves into instruments of horror. I felt as though I were inflicting that on Natalie, somehow. Bringing depravity with me like a rank scent into the garden, lurking beneath the perfume of the lilac, something rotten.

In the autumn of Paul Bernardo's imprisonment, I took a studio apartment in New York's West Village to complete some reporting for a book on violent women. The spectre of horror was everywhere, taking its stylish turn through the culture, spooking me as I came around corners. I went to see *Seven* at the suggestion of a friend and exited the cinema in a state of speechless psychic jitters. The film's savagery was thought to be clever: how often do you see a victim forced to eat until his stomach explodes? Or a man made to bleed to death by cutting a pound of his own flesh? Dazzling innovations for a crowd grown bored by gunfire.

I wandered into the Guggenheim and came across an exhibit of still lifes with Mexican corpses and fruit. The photographer, Joel Peter Witkin, had purchased bodies from coroners, dragged them to his studio, and dressed them in hoop skirts. Patrons were gazing appraisingly at severed feet on platters surrounded by pears.

One evening, I picked up the phone to hear an ululating wail, no introduction, then the announcement: "Lionel buried Jeffrey's brain!" It was Jeffrey Dahmer's mother, who hoped I would ghost her autobiography, calling to update me on the custody battle with her ex-husband over their son's remains. Dahmer had photographed corpses, not unlike Witkin. When his traumatized mother went shopping, people unwittingly told her Dahmer jokes.

I ran into someone at a party who knew Brett Easton Ellis, author of *American Psycho,* a novel much loved by Paul Bernardo. Ellis had apparently read up avidly on Bernardo's trial. In Toronto, the parents of Bernardo's victims began fighting passionately to have the tapes destroyed as child pornography. They weren't just courtroom evidence, the parents argued, because the distinction between justice and entertainment could no longer be trusted to hold. Someone would seek out the tapes, some author with a fat book deal; someone would disseminate their daughters' agony for profit.

In studies of exposure to trauma, one occasionally finds the question posed as to who survives the trauma most intact, and why. Of psychologically healthy Vietnam vets, the authors of one study note: "These men had consciously focussed on preserving their calm, their judgment, their connection with others, their moral values and their sense of meaning." Ah, their sense of meaning, that catches my eye. That is the point of vulnerability for my generation. In my West Village flat, I succumbed to insomnia, sitting dully through each midnight with an ashtray.

What is the definition of a crime? What does the criminal confess to? The breaking of a law, or to something else, to a criminal indifference, to the breaking of a heart? I encountered two mothers that autumn whose children had died at their hands. One was a Long Island high school student whose confession had been videotaped. The district attorney's office made me a copy, which I watched in my flat. This girl was wary of her interrogator, alarmed by his interest in her teenaged affairs. She tells him, because he asks, that she gave birth to a son, the one swimmers later found entangled in the reeds at Laural Lake. She stuffed her son into a garbage bag, because that was where a mess belonged, and drove around for the day paying visits to pals, announcing to those who knew she'd been pregnant that she'd had a miscarriage. She omitted the fact that the child was in the back of her Toyota, packed in a two-dollar cooler, awaiting disposal under cover of night.

A crime of utter disregard. For which she was eventually sentenced to two years.

I met the other mother at Bedford Hills Prison in Westchester County. I didn't know she had been a mother. I had gone to see her because I'd read her writing in a prison journal. We met in the visitors lounge to talk about prison culture, on which she was an expert, having ticked off fifteen years of a twenty-five-year sentence already. She was exceedingly thoughtful, this woman, and generous, not wanting to know what was in it for her to assist me. We ate vending-machine popcorn and spoke for a long while perched on our hard plastic chairs. We spoke about child abuse, and I offered that I was sometimes apprehensive about having a child, that I wasn't certain about my temper, that sometimes in the moments of just-waking I was seized by wild fury and had, on occasion, swung my fist at my lover. And then she judged it important to tell me that she had killed her three-year-old daughter. The girl had been having a temper tantrum in a restaurant restroom. Frantically exasperated, the young mother had finally backhanded the girl, sending her flying into a pipe beneath the sink. She lost consciousness, and after two agonizing weeks in a coma she died.

This is a confession told in confidence, the prisoner's eyes brimming with tears, her body rigid with the effort of staying composed. A crime of passion. A passionate lifelong grief.

Toward Halloween, I was wakened before dawn by a lacerating pain in my abdomen. I rolled over startled and realized that I was bleeding. The blood warmed my legs and then, as I pulled myself up, began to soak me. It was gushing. Frightened, I scrambled to the bathroom, but the accompanying cramps grew so bad I nearly passed out from the pain, dropping to the bathroom floor with an Aspirin bottle in my clutch, rocking and gasping. It flew through my mind that I was bleeding to death, like the character in *Seven*. Crouched over, squeezing my legs together and swearing, I dashed to the desk and rifled through my bits of paper for my out-of-country insurance. What did it cover, what, what? I called their 1-800 number and delivered pertinent information about my employment status and postal code between bouts of projectile vomiting against the wall. It appeared I was allowed to stumble off to a hospital for "emergency treatment."

I phoned around to friends, but nobody answers at 7:00 on a Sunday morning; you can't penetrate the blanketing perimeter of their call-answer systems, you just howl into cyberspace. I called an ambulance and was instantly ashamed. I ran around the apartment looking for my pants and wondered if I should lie on the floor to make the call more legitimate, somehow, to validate the drama. I didn't know the etiquette of rescue. I'd never even broken my thumb.

A noisy train of paramedics and cops came lumbering up the stairs of my genteel walk-up, walkie-talkies crackling. Oh no, a scene! WASP Hell. The female paramedic wore reflecting shades and smoked a Marlborough while she piloted the ambulance through Greenwich Village. Please feel free to smoke through my medical emergency. St. Vincent's was quiet. They stuck me in a room on a cot. Someone took blood. I slept fitfully under my coat. Finally, a young, wan-faced German resident came in and prattled away about the difference between Aspirin and Tylenol and how Aspirin was a "little bit of magic" when you're elderly. As an afterthought, he decided to examine me, extracted something, some object, and blurted, "It's a product of conception," and fled like a startled deer. Ten or fifteen minutes later, a gynecologist flipped aside the curtain and stepped in. He asked a few questions, decided to do his own exam, and said, "I have to get a female." A female was fetched to act as chaperone. The examining lamp didn't work. Much muttering in irritation. The final decision: I'd had an incomplete D. and C. They needed to do another blood test and a sonogram. On Tuesday.

I returned to St. Vincent's on Tuesday and sat there interminably, on a blue plastic chair between a cheerful teen with a six-month-old cutie in a stroller and a crack addict with bulbous eyes and missing teeth who kept scratching her bare midriff. Finally they called me into an exam room. "And this is a post-pregnancy checkup?" asked a nurse. No, no. I confess that I had been pregnant that summer, not by conscious design, and had distanced myself instantly from my womb. I smoked, I drank, I thought, I am not behaving like a mother. I terminated the pregnancy; I believe that's the medical term.

"So, what you passed at emerg was a clot?" That would be understating it, I said. I was suddenly desolated by this game of tag between anonymous health professionals, each one beginning with the assumption that nothing much was up. None of them grasping, remotely, the enormity of this to me. Sorry, so sorry, for the little twins who died with such violence; don't tell me otherwise, I saw what was left behind, what came out in the hospital, a bloody *chunk*. A "product of conception."

I watched a blond-haired pair of twins, six or so, boy and girl, try to balance themselves along a ledge in Union Square. Products of conception grown a little taller. Loved. Lives lived. I prayed for the twins at the Cathedral of St. John the Divine, though I have prayed perhaps only a dozen times in my life. I dream about them as the little persons they were about to become. They had no funeral. Don't speak to me of clots.

I turn my traumatized attention to my violence, to my body. I am flesh bereft of spirit, like Witkin's chopped-up props, a friable self, grotesque. I get an AIDS test. I have my moles checked. I grow suspicious of pains in my back. If I'm nauseous, I worry about cancer and start reading up obsessively on symptoms. I lie in my bed whenever I can, trying to shut up the clamour of terror with sleep. When I sleep, I dream that my house is burning down.

My parents flew into town and tried to divert me with the theatre. But I spied a young man in the audience who looked edgy and furtive; he was carrying an uncommonly heavy knapsack. I grew certain he was planning to mass murder the patrons during Act I. I fled with my heart pounding in my ears.

Someone suggested Christmas in the country. We gathered together dear friends and ventured into the hills of Quebec, to my grandparents' cottage. The snow was a blanket of white velvet. The maple trees sparkled with ice. The woodstove in the cabin made our faces glow. Here, there need be no fear. Here, there should be giddy happiness as we tromp about ineptly on snowshoes to much laughter, then warm our bodies with roast turkey and wine.

But the fear is fierce, and more piercing than cold, and I keep it to myself because I have no explanation. I take a solitary morning walk along the road and hear the sound of footsteps crunching. They come from behind me, crunch, crunch. There is only that sound, not even distant traffic, not wind.

A slowing of the steps, a hesitancy, another crunch. My mind cartwheels through the options. If I scream, will my friends hear? Should I talk my way out of the encounter? I know from my reporting that rape victims can luck out either way. But it's *either* way. It depends on the rapist.

Buzzing with adrenaline, bracing, I stop and turn. I see a little girl, eight or ten, stomping balls of ice beneath her boots. After she passes, I stand there for so long that the shadows shift. I am silenced by amazement. Not at my fear, but at the girl. It's a fact that I cannot quite get through my head. That she can walk alone through the woods, that she is not afraid.

I get into my small white Mazda and try to drive to Ottawa, to where my loving sister lives. She has a beautiful voice, my second-eldest sister, melodic and gentle; I want to be with her. But the temperature outside has dropped steeply. The white winter light blazes through my windshield, blinding me as I climb the hill of the cottage turnoff road and try to reach the highway. It's too cold, the frost is clouding upward on the glass; I won't be able to stay in my lane. I have to drive slowly. I have to put the hazards on and clench my muscles taut and try to progress, mile by mile.

Katharine's son bounds gaily all around her, putting together his Christmas train set, beckoning for our assistance. My sister and I share a fine talent for masking fear. People rarely see through poise. I don't know why. There's a certain kind of silence that comes across as calm. We even fool each other, we sisters, that's the surprise. We contain our terror as if we're entrapped under ice.

So she's not expecting it, when I go to my car and realize, with an awful, shocked dread, that if I turn the key in the ignition, the car will explode. "Oh God," I whisper, and fetch her, cutting in on my nephew, speaking sharply to him, "Graeme, damn it! This is not a joke!" Gamely, she sweeps the snow from her station wagon and follows behind as I inch my way toward Murphy's Garage, panting, barely able to swallow, my eyes as round as the eyes of a woman I once saw in a Polaroid photo, snapped by her killer in the beat before oblivion.

I cannot say that I wanted this madness to end, because a part of the madness was my inability to want without apprehension, to envision a life without calamity, to make a simple wish. "To cease wishing is to be dead," Rollo May once wrote, "or at least to inhabit the land of the dead, for without faith, we cannot want anymore, we cannot wish." May quoted Eliot: "What shall I do now? What shall I do?… Pressing lidless eyes and waiting for a knock upon the door."

Can I wish this much, I ask myself one night, having sat in arid terror in the bathtub for an hour, to rise from the cooling water and walk into the living room and listen to music that moves me? I need to wish this much, and I know it. I get up on shaking legs. I pull out the CD *Grace* by an emerging singer, Jeff Buckley. His voice is peculiarly beautiful, suffused with a sorrow rarely articulated in my vernacular, for my age. He sings of attending a funeral.

"I wish they hadn't died," I say aloud to my empty living room, trying to think of things to wish. It is an odd, uncertain sentiment that grows, as when a dry bit of etiquette unexpectedly swells with meaning. Curled into my hand-me-down futon, I feel the tension in me snap and grief break through. I weep for the girls who wailed for my help, for the boy left strangled beneath a tree, for the mother hurled on the kitchen floor, for the woman in her prison and her child beneath the sink, for my twins, for the absence of consecration, letting the tears slide blindly through my hands. I can't stop, I do not want to. I weep for hours.

Near the house I bought last year is a park. It has a little zoo. The zoo has two horses, six pigs, and five cows. The people who work there wear red T-shirts. "I want to work at the zoo," I tell my husband.

"That's fine," he says. "But you'd have to do chores."

"Oh, that's true. Never mind."

I walk across the grass with my daughter on my hip.

My love is my weight, wrote St. Augustine. Because of it, I move.

1998

Join the Revolution, Comrade

CHARLES FORAN

WHY DO I THINK ABOUT CHINA SO MUCH?
Because, I suppose, my life wound up shaped and directed by
the Tiananmen Square massacre. Because my wife and I were living
in Beijing in 1989, and witnessed the six glorious, unbuttoned
weeks of the student movement, often in the company of friends at
the college where we taught. Because on the night of June 3, we
stood watching locals, armed with rocks and bricks, attempt to
block an army convoy storming into the city past our gate. Because
for the thirty-six hours that Beijing lay under siege, people com-
mandeered our apartment as a media centre, listening to Voice of
America and BBC reports on short-wave, contrasting the freshly
minted propaganda being broadcast on television with the truth of
what they had just seen with their own eyes. Because, having left the
city five days after the crackdown, we returned to the same college
and the same jobs, and to many of the same friends—whose association with us in 1990 involved greater risks than before—to experience the aftermath. Because what we observed that second year, the
courage and composure, desperation and despair of individuals
struggling to maintain their sense of themselves in a nation hostile
to any ambitions, thoughts, or personalities that strayed outside the
narrow, prescribed norms, jarred my sensibility in a way that I
thought nothing, aside from a birth or death, could do.

I think about China because of our friend Gao Gianbao, a classics teacher with an opera mask for a face and a bum leg, due to childhood polio. On campus, Gao was known to colleagues and students alike as "the cripple." Probably the brightest person I have met, and certainly the most extravagant, delighting in excesses of food and drink, indifferent to people's opinions of him, he used this pitiless moniker as a prop in his own theatre of the absurd. At a track meet, Gao insisted on running in a relay race with his department. As the various squads paraded around the grounds, he limped along with a sign describing the classics team as "An Old Man, a Woman and the Cripple." Nearing the finish line of a race a half minute behind the rest of the heat, he broke into a grin and, turning to the bleachers, imitated a champion surging into the red tape, chest thrust out, features wrenched in agony.

I think about China because of Shen Hong, a student of my wife's who spent hours in our apartment, avoiding her unheated classrooms and on a break from her grotty six-girls-to-a-room dormitory. Hong's favourite pastime was reading in her bunk, under her coverlet. Being a pupil of English, she might be expected to concentrate on Western novels in the original. Once, I asked my students what they'd read over the summer in their second language. One young man claimed he had devoured the works of Ernest Hemingway in the original: *The Old Man and His Fish* and *Goodbye, Arm*. Another boasted of having plowed through the five hundred pages of John Steinbeck's masterpiece, *The Angry Grapes*.

Shen Hong loved English novels, but only those, she freely admitted, that had been translated into Chinese. The longer the novels, the better, she explained to us after offering a rapturous plot summary of *Gone with the Wind*. "What else do you read?" I asked her. "Nothing else. Only long novels. Many days we stay in our dormitory and read. It is better than going outside." "Outside the campus?" my wife wondered. "Outside the room," Hong answered in her soft, shy voice. "All six of you in the room, all day?" "We forget together," she replied.

Finally, I think about China because of Liu Junhui. He was a colleague at the college, a teacher of English grammar and film studies, but really he was an artist as yet undiscovered by his art. Dismissed by many as a *liu-meng*—designation for the urban underclass of punks and petty criminals, nihilists, and existential heroes—he wandered about campus dressed in shabby clothes, hair long and unwashed, pores oozing too little sleep and too much alcohol. "I cannot imagine my life without beer" was Liu's favourite refrain. He adored all things Western, and his dreams were variously to escape to the West and become a filmmaker, or else to dissolve—literally, like melting snow—into the wilds of Tibet, where a friend had vanished a few months before, taking with him a film camera, the gift of a German fleeing tanks during the massacre. Liu Junhui, who had been peripherally involved in transporting the Goddess of Democracy statue from the art institute over to Tiananmen Square, had dodged tanks and soldiers on the night of the massacre and then guided an American network crew around the city in the dark hours. We had spotted him whizzing into town on a bicycle shortly before the crackdown. "What are you rebelling against?" I asked him, thinking of Marlon Brando in *The Wild One*. "Whattya got?" he answered.

Liu had even acted in a movie. A few years before, the production crew for Bernardo Bertolucci's *The Last Emperor* had put out a casting call for young Beijingers with slangy English. He had fit the bill, and had been not only cast as one of a thousand extras, but given a line of dialogue. His role was of a Red Guard marching a disgraced teacher through the streets of the capital during the Cultural Revolution. Among the spectators was the last emperor of the Qing Dynasty, Pu Yi, now a gardener in a public park, who had been re-educated decades before by that same teacher. Pu Yi steps into the parade to testify to the man's character. Liu Junhui intercepts him, listens to his plea for compassion and a sense of historical perspective, and then says, "Join the revolution, comrade, or else fuck off!"

He practised the line for six weeks. Over and over, with friends and family, strangers in the street. The day of the shoot was the happiest of his adulthood. Cameras and action, free food on the set. Four years later, Liu was still employing the dialogue as a catch-all summary for the illogic of his life, and of China. A question as complex as "How long can the government maintain its fiction about June 4?" or one as simple as "What will you do if they arrest you for your activities last spring?" would both be answered using the mantra.

"Join the revolution, comrade, or else fuck off!"

That is why I think about China so much.

A country of weaklings, even if they have guns, can only massacre unarmed people; if the enemy is also armed, the issue is uncertain. Only then is true strength and weakness revealed.

Lu Xun

I was reading a lot of Lu Xun in 1990. Lu (1881–1936) is China's greatest modern writer. Everyone agrees with this assessment, rare in a nation where the back half of the century—i.e., the People's Republic of China, established in 1949—has little good to say about the front half. Communist China or, more precisely, Mao Zedong, had only praise for Lu Xun. In 1940, while still a rebel leader, Mao enshrined the dead writer in his pantheon of revolutionary heroes. His essay on Lu was subsequently read and reread, committed to memory, and recited in dreams by generations of Chinese. Lu Xun's short story "The Real Story of Ah Q" has appeared on every curriculum in every high school in the country for the last fifty years. According to the party line, typified by a capsule summary of the official English-language edition, "The Real Story of Ah Q," a savagely ironic tale of a foolish man so befuddled by his allegiances to various unworthy masters that he winds up cheering at his own execution, "bitterly criticizes the bourgeoisie, which led the 1911 Revolution and failed to arouse the peasants."

Lu did become a communist late in life. Still, he would have been amused by the embrace of Mao Zedong, no friend to real authors or thinkers. A writer steeped in irony, he would have smiled at how earnestly his fiction came to be "read." A translator himself, he would have shaken his head when the English translator of his stories, instructed to fan the revolutionary flames, rendered the book title *Call to Arms,* instead of the more accurate *Cheering from the Sidelines.* Lu, a private, unflashy person, would have rolled his eyes at the statues of him all over China, the museums dedicated to his life and work, his surviving pens and cigarette cases, robes and toiletries, now under glass in Shanghai and Beijing. Had he survived to witness 1949, by then an elder of sixty-eight, he would surely have begun almost at once to criticize the new regime for its extermination campaign against rural landlords. A critic of false language, he likely would not have waited long before commenting on how closed doors seemed to be to "the peasants" in this new "dictatorship of the proletariat." A hater of despots, he would have wondered aloud about the growing deification of Mao Zedong, a process so similar to the exaltation of emperors. He would, in short, have noted the same old national characteristics bubbling up to the surface of the revolution, threatening to render it no more than a skewed version of the venerable Chinese cycle: absolute power, once solidified, absolutely enforced.

Lu Xun would have said all this and written it down with his usual candour, sending his essays to the dwindling number of newspapers that dared publish them. Then, still wryly bemused—if also appalled—he might have gone on to predict his own imminent arrest and denouncement by, or on behalf of, the same Chairman Mao Zedong who had previously called him immortal. I doubt Lu would have fled China. I suspect he would have died in disgrace, possibly in prison.

Lu lived, in other words, a free man. He was born Zhou Shuren—most Chinese writers used pen names—into a middle-class Zhejiang province family that had fallen on hard times. His early life coincided with the dimming of the corrupt and inept Qing Dynasty. While a young adult studying medicine in Japan, Lu had an epiphany. Unless China was dragged into modernity, it would never be free of internal tyrants or external aggressors. He quit medicine in 1907 to begin an itinerant career as translator, teacher, and author. The first decades of the new century witnessed endless upheaval in China, and when Lu wasn't relocating for a job, he was fleeing warlords incensed by his writings. He eventually found sanctuary in the international concession of Shanghai and lived the last nine years of his life there, protected from prosecution—and summary execution, most likely—by the reality of a Chinese city carved up by foreign occupiers, where the laws of the land and their enforcers had no authority.

Though Lu's fiction made him famous, his brilliance was best served by the short essays he wrote for newspapers and magazines. He more or less invented the form called *zawen,* a cross between a personal column and an epigrammatic philosophical essay. In the spring of 1990, I was rereading his *zawen* "Some Notions Jotted Down by Lamplight," a piece first published in 1925. Lu begins with an anecdote: how, during a period of hyperinflation in China, he traded his own plummeting currency for silver at some forty per cent of its face value. Later, when offered fifty per cent, he felt grateful to take only a half loss. "How easy it is for us to become slaves," he concludes, "and to revel in our slavery!"

Three thousand years of Chinese history are condensed into two categories. The first, eras of social disorder and even anarchy, are dubbed "the periods when we longed in vain to be slaves." The second, those epochs when the country was unified by a strong, generally ruthless leader, Lu calls "the periods when we succeeded in becoming slaves for a time." What period, he asks of the 1920s, is China in now? He knows many citizens are nostalgic for the good old days of being outright slaves. Lu offers them hope. "Those who hanker after the past need not feel pessimistic. To all appearances there is still peace; for though there are often wars, droughts and floods, have you ever heard anyone raise his voice in protest?"

Suddenly, he shifts metaphor. "Our vaunted Chinese civilization," he writes, "is only a feast of human flesh prepared for the rich and mighty. And China is only the kitchen where those feasts are prepared." Cannibalism was Lu Xun's most outrageous weapon. He used it sparingly, but unflinchingly. In the short story "Medicine," a poor family, at the mercy of superstition and ignorance, hands over its life savings to feed its dying child the blood of another human being. In "Some Notions Jotted Down by Lamplight," he disavows even the metaphorical protection of "Medicine." The Chinese, he says outright, are "intoxicated" by their own civilization. In a way, being Chinese keeps people from acting human. Thus, "they cannot feel each other's pain; and because each can hope to enslave and eat other men, he forgets he may be enslaved and eaten himself." He ends with a warning: "Feasts of human flesh are still being spread even now and many people will want them to continue."

The essay issues a plea to foreigners who interact with China. Westerners, Lu complains, are forever lauding the Chinese for their excellent culture and enigmatic but splendid ways. He decries the tendencies of outsiders not to comment on or criticize China. By keeping aloof, the rest of world is, by default, encouraging the country to remain in bondage. He gives an example. The British philosopher Bertrand Russell had recently visited the middle kingdom. According to Lu Xun, Russell "praised the Chinese when some sedan-chair bearers smiled at him." Of this tiny incident, he makes two requests: that the "chair bearers stop smiling at their fares" and that Westerners quit automatically admiring all things Chinese, including impoverished rickshaw boys. That kind of admiration, he implies, masks either condescension—the secret view that China is so inferior as to not be worth engaging—or else represents a hangover from the nineteenth-century European fashion of oriental exoticism, which objectified the nation as silky and refined, mysterious and barbarous, a travel destination that promised plenty of moral, social, and even sexual frissons.

I sat up at Lu's twin directives. "Some Notions," born of rage at the way authority was exercised and dissent suppressed in 1920s China, might have been written about the democracy movement and June 4. Deng Xiaoping and his carefully chosen generals—old men, one and all—had feasted on their own children. Worse still, their paranoia had trickled down into society, even to the students themselves. Three young teachers who tossed ink-filled eggs at the portrait of Chairman Mao on Tiananmen Square during one demonstration were turned in by student leaders who feared the men were undercover agents, their actions calculated to bring disgrace upon the movement. The teachers were given lengthy jail terms, including a life sentence for the instigator, a twenty-seven-year-old named Yu Zhijian. After the massacre, a Beijinger volunteered what he witnessed—clashes between military and civilians, soldiers shooting protestors in the back—to an international TV crew. Next day, Chinese television flashed a clip of the interview, urging citizens to turn in this enemy of the state. Less than twenty-four hours later, the evening news showed the man, handcuffed and worse for his arrest, apologizing for spreading lies and counter-revolutionary propaganda. Two frumpy women smiled for the camera, proud of having ratted on their neighbour, done their duty for China.

Lu Xun's essay may have been addressing Bertrand Russell and his fellow early-century visitors, but his argument about foreigners applied equally to us, and to how we should respond to the Tiananmen massacre. Our friends in Beijing were hardly smiling for their fares. My wife and I hoped we were seeing these people for who they were: Gao Gianbao the joker and Shen Hong the reader of foreign novels, Liu Junhui who could not imagine his life without beer. Nothing inscrutable about them. Nothing oriental exotic. Quite the opposite: the way this generation of urbanites—the only Chinese people we knew, in effect—had gone about expressing their will and individuality struck a familiar note. Television series like *River Elegy* and films like Chen Kaige's *Yellow Earth,* the music of Cui Jian and poetry of Bei Dao, the novels of Wang Meng and Wang Shuo, all adopted attitudes and stances, aesthetics and convictions, that showed the clear, happy influence of Western artistic and intellectual modes. Cui Jian blended folk melodies with rock and roll and reggae, ska, and jazz. Wang Shuo wrote streetwise novels about dropouts that had more in common with Kerouac and Kafka than any of the Chinese classics. Chen Kaige's early movies, like those of Zhang Yimou, his fellow former Red Guard and member of the group known as the Fifth Generation filmmakers, presented China onscreen as no one had before: a country trapped in the nightmare of its own myths and traditions. Likewise, *River Elegy* used the Yellow River, with its meandering trajectory and unpredictable, often disastrous, siltings as a metaphor for the course of Han civilization for the last several thousand years.

I could watch these movies and listen to this music, read these books in translation, and connect with their spirit. (Could an image have been more accommodating than the Goddess of Democracy, modelled on the Statue of Liberty in New York's harbour?) I could connect with those Chinese in the thrall of such a courageous, even reckless cultural awakening. Among this group, the words "Confucius" and "family values" and all the old truths of Chinese thinking, the emotional verities of sentimentality and fatalism, came up only for discussion. Friends were equally disinclined to dwell on personal histories. Most had grown up during the Cultural Revolution and witnessed appalling degradations within their communities and, often enough, their own homes. Still, they weren't interested in viewing themselves as victims or categories or even just one more jaw-dropping Chinese story of suffering and survival. Multi-generational memoirs and Amy Tan opuses may have begun their assault on Western readers, but back in China—or, again, among the young Beijingers we encountered—there was scant enthusiasm for such narratives. These Chinese had other things on their minds. Their heads were filling with alternative notions of self-definition.

No disrespect was being shown to the deep structures of the civilization, and certainly no one was calling for the old culture to be obliterated, as Mao Zedong had done, for his own twisted reasons, two decades before. The issue was the same as it had been for Lu Xun in 1907: to drag China into (post) modernity, to expand and enrich the national debate, to forge a new, more inclusive polity.

That had been the fuel that fired the democracy movement—more a movement of consciousness—in 1989. That had been the challenge that the authorities, especially once the goddess was wheeled onto the square, had responded to with such ferocity. (The statue was a tactical error, and perhaps too confrontational—or simply alien—an image.) Even one year later, with all concerned reeling in the aftermath of the crackdown, it still seemed the fire could be kept lit.

In April 1990, my wife and I attended a performance in the Beijing Concert Hall. On the bill was the violin concerto *Butterfly Lovers.* Friends insisted that if we wanted to understand China, we had to hear the concerto performed live. *Butterfly Lovers,* composed in 1949, had already suffered for its nation. The piece had been an immediate hit. The central melody borrowed from a sorrowful folk song. The story, told mostly by a dolorous violin, was a local version of Romeo and Juliet: star-crossed lovers and tragic love, everyone dead at the end. The piece was lush and emotive, unashamed of its tug on the culture's heartstrings. Judging from the twelve hundred Chinese who sat hushed and enthralled that night, so moved they could barely applaud at the end, the music had tugged hard indeed. Just the same, the concerto had been banned during the Cultural Revolution and then resurrected in the early 1980s. Programmers had apparently hesitated to schedule it in the wake of June 4, and were only now willing to risk letting audiences in the capital hear it again.

All this could mean one thing: the significance of *Butterfly Lovers* went far beyond its notes. Zealots feared the music. Self-censoring instincts warned of its powers. My ear heard a sweet, if conventional piece that wore its emotions on its sleeve: a cross between Pachelbel's *Canon* and Williams's *The Lark Ascending*. My heart, however, being tone deaf, declared the concerto to have an entirely different sound. Chinese and foreigners alike in the audience were in agreement, I decided, about the experience of *Butterfly Lovers* that evening. We agreed on the musical form we had just heard: a charged lament. We agreed on the subject of the lamentation: the Tiananmen Square massacre. We even agreed on the context—the injustice of a society forever at the mercy of its despots—and a way out: not taking it anymore.

In 1992, back in Canada, I published a book of my experiences in China called *Sketches in Winter*. For an account of the student movement, I used quotes from Lu Xun's essays as a guide. For the bulk of the text, I relied on the personalities of our university friends, and the drama of the 1989 to 1990 period, to craft a tale that would show the David and Goliath conflict between the two visions of China's destiny. Not content to let the narrative do its job, I ended several chapters with images of the cooking and eating of human flesh. I wanted to make Lu's fierce point; I wanted to be the sort of foreigner that he would have declared a genuine friend to China. When the typeset manuscript came back from the copy editor, the material had vanished. I read the text twice before even noticing the cuts. Still, I called my editor for an explanation. The metaphor wasn't working, she apologized. It seemed over the top. Outraged, I went on at some length about how fundamental cannibalism was to the book's schema. How outsiders had to understand this about the country. How so few really did. My editor suggested I sleep on it. I did sleep, until a thought jolted me awake: *Why hadn't I noticed the material had been deleted? Because it wasn't working? Because it was transparently tacked on?*

I let the deletions stand. There were some things I could not claim to know. There were some places I simply could not go.

> *A handful of people first staged turmoil, which later*
> *developed into a counter-revolutionary rebellion. Their*
> *aim was to overthrow the Communist Party, topple the*
> *socialist system, and establish a bourgeois republic.*
>
> Deng Xiaoping, June 9, 1989

The Chinese government filed June 4 as a treasonous uprising and has since refused to reconsider its verdict. The state offered its urban population, especially the generation that succeeded the one shattered by the massacre, a deal: material prosperity in exchange for pretending the past had not occurred. The media got behind the revision, and the spring of 1989 wound up virtually erased from sanctioned memory, the way purged leaders were once airbrushed out of photographs. Student leaders fled into exile, sometimes after serving prison terms, and now live in the United States and Canada, France and Taiwan. Artists either left China or else shifted away from contemporary topics and problematic metaphors. (Only a few, like the musician Cui Jian, have managed to remain both vital and at large inside their homeland.) Our Beijing friends now mostly reside in the West. One works for a software company in San Francisco. Another lives in Toronto. Gao Gianbao spent the 1990s in northern Europe. Shen Hong enjoys the half-in, half-out life of a secretary in the special administrative region of Shenjen, near Hong Kong. Liu Junhui, who counselled friends and strangers alike to join the revolution, comrade, or else fuck off, has disappeared. Efforts to locate him have failed, and when I returned to the college in 1998, I found no one who even remembered the film teacher. The entire English department faculty had changed in less than a decade. The names I tried on a secretary drew blanks or else vague recollections of that woman taking a job with a company in Shanghai, that man accepting a scholarship in Texas and never returning.

And the Yellow River resumed its meandering and silting.

And what period was the 1990s: one of being slaves or of longing to be slaves?

And though I dare not speak of cannibalism, Yu Zhijian, the young teacher who threw ink at the portrait of Mao, is still serving his sentence, which the government eventually reduced to a mere seventeen years, on account of the prisoner having shown "an attitude of repentance."

My wife and I spent 1997 to 1998 in Hong Kong with our two daughters. We wanted to get back to China. We wanted to witness the first year of mainland rule for the former British colony. I wound up staying an extra month and attended a concert one night in July. The program offered a selection from the score to a popular television adaptation of *A Dream of Red Mansions,* the novel considered the greatest work of literature in the Chinese canon.

I had the read the book years before. Written in the mid-eighteenth century by Tsao Hsueh-chin, *Red Mansions* sprawls for nearly two thousand pages without often leaving the confines of the houses—palaces, really—of four wealthy families. Little happens inside the compounds, aside from countless small acts of cruelty, and the many, many characters are all very, very unhappy. The red mansions, of course, are China itself, imprisoned by its feudal skin, doomed never to step outdoors. (Zhang Yimou used the same metaphor in his 1991 film *Raise the Red Lantern.*) I appreciated the theme and, though receptive to it, still found the novel stultifying. Most Chinese love *Red Mansions* more for its overripe characters than grand metaphors. A mood of profound melancholy clouds the narrative. Fate keeps lovers apart, dreams go unfulfilled, and people living in close proximity still never manage, over the course of decades and hundreds of pages, to say what is on their minds.

The score to the adaptation, naturally, was two-hanky material. To my own astonishment, I loved every note of it. I adored the pinched-nose vocals of traditional singing styles. I couldn't get enough weepy *erhu*—a two-stringed instrument with a sombre tone—counterpointed with a full string orchestra. Mindful of my earlier misreading of *Butterfly Lovers,* I let the music be, allowing it to wash over me as it would any other audience member. As in Beijing, the waves of sentiment and plangent emotion visibly affected the crowd. Young lovers squeezed hands. Women quietly sobbed. An older man's eyes welled up, though he held back tears. Among the Chinese, I presumed, the music triggered both general emotions and personal stories. Hong Kong, after all, was a refugee colony; just about everyone had left some place, someone, behind. Silence greeted the conclusion of the final selection, which featured four vocal soloists, the orchestra, and a choir of eighty men and women, but soon the hall had climbed up to its collective feet. Though aware that I probably hadn't been overwhelmed by the music for the same reasons as the others, I joined in.

Next day I bought the CD and listened to it obsessively for the rest of the month. Back in Canada, I shared the discovery with my wife. The music *A Dream of Red Mansions,* I explained to her, captured the essence of the Chinese world view. Not the view of our friends in Beijing, necessarily, or of their generation, or even of Lu Xun, but of the other China, the one rooted in family ties that bind and fates that cannot be escaped. The one that hears *Butterfly Lovers* as the once and future tragedy it is, rather than a trumpet to present change. The China, in short, that everyone has been telling us about in different films and music, all those memoirs and best-selling novels. Finally, I had come upon that place. Finally, I had recognized that country.

I need to think about China a lot more.

1999

If the Nail Sticks Out, Hammer It Down

(Japanese Proverb)

ERNA PARIS

I HAVE ALWAYS BEEN FASCINATED by traditional Japanese architecture, by those simple wooden houses with wide screened doors that slide open to reveal the whole, or merely a part, of what is outside. The reality of "out there" can be framed through those movable screens, according to inclination. If there is a formal garden attached to the house, as there often is, one can observe it from different perspectives simply by adjusting the aperture of the screen. I have imagined the experience to be a powerful one, for like a god, one shapes reality. Metaphysical too, since the very idea of movable, fluid space raises all those unresolvable philosophical questions about what is truly "there."

Recently, I have begun to practise "seeing" from different perspectives. First I look only at shapes and lines. Then I look only at shades of colour. Afterwards I try to put it all together. This is new for me because I am neither a painter nor a photographer, but I have of late grown intrigued by the idea that separating out the elements of an experience, then putting them together again, may help me understand other things that seem impossibly, dauntingly, difficult. I am trying to grasp what is at the essence of things that have already happened, of historical events. This strikes me as important, even urgent, because what we believe about our past dictates what we think about the present, and our expectations about the shape of the future.

The question is, Who decides what actually happened yesterday, or the day before? Who, in other words, gets to write history, the to codify it as "fact" for the generations to come? From the spin imposed by opinion makers to the careful creation of national myths, the struggle to shape memory is a deadly serious business. Dire conflicts endure. Take, for example, the Second World War. Fifty years later, the tragedy of the murdered Jews of Europe remains subject to outright denial and powerful propaganda campaigns designed to capture and reframe the tale for future generations. A Canadian television documentary about the war unleashes a whirlwind of accusation from veterans who were on the spot, and whose commemorative approach to memory seems not to include sojourning in the archives. And in America, the memory of the attack on Pearl Harbor continues to impose itself with such power that a proposed 1995 exhibition at the Smithsonian Institution about what happened to the peoples of Hiroshima and Nagasaki when atomic bombs were dropped on their cities is cancelled amid cries that the curators and historians are liars and "anti-American." There is much at stake in these passionate debates: national pride, personal honour, and the maintaining of mythologies. But underneath the noise and diversion lie the bleached bones of fact and truth.

American perceptions about the conflict aside, Japan truly is a case in point. During its fifteen-year war of expansion (1931–1945), that country committed atrocities that are little talked about in the West, such as the so-called Nanking massacre, during which thousands of Chinese civilians were hacked to death or destroyed in other imaginative ways by soldiers who were loosed on the population to indulge their murderous fantasies. Crimes such as these were either unknown or displaced from the centre stage of memory by the horror of the atomic bomb attacks: for fifty years, these have commanded the exclusive attention of both the Japanese and ourselves. Selective vision, perhaps? Or the magic of sliding screens that train the eye on one part of the garden, obscuring the rest?

I learned about what happened in Hiroshima many years ago, in a moment I can summon on a private screen of memory whenever I choose. Through a distant lens I see my child-self curled up in the family reading chair, flush beside the wall of books I was trying to ingest one by one. Our imposing *Webster's* stood there, alone and aloof on its regal stand, my gateway to language and silent home to legions of my pressed flowers, including a veritable four-leaf clover I had recently discovered in the park down the street. The book I held in my hand that day had been picked off the shelf at random.

When I opened *Hiroshima,* John Hersey's seminal reportage on the calamity, my knowledge of the Second World War was limited to having learned to use a pencil by printing large, looped words of encouragement to our soldiers across the sea, and to having chanted skipping-rope ditties that exhorted young maidens to "turn your backs to the German submarines." As for human suffering, well, let us say I had been protected. That long afternoon of reading ended innocence as images printed themselves indelibly on my memory. Drowning people clogging the Ota River that traversed the city, gasping and clutching at falling debris while the nuclear fire devoured their streets. Melted eyes running down faces. And the horror of the verb Hersey used to describe what was happening to those who had survived the initial seconds. Their skin, he said, "sloughed" off their bodies.

All this came to mind recently when an invitation to Japan arrived at our house—addressed not to me, but to my husband, as it happened—holding a promise of two plane tickets. I hesitated at first. It took me a moment to remember that the Hiroshima of childhood memory and repressed imagination was actually located there, and the prospect of confronting the reconstructed city in present time and real space felt strangely daunting. On the other hand, I had spent years exploring the broken patterns of human cruelty and kindness from more distanced perspectives, and the chance to follow through on John Hersey's work, half a century later, drew me irresistibly. I knew, for example, that some survivors of the Nazi Holocaust, that other previously unthinkable catastrophe of our era, had been able to piece together an emotional existence, while others lived a death-in-life, and that the denial of their historical experience caused unimaginable despair in all. How, I asked myself, did the nuclear survivors of Hiroshima understand *their* suffering? Nazi death-camp survivors could look to written histories that traced the path leading to their tragedy. Was there a similar context to events in Japan?

Might I glimpse the "screens" that contour history? Had fact and memory converged?

The Shinkansen Bullet train speeds and rocks along its track heading south out of Osaka. Yesterday I walked broad streets amid hundreds of businessmen identically dressed in dark suits, white shirts, ties, black shoes—most of whom were carrying cell phones and briefcases—and uniformed schoolchildren on outings, marching dutifully behind stern-looking teachers who barked authoritatively into bullhorns. In Namba, "pleasure quarter" of the city, yellow, red, and white neon flashed incessantly, advertising largely in English, though curiously no one seemed to speak the language. Ornamental snob-English, as a friend put it, with sometimes curious results. In an attempt to communicate "snooty" class appeal, one women's hairdressing salon had proudly named itself Miss Snot.

Raucous, Western music poured out of cavernous pachinko parlours in which people of all ages could be seen staring mesmerized at video screens of dancing pinballs, some working the levers with gloved hands. Back-to-back restaurants advertised dinner with life-sized plastic moulages, and miniskirted hostesses literally chased after groups of salarymen who were preparing to do business after hours. This was Japan in 1996: rich, and apparently Westernized.

The contours of the Japanese landscape float by the train window, ugly urban sprawl linking city to city for hundreds of kilometres. Then intriguing hints of transition. A rice paddy surrounds a low-lying, traditional home with a pagoda-style, red-tiled roof, but it is sandwiched on either side by fat, industrial chimneys that belch columns of noxious smoke into the sky. The Japanese have a highly developed aesthetic, as displayed in their magic screens; their carefully structured gardens are admired; their appreciation of visual and literary artistry is perhaps unrivalled. Yet outside this train the land looks blighted and unzoned.

This strange juxtaposition of rural rice paddies—the landscape of old Japan—with unregulated, post-war growth was a striking metaphor for the identity transitions I had been reading about. The old and the new flat up against each other, without space for reflection or perspective—and certainly without screens to highlight or conceal aspects of reality. No surprise, perhaps, that the Japanese seem constantly to wonder who they are or, more to the point, who they ought to be. Are they a "Western" nation? They have a constitution and a democratic political system, so perhaps they qualify in that respect. And they are, at least for the moment, the richest, most technologically advanced nation on Earth. Certainly, no population uses more cell phones, although the vision of a lone businessman smiling broadly and bowing vigorously on an Osaka street corner as he presumably clinched a deal over his phone was hardly a Western sight. McDonald's and Burger King recently registered the highest restaurant sales in the country, elbowing out purveyors of sushi, sashimi, and tempura. Is this is a sign of Westernization?

I must also point out that the Japanese consume large amounts of chewing gum, an American habit they picked up from the US soldiers who occupied their country from 1945 until 1952. More than one writer has reminisced nostalgically about the discarded silver wrappers that glittered in the streets of his or her childhood, and the first person to welcome me when I arrived here immediately offered me a stick of the stuff, presumably to make me feel at home. Perhaps Wrigley's gum stood for freedom, or democracy, as these ideas were understood, or, at the very least, for a new world in which people could be independent and need no longer vow to give their lives for an emperor who was believed to be descended from a god, as they did during the Second World War. Emperor worship was a brief phenomenon in the context of a millennium of Japanese history, but it was powerful and reassuring; within his symbolic self, the emperor embodied and protected the essence of his people. Adolf Hitler has been described by German psychologists Alexander and Margarethe Mitscherlich as "an object on which Germans depended, to which they transferred responsibility." This was even more the case in pre-1945 Japan, when Emperor Hirohito was also "divine."

The frenetic consumerism that marks Japanese society today—matched in my observation only by Hong Kong, where there is no rest from buying and selling—is in itself a source of cultural tension. For until the end of the war and the advent of Wrigley's, Japan thought of itself as a place of *spirit,* as opposed to the crass materialism of the West. "Spirit" had many uses. For example, it informed the building of the houses, that contained the screens, that shaped the view of the garden. According to feng shui ("wind and water"), an ancient tradition borrowed from China, a Shintoist priest "reads" the land on which a house is to be built to ensure favourable conditions that will not disturb the gods. Intriguingly, wind and water—spirit elements both—had figured in each of John Hersey's survivor's tales: just after the explosion, a blast of wind travelling at a speed of 440 metres per second seized the city, followed by the crush of the wounded as they stumbled toward the waters of the Ota River.

Spirit. It was this emphasis that made it possible for an entire nation to give itself up to the perceived holy will of the god-emperor and to work together in the war effort as a disciplined colony of antlike humans who operated according to a hierarchy of status and designated place. In her classic study of Japanese culture, *The Chrysanthemum and the Sword,* anthropologist Ruth Benedict describes how the authorities propagandized the dominance of spirit over matter at the most literal level. To a population exhausted by bombings and twelve-hour working days, they announced, "The heavier our bodies, the higher our spirit rises above them … The wearier we are, the more splendid the training." To people with too little to eat and nothing to keep them warm, the authorities pre-scribed body-heating calisthenics. Only materialistic Americans needed to worry about physical deprivations, they said.

Not surprisingly, the very Westernization that has turned Japan into a rich land of imported BMWs and cell phones continues to coexist in subterranean conflict with the old spiritual values that were ostensibly tossed out the window in favour of the post-war so-called economic miracle. I say "ostensibly," because just behind the veil of Westernization—admittedly opaque though it may be—the old culture is still visible, like the rice paddy beside the smoke stack. Take the salarymen in their interchangeable dark suits and ties with matching briefcases. An acquaintance suggested laughingly that they are, in effect, the new ruling samurai. The samurai, he explained, were compelled to dress in a costume that denoted their class and their status within the group. Today, the ruling class of businessmen conforms to similar expectations.

A theory, of course, but to my eyes, group conformity was emerging as the most strikingly *non*-Western aspect of Japan. Blue-collar workers all wore uniforms denoting their position and com-pany; and the so-called office ladies—young, unmarried women who do clerical work and make tea—wore a female version of the dark suit and buttoned-up white shirt. The uniforms of the school-children were the most interesting and ambiguous. Although Japan does not have an official army—the famous Article Nine of their US-imposed constitution expressly forbids this and is referred to in tones of hushed reverence by liberals and leftists who continue to mistrust their own country—the legions of students in railway stations and on city streets are dressed in what look distinctly like military uniforms. The boys wear buttoned-up "army jackets," and the girls wear the middy blouses of the navy. State public schools dictate hair lengths and what, if any, jewellery can be worn—difference of any kind is not much appreciated. In Nagasaki, for example, the one Japanese city with a history of foreign settlement, children with curly hair have been subject to attacks in the schoolyard, and families with mixed blood dating from the presence of the Dutch in the last century have been known to worry anxiously lest someone with a "long nose" be born to them.

I had been talking to an acquaintance about this, and she recited an ancient national proverb: *Derukui wa utareru*—If the nail sticks out, hammer it down. Such discomfort with individualism and minimal diversity is an unpleasant reminder of Japan's formerly notorious racial preoccupations, and because I was headed for Hiroshima, I began to wonder how the survivors of that terror had seen themselves and been seen by their compatriots. A human being who has been pumped full of gamma rays, or whose face has been burned off, could hardly be more "different."

In the West, the survivors of Hiroshima and Nagasaki were caught, collectively, in the amber of memory, including my own, of course; but simultaneously over the decades they have receded into amorphous symbolism. They and their bombed cities metamorphosed into stand-ins for end-games and a half century of brinkmanship during which doomsday clocks ticked off the moments to nuclear disaster and puffed-up leaders strutted across the world stage. From time to time, we were informed that the survivors suffered, still, from radiation sickness, into the second generation, but while worldwide movements arose to ban the bomb, the survivors themselves seemed to have been eclipsed. Perhaps they were bypassed by the emerging story of the Holocaust and the Jews. Or obscured by the enduring memory of Pearl Harbor, an act of Japanese aggression that brought the United States into the fray and "justified," according to some, a nuclear attack on civilians. Whatever the reason, they seemed to have dissolved into abstract symbols of the anti-nuclear peace movement. What I already knew before arriving in

Hiroshima was that a massive, government-endorsed, anti-nuclear movement had grown there. What I did not yet know was whether it was connected to any historical memory of war.

The young woman wearing the uniform of Japan Railways carries her tray of goodies up the aisle; she turns to bow deeply and thank us before she leaves the car. *Arigato, arigato gozaimasu.* Thank you, thank you very much. The forms of the language are deeply courteous. Then an announcement over the system: next stop, Hiroshima.

I am breathing a little faster and am acutely aware of the child who once sat curled up in the safety of her parents' home, reading John Hersey. I am aware of the images that were burned into memory that day. Thinking of the screens that shape perception.

The taxi approaches the famous Ota River and an image of burnt, drowning people passes before my eyes. I flinch, look away. I am angry at myself. I have come to see and I cannot look. River of myth and death. The astonishing Canadian director Robert Lepage has mounted an opera on the theme of this river and the memory of survival. Others, exploring the aftermath of the bomb in fiction, film, or documentary, have featured the Ota as central to the tale. In real time and space, it happens to be evening rush hour in Hiroshima, and the rebuilt modern metropolis is at its busiest. It suddenly occurs to me that I may be the only person in the city who is thinking about that long-ago August day.

The taxi crosses the bridge and I compel myself to look. The Ota is beautiful. It cuts through the centre of the city in its several branches and is surrounded in places by parks. There are people sitting on the banks enjoying the late-afternoon sun.

My interpreter, Keiko Ogura, is a no-nonsense professional who is accustomed to ferrying foreign visitors about her famous town in her white BMW. Most visitors from abroad come to explore the "Hiroshima spirit," she tells me. The "Hiroshima spirit" stands for the anti-nuclear movement that has made this city a pilgrimage centre for peace activists all over the world. We drive past Hiroshima Peace Memorial Park. It is a huge tract of green studded with monuments built around the hypocentre of the explosion. There are hundreds of uniformed schoolchildren on the grounds along with their megaphoned teachers.

The business of Hiroshima wasn't always peace, although few official spokespeople for the city are likely to dwell on that. Hiroshima was an important military centre from the time of the restoration of the Meiji emperor in 1868. The Imperial Headquarters, Japan's supreme military command, was moved here to direct operations during the Sino-Japanese War of 1894 to 1895, and Hiroshima was a main launching base for attacks during the Pacific War. On the day of the A-bomb, there were approximately 350,000 people in the city, including at least 40,000 soldiers, and although the target of the *Enola Gay* was originally meant to be Fukuyama— a city up the coast on the Inland Sea—there seem to have been plenty of military reasons to have chosen Hiroshima.

The war-focused community of Hiroshima acted as one in the spirit of national service. Neighbours watched neighbours to make sure everyone pulled his or her weight. No one doubted that the war would be won, because military battle was an outward expression of the mystical Japanese spirit. Yesterday, the sword of the samurai; today, guns and naval boats. Incessant propaganda reinforced this thinking. In the 1930s, General Araki, Minister of War, wrote a pamphlet addressed "To the Whole Japanese Race" in which he stated that the mission of Japan was "to spread and glorify the Imperial Way to the end of the Four Seas. Inadequacy of strength is not our worry. Why should we worry about that which is material?"

To counter niggling doubt on the part of ordinary folk who did, indeed, worry about such things as sending a beloved son to war or the possibility of being commanded to pilot a kamikaze suicide bomber, propaganda broadcasts announced that the

Japanese spirit could conquer death itself: the spirit could be trained to survive by self-discipline. Extravagant? Perhaps only to determinedly secular, Western ears. In a Buddhist-Shintoist nation where self-control, meditation, and the quest for spiritual enlightenment were an ancient way of life and where houses were built so as not to offend the gods, the transfer of religious values to the political arena was not as big a leap as it might seem.

Early in the morning of August 6, 1945, the *Enola Gay* lifted off the runway on Tinian Island in the Pacific. The American B-29 was carrying a 10,000-pound atomic bomb named Little Boy. At 8:15 A.M., the crew of the aircraft released its cargo over Hiroshima. The bomb exploded with a brilliant flash, followed by a deafening blast, and a powerful shock wave releasing radiation in all directions. A fireball roared over ground zero until temperatures approximated those of the sun; a giant mushroom cloud reached toward the sky. Within seconds, half the population was dead and the city was destroyed.

Fifty-one years later, Mrs. Chiyoko Watanabe extends her hand in the lobby of one of the city's best hotels. White hair floats about her face and her expression is open and warm. She has dressed up for this occasion in a carefully pressed print suit and an amber necklace. A large scar marks her forehead. Today is her seventy-fourth birthday.

One of the survivors John Hersey followed was a doctor who worked at the Red Cross Hospital, the largest medical facility in Hiroshima. Of 150 physicians in the city, 65 were killed instantly and most of the rest were wounded. Of 1,780 nurses, 1,654 were dead or too hurt to work. Chiyoko Watanabe was one of the 126 surviving nurses able to help that day. She too worked at the Red Cross Hospital, just 1,650 yards from ground zero.

She was twenty-two years old and already a widow. Earlier she had answered the national call to write letters to lonely young men at the front. After several years her correspondent proposed. She accepted, and he came home for their wedding. The marriage lasted three days. He returned to duty and was shot down over China.

At 8:15 A.M. on August 6, Mrs. Watanabe was in her office on the second floor of the hospital, standing in front of her desk. A young trainee was writing something at the next desk. Suddenly there was a blinding flash followed by a boom, and what felt like a tornado whipped through the room. Mrs. Watanabe was knocked unconscious, and when she came to about fifteen minutes later, her colleague had disappeared. Blown away, or vaporized. No one ever saw her again.

Glass shards had speared Mrs. Watanabe's face. The biggest one was lodged in her forehead, and the blood flowing from her wounds blinded her. She ran to the bandage room, but everything had been blown away. A towel remained in the toilet. She wrapped it around her head.

The hospital was in chaos. Walls and ceilings had fallen on patients, and the wind following the blast had shattered windows. Blood splattered every room. Patients were dead or running about screaming. Miraculously, all of Mrs. Watanabe's soldier-patients had survived. She had been especially proud to be assigned to this group of men. To be a nurse had been her dream since childhood; to nurse wounded soldiers in the service of the emperor was her joyful duty.

The wounded were crushing the entrance to the hospital; more than 10,000 people would make their way there that day, to an institution that had only 600 beds, almost all of which had been destroyed. People lay on the floor, huddled on the stairs, collapsed on the sidewalk entrance; they vomited, bled, screamed, or lay quietly in shock. Some were burned black. It was impossible to know whether they were male or female.

The fire that started about an hour after the explosion quickly became a roaring inferno as the city's wooden houses fed the flames. Mrs. Watanabe now found herself the sole nurse in the hospital; all the others had run away. The post office next door caught fire, and it was urgent to move patients from the possible reach of flames. Mobile patients helped her move the stricken on canvas stretchers. They ran back and forth. There was no medical treatment, with the exception of Mercurochrome; several bottles had somehow survived.

The hospital did not burn, but by evening the remaining staff of about ten people were exhausted. No one had eaten (emergency hard tack would arrive only the next day), and dead bodies were beginning to putrefy in the heat. Frighteningly, people who had seemed relatively well earlier in the day were now dreadfully sick; some were dying. They had radiation sickness, a condition no one knew anything about.

In the foyer, the wounded and the dying pulled at Chiyoko Watanabe's legs as she passed, crying for water. One of them pleaded, "Stay with us. If you stay, we will be all right." For the first time in twelve hours she was overcome by hopelessness and desolation. "We will die here together," she promised him. Then she made a place for herself on the floor.

Mrs. Watanabe is deeply engrossed in the telling. Her eyes have filled with tears as she remembers, and she waves her hands as she speaks. I too am overwhelmed—by the strength and courage of this woman who was then a girl of twenty-two. I spontaneously take her hand, an old, gnarled hand that is shaking with emotion. I look at her so long and so deeply that for a moment I seem to lose myself. I am remembering a man named Menachem whom I met in Israel. When he was a boy he escaped the forced march from Auschwitz because a person like Mrs. Watanabe was entirely committed to saving him. Menachem's older brother ran for both their lives, carrying Menachem on his back.

Mrs. Watanabe developed radiation sickness and her white blood cell count fell to half the normal level, but, unlike many others, she never reported her illness. She is vague about this, but I gather she was too proud—or perhaps she was ashamed. Strange as this may seem, many people felt shame at being among the wounded. Women, in particular. During the years that followed, some never left their houses in daylight so as not to inflict the sight of their burnt, disfigured faces on others.

During the fifty years between then and now, Mrs. Watanabe has never thought about the bombing of her city in anything but personal, or perhaps local, terms. The second most terrible event in her life happened just nine days after the attack on Hiroshima, when Emperor Hirohito addressed the nation on radio and told his devastated subjects to "bear the unbearable." Japan was surrendering, he said, and furthermore, he was not a god. To a people for whom surrender meant unparalleled humiliation, the emperor's speech was, quite simply, unthinkable. Mrs. Watanabe says she "lost her will" that day, and that the strength that had carried her through—the idea that the bomb was but a terrible moment in a war that would eventually be won—seeped out of her and took a long time to return. All these years later she still "adores the emperor." "He is not the only one at fault, and he was never forced to admit to anything. So why should the Japanese people blame him?" she asks.

I was to hear this many times again, for Chiyoko Watanabe was offering the standard response to the unresolved, hanging-in-the-air question of national war guilt: the crimes committed in the name of the all-embracing leader. There *was* no historical context to Mrs. Watanabe's personal story of heroism and suffering. It was wartime, she said, and "it couldn't be helped." This common Japanese expression carried with it a deeply ingrained fatalism; I was later to learn that many individuals identified the atomic bomb attacks as one of the innumerable natural disasters Japan has been subject to over the centuries. This was one way of seeing, one way of angling the screen of reality. It was the way Chiyoko Watanabe understood her suffering.

She has lived the rest of her life in a highly structured society where unmarried, childless women have no identifiable place. She has suffered from a form of blood cancer for fifty years. What, I asked, has saved her from bitterness and despair? She answered without hesitation. "I have lived without a child, but I have been a nurse, and I think I have helped others," she said softly.

That night Mrs. Watanabe invites me to celebrate her birthday over dinner. We eat in the restaurant of my hotel, accompanied by the manager (acting as our interpreter), who listens attentively as she animatedly tells him her life story. "How do you stay healthy?" he asks her. This is the Hiroshima question. She orders the most expensive sashimi and tempura meal on the menu with much sake and beer. She looks happy and beautiful.

"She says you have a deep insight into what happened to us here and she is very moved." Mrs. Watanabe smiles broadly as he translates. Do I? *Arigatō gozaimasu,* thank you. But I'm not sure. What seems more likely is that Chiyoko Watanabe is alone in her seventy-fourth year, and a stranger from another country has listened with intense sympathy as she remembered the most difficult days of her life.

Sunao Tsuboi was a twenty-year-old university student on his way to school when he saw the flash and felt his body hurtling through the air. When he recovered consciousness, his sleeves and trousers were burning and his shoes had been blown away. He was bleeding from his left shoulder and hip, and his hands and feet were badly burned. The sky had turned black.

He began to run wildly, his shirt burning on his back. All around was silence. Tsuboi was close enough to the hypocentre to experience this strange initial quiet. Only at farther distances could sounds be heard.

He was running for the Ota River, whose floating, dying, human detritus John Hersey was to describe so vividly; and en route he saw terrible things that have never left his dreams. A schoolgirl whose right eye had popped out and whose hair was burning; a woman with a three-inch spear of glass in her head, running, like him, toward the river; another who was trying to push her intestines back into her body; an old man with a shard of glass in his lung, which was sliced open, so that every time he breathed, Tsuboi saw the lung move.

The fire in the city started, and a child trapped in a house was screaming for its mother. She was outside, in a panic, unable to help. Tsuboi suddenly felt cool and collected. "The war is just beginning," he shouted heroically. "Have courage, for the sake of the emperor!"

Tsuboi has a sense of irony. "I was abnormal," he says bitterly.

Eventually he reached one of the bridges over the river, but it was burning. Exhausted, burnt, and bleeding, he lay down on the road. With a piece of brick he carved "Tsuboi died here" into the pavement. But someone on a truck picked him up and took him to one of the ports. They took him because he was a young man who had had military training and might still be useful for the war effort. The old men, women, children, were left to die.

"Then, I was happy to be saved, but I am angry now," Tsuboi whispers, looking away. "They had no humanity."

He suffers debilitating guilt because he made it through and others did not, as do the still-preoccupied survivors of the Holocaust. During his thirties and forties he continually asked himself why he lived and by what right. Still, at age seventy-two, he dreams, and always someone is crying for help. He is accused. "Tsuboi!" shout his tormentors. "Why did you not help? Why, when you were chosen for life, did you not plead with your rescuers for the lives of others?"

We are talking across a table at the back of a makeshift storefront operation he heads called the Hiroshima Sufferers' Welfare Organization, which helps survivors with practical advice about medical referrals and how to access the tiny compensation the Japanese government provides. How apt the name, I think to myself: Hiroshima Sufferers. At a partially curtained-off table several feet away, a hunched, anxious-looking old woman is answering questions from a counsellor while her daughter sits beside her holding her hand. As for Tsuboi, his physical pain has largely abated, though the scars on his hands, face, and arms are terrible to see. Hiroshima survivors speak of "scars of the heart." Tsuboi has these as well.

In his final moments, he too was saved by friendship. The soldiers had left him at one of the ports along with 20,000 other wounded men who, if they survived, might eventually be taken to Ninoshima Island, where medical care was available, when he was discovered by a classmate. He is still overcome by the memory: "He recognized me in spite of my wounds." Although his friend also was seriously wounded, he carried Tsuboi to the pier and onto the ship.

Tsuboi slipped into a coma that lasted forty days, during which all his hair fell out and his skin peeled off. He breathed with difficulty, and for two months the doctor told his mother, who had somehow found him, that he was unlikely to survive the day. When maggots invaded his "dead" flesh, his mother removed them with tweezers. Later she told him his ears had literally been hanging from his head.

On January 10, 1946, Tsuboi sat up in bed for the first time. In 1948 he tentatively resumed his life.

The suffering of the survivors of Hiroshima did not end with partial physical recovery. They lived, and continue to live, in fear of radiation effects. They were different in a society in which no "nail" was allowed to stick out. Some of them were badly disfigured and were shunned. Parents conducted careful research on their children's prospective mates—survivors were unwelcome. Having been exposed to radiation, it was assumed they would die young and leave their spouse widowed. Or that they would pass on mutated genes to their offspring.

Tsuboi fell in love, but his girlfriend's parents refused to accept him. The couple decided to meet secretly, but her parents found out and told Tsuboi's mother that her son was trying to kidnap their daughter. Seven years later they relented, but only after their daughter threatened suicide.

They were married more than forty years. She died in 1995.

Tsuboi also suffered discrimination in employment. Because it was assumed (rightly, as it happened) that he would spend much of his life in hospitals, he was unable to find work in his field of engineering. He became a schoolteacher at the junior high level, but was promoted only toward the end of his career. In fact, he was lucky. Seventy to eighty per cent of people exposed to radiation never worked again, and those who did find employment were paid less than the norm.

Unlike Mrs. Watanabe, Sunao Tsuboi soon fell out of love with Emperor Hirohito and all that he stood for. He says now that he was "confused about everything" for about ten years. "When the emperor abandoned us I didn't know how to live." He began to read history. Now he believes in "democracy and equality" and that "the government should apologize to the Japanese for the years of war it subjected us to, and for what happened to us. They should also apologize to the foreign countries we invaded and assaulted."

Tsuboi thinks many anxious thoughts about the atrocities his country committed during the war and about the fact that little is discussed and nothing is recognized, but he doesn't do or say anything public. In Japan, it is the height of courage to voice an opinion, even privately, let alone to lobby government. What he does do publicly is sanitized and sanctioned; indeed, it is the official "work" of Hiroshima. He is an anti-nuclear peace activist. He has even been on a sponsored peace mission to New York.

He says his anti-nuclear work has helped transform his feelings of helplessness, but unlike Chiyoko Watanabe, Tsuboi is not at peace. Anti-nuclear activism in the bombed city has been detached from a taboo past where truth seems less disputed than erased. This too is an angled view through a framed screen, and it has increased, not decreased, his suffering.

The Hiroshima Peace Memorial Museum was created in 1955, three years after the US ended its occupation of Japan. The Americans had imposed total censorship on the Japanese. It was impossible to speak or write publicly about the effects of the atomic bombs on Hiroshima and Nagasaki, which meant that those of us living in the West knew what had happened—through the auspices of John Hersey and others—a lot sooner than the Japanese themselves. During these years, a professor of geology in Hiroshima took it upon himself to collect remnants of the disaster. He squirrelled away pieces of melted iron, torn clothing, and broken pottery. His neighbours thought he was insane, but it was his collection that formed the basis for the museum.

The tribes of schoolchildren are here as well. They giggle, push, and jostle, and are hushed by their teachers, for in addition to being a place of physical record, this museum is a holy shrine. The geology professor's collection is in evidence: twisted bottle caps and burned roof tiles. There are glass display cases of burnt children's clothing donated by grieving parents. And a horrific life-sized wax display of a wounded family staggering forward, their arms raised to alleviate the pain. This was reality in the aftermath of the bomb: thousands of people moving, mostly toward the river, holding up their burnt arms. The skin of the wax figures has sloughed off—yes, Hersey had the right word—and is hanging in shreds, but faces have been cleaned up to protect the schoolchildren. No eyes stream out of empty sockets. No one has charred black skin.

The unmissable message of the Hiroshima Peace Memorial Museum is contained in the second word of its name: Peace, which means *universal* peace. All the wartime suffering of the Japanese has been swept up and funnelled to this place. Yes, atomic bombs were dropped, and we in Japan were the victims of those bombs, but now we must turn our minds to peace for the sake of all humanity. The inscription at the A-bomb cenotaph says it all: "Let all souls here rest in peace, for we shall not repeat the evil." However, lest anyone think that the potentially ambiguous "we" includes Japanese war guilt, an explanation is offered: "[The inscription] summons people everywhere to pray for the repose of the souls of the deceased A-bomb victims and to join in the pledge never to repeat the evil of war. It thus expresses the 'heart of Hiroshima,' which, enduring past grief and overcoming hatred, yearns for the realization of world peace."

For all its shock-appeal and fine intentions, I am surprisingly unmoved by the museum and the inscription, possibly because the noble ideal of peace seems to have been abstracted from any context. Although my child-self was marked forever by the images in John Hersey's famous book, I now ask, where is the record of mutual aggression that led to this atrocity? Is it enough to say, albeit sincerely, that war is really, really bad and we will never, ever do it again? History suggests the contrary—we *will* do it again; and there is nothing here to move the visitor beyond the well-meaning cliché. Naturally there was discussion about what would appear in this museum, but the conservatives won out. Their message is that what happened in Hiroshima and Nagasaki concerns those cities alone and is unconnected to the larger history of Japan. Hence the convenient abstractions of universal peace in a vacuum. Hence the happy Japanese consular official on the other end of my telephone after I have returned home, asking if I will write something "light and upbeat" on Hiroshima as a "peace city" for their next newsletter.

Dr. Kohsoh Matsuo doesn't want to talk about what happened to him on August 6, 1945, except to say he was made sterile and never fathered a child with his wife. Instead he hands me a stapled manuscript replete with scratchy cross-outs, translated by himself into something approximating English. The title is "Too Much Worry Recently."

Dr. Matsuo worries about many things. "Why did the United States not warn Japan about the possible nuclear bombing of human beings?" he asks me, apparently expecting an answer. He has met Americans and he thinks they feel guilty about this. "I know Japan did horrible things to others, but then there were the terrible air attacks on Tokyo. Wasn't that enough? Or did the A-bomb represent some sort of balance of victims? Maybe this bomb was necessary. Maybe it couldn't be helped."

There was that fatalistic idea again: "It can't be helped." And my first, but not last, encounter with the startling idea that the bomb might have been "necessary" to bring "balance" into the conflict. Dr. Matsuo agonizes over questions of morality. He wants the Japanese government to apologize to the Korean "comfort women" who were forced to service Japanese soldiers at the front, and to pay them from government coffers to indicate official remorse on behalf of the Japanese people. (At the time of our meeting, the government was attempting to raise private donations to recompense the women.) He wants to build schools in countries Japan invaded in which truthful history will be taught. He wishes Japan were a "real democracy" where people were free to think independently and voice their opinions. "We only want to forget," he mourns. He shows his tortured writings to his friends in the Hiroshima Lions Club, but they never say anything except "Oh, what a fine writer you are. Such excellent style!" As for the younger members of his family, they dismiss him as a silly old man with boring memories of bygone times.

"Just how necessary is it to have opinions that conform with other people's?" I ask. He looks perplexed. The interpreter must look up the word "conform." I explain: to conform means to act and perhaps think in the same way as others. "Ah," she says after a moment and writes down the Japanese word *wa* for my edification. *Wa* means harmony. *Wa o tohtobu* means the harmonious whole. She nods vigorously as she explains. "It means 'Let us discuss things, but aim for the harmonious whole.' We will *endure* discussion if we must, then we will return to *wa*."

"We will *endure* discussion." Here was a key to the reluctance to debate, let alone resolve, the fifty-year-old problem of wartime atrocities, and an explanation for the evasive response of Dr. Matsuo's friends in the Lions Club. Here was a glimpse into the underpinnings of ancient attitudes that live behind the veil of Westernization. As the culture of Buddhism and Shintoism made it possible for army propagandists to suggest that spirit can conquer physical death in war, so the religious-cultural ideal of *wa* made sustained, open dissent virtually impossible.

One man challenged *wa* and almost paid for it with his life. In December 1988, as Emperor Hirohito lay dying of cancer, Hitoshi Motoshima, the mayor of Nagasaki, was asked by a left-wing member of his municipal government whether he thought Hirohito was guilty. "Yes, I do believe the emperor bore responsibility for the war," he replied.

Although Hirohito had long abandoned his god-descended status and donned a civilian suit, he remained the embodiment of the nation, especially for right-wing conservatives, and in their lexicon, Motoshima's words amounted to treason. Sixty-two groups of extremists from all over Japan descended on Nagasaki in black armoured vans to cruise the streets and broadcast a call for death. On January 7, 1989, the emperor died. And on January 18, 1990, a lone gunman shot the mayor through the lungs. He survived.

I travel to Nagasaki to meet the small, somewhat crumpled man himself in his messy office. He is perhaps the only male in Japan not wearing a tie at 2:00 on a weekday afternoon. Large glasses tend to slip off his nose. He looks tired. He tells me he has never recovered his energy.

Motoshima's critics do not exactly deny the truth of what he said about the emperor's war guilt. They argue, instead, that he does not have "a Japanese mind." By this they imply that he thinks like a "Westerner," which in turn seems to mean that he insists in seeing the A-bomb attacks in the context of Japanese military aggression—therefore possibly implicating the emperor—and not as related only to the two bombed cites. Noburu Tasaki, the director of the Peace Museum of Nagasaki (which has gone a mini-step further than the Hiroshima museum in demonstrating Japan's contribution to the war and occasioned serious criticism), put it this way: "The Japanese do not want to believe that Japan did such cruel things. We are living in harmony with other peoples." So it appears that Motoshima committed an "un-Japanese" act by disturbing the harmony of life. He disrupted *wa*. That is why he was punished.

Furthermore, Motoshima is a Christian—with some quite surprising ideas. During our conversation he suggests, following Nagai Takashi, the famous author of *The Bells of Nagasaki,* that the bomb that fell over Nagasaki was "God's will." Motoshima now calls the nuclear bombing an "act of grace" that must be "joyfully accepted."

This journey into religious mysticism is relatively new for him—as mayor he was known best as a shrewd politician deft at hammering out compromise deals with his opponents. But his Christianity has angled his outlook vis-à-vis his Buddhist and Shintoist compatriots. Motoshima believes deeply in sin, guilt, and personal responsibility—ideas that have led him to the notion of national responsibility and to the truth about the emperor.

He is on a collision course with many of his compatriots in other ways as well. From the train window I had been struck by the rice paddy next to the smoke stacks: the old Japan next to the new. Motoshima represents the new, and he has no tolerance for those who represent the old, or who want to incorporate tradition into contemporary Japanese life. Tradition is *wa,* the stifler of memory and debate; tradition is the ongoing hierarchical organization of society where ideas and orders emanate from the top; tradition is keeping silent and controlling the expression on one's face; tradition is a religious culture that says no one is to blame because "it can't be helped." Tradition is hammering down any nail that dares to stick out.

Motoshima scoffs. What *he* embraces is the openness of Western democracies, the diversity of populations, the freedom to speak one's mind, the search for factual truth in history. He hates conformity. "What is democracy like in Japan? Well, true democracy is a recognition of human rights, of difference, but in my country difference is not allowed. People dress the same. And they think collective opinion is a good thing. Children are not taught history. They do not ask questions in school, even in the universities." He fiddles with his pencil and looks disgusted. "Democracy is a short person looking up at a tall person and speaking his mind," he adds, looking at me with a sly smile. I laugh. Hitoshi Motoshima is a short person.

Like Dr. Matsuo in Hiroshima, Motoshima struggled with suppressed history, with the need for national resolution and justice, with the substance of democracy, and with a possible religious meaning to the devastation that was visited on his home city half a century ago. His anguish felt raw and poignant. He was committed to the liberalism of Western democracies—to the political system on which modern Japan is based, but he had broken an unspoken code by aggressively pushing through cultural limits. He was courageous, tragic, and out of step.

With the exception of Mrs. Watanabe, whose attitudes reflected *wa* and were therefore not disturbing to her, the survivors I had met were still suffering, physically and morally. The wide-screened view of history they sought to memorialize and maintain kept shifting before their eyes. Truth was there, but it seemed ungraspable within the context of their culture. And dangerous. Hitoshi Motoshima had dared speak out forty years later and he had almost died in the attempt.

I am travelling north again, away from the bombed cities of memory and forgetfulness. It is evening, and as the train rolls along, metropolis after metropolis illuminates the sky with neon, like a beckoning fairground. Japanese cities glitter at night—promising pleasure. Riding high over Osaka, we look down on two national obsessions: dozens of men lined up at a golf driving range under the night lights, and hundreds more inside an open pachinko parlour, its garish neon flashing "Paris, Paris" under a giant, twinkling Eiffel Tower.

When the bubble bursts and the extravagant riches are no longer within easy reach, what will happen to pleasure and glitz? The extreme right that tried to kill Hitoshi Motoshima is still marginal but on the move, as the struggle between nationalist spirit and Western materialism remains unfocused and unresolved. As one with an admittedly "Western mind," I am left wondering how a nation that stifles dissent according to the dictates of *wa* will defend the democracy it claims to cherish, should the need arise. I am left wondering about a "Hiroshima peace culture" that has dissolved the bilateral horror of war into a sentimentalized abstraction in the name of all humanity.

Hitoshi Motoshima, Kohsoh Matsuo, and Sunao Tsuboi may one day prevail in their quest for truth; but for now, memory has been interred. A screen of oblivion separates today from yesterday, and it has been angled to hide the dark.

1996

Still Life:
Reflections on Running,
Walking, and Standing

CATHERINE FRAZEE

RUNNING

IT WAS ONE OF THOSE RELENTLESSLY
wet February days for which Halifax winter is known. As we were
heading home from the tavern, my friend Nancy ran ahead to start
the car. Perhaps it was something about the way a light drizzle can
change the quality of sound in the air or perhaps it was the way the
fog stripped away the background elements for a moment, but I saw
Nancy and I saw running in a way that I had never before understood.

Her sneakers barely touched the ground. I could detect no
weight, no force, no resistance. The very act of running, without
question, took far less effort than the act of not-running. It was a
gesture that spoke less of speed and more of the confidence of having all the time in the world. I understood freedom and youth and
joy crystallized in that moment.

*Running has never been part of my repertoire. Racing, yes, as in
the race against time, the rush to finish my Christmas shopping,
the pressure to begin another sentence before my screen saver
appears, the heart-pounding velocity of a runaway wheelchair. But
running—purposeful, controlled, concentrated—I've not been
there. I've not done that.*

> *I've never run. Nor have I ever walked. Nor, for that matter, have I ever stood still. The force of gravity, now compounded by forty-five years of inexperience, has made all of these postures impossible.*

Before that particular moment in February of 1980, what I knew about running was pure theory. Brain transmits signals, muscles respond, body hurtles through space. Then, in one of those rare moments of receptivity when the mind is caught off guard and the senses have a direct line to consciousness, I caught a glimpse of running. Running not as transportation, but as a form of expression that uses the body as its instrument. Nancy had illuminated running in such a way as to free it from the distortions of intellect. Seeing Nancy had made it possible for me to let go of the *idea* and, in so doing, to grasp the *experience*.

The intellect puts Running-like-Nancy in the same category as what the hamster does on the wheel in its cage. Running is defined by measurable physiological criteria. Through the lens of intellect, running is a matter of biology and physics. The body knows when it is running by the way the heart pounds, the lungs burn, the sweat pours. The mind understands running as an elaborate fusion of arcane forces—calories, energy, gravity, momentum. For the average, garden-variety runner, running is an act of mind over matter—runners *will* their bodies to run, controlling for speed, direction, form.

But the experience of Running-like-Nancy is more than body, mind, and will, for what we understand of any human experience through these apertures alone is but a part of the full story. Running-like-Nancy transcends mind and matter both. It begins somewhere in the body—who knows where—when some essence that is neither body nor mind rises up and takes flight, carrying all along: runner, body of runner, will of runner, thoughts, words, and imaginings of runner and witness alike.

In the not-so-flattering language of medicine, I am called a "flacid paralytic," meaning that my body has the consistency of overcooked pasta. All my parts are in working order, but the current that powers them runs at about 10 volts instead of 110 or 220.

For the purposes of function and expression, my body-instrument offers a small clear voice without much wind behind it, more or less full facial movements, such subtle shifts and turns of head as can be made upon a floppy neck without engaging gravity full force, one hand that can finger-crawl around the radius of its wrist, and another —my chief spokes-hand—that is mobile from the elbow to fingertip with the aid of a spring-loaded steel support.

The matrimonial arrangements between my body and will are perhaps more egalitarian than many. Neither partner serves the other. Instead, every exchange in this marriage is negotiated. Roles are fluid, according to circumstance. If a mosquito lands on my chin, my hand will respond, deftly but slowly and probably not with murderous force. If a mosquito lands on my forehead, it is the will that must respond: swiftly recruit a Samaritan or find a tool light enough to lift and long enough to reach or, failing these, deliver me into the zen of a different moment, seizing me with thoughts of distant places or ideas of greater consequence than a biting insect.

Egalitarian though it may be, my marriage of body and will is often frowned upon. Instead, it is said that I am "trapped in a helpless body." Retreating to that reflective state where wounds seek comfort, I wonder if for those who hold this view, the greater tragedy is that of "being trapped in an active, vigorous body"—fleet of foot but slow to connect with the force that rises up and Runs-like-Nancy.

Bodies feed us and keep us warm. They take us to most of the places we want to go. But sometimes, like a loving parent, a designer suit, or a house in the suburbs, they can get in our way. Sometimes things are just too perfect, seducing the occupant with the illusion of completeness. Our thinking gets flabby, our passions lose their tone, our ambitions grow mould. When it is all handed to us—fitness, vigour, capacity of intellect, and body—it's easy to settle in, easy to lose our edge. When body and mind are able to serve, responding to every command, bestowing their gifts of useful function and entertaining performance, there may be fewer points of entry for the impelling call of the quest, the prod for us to attend to other voices. What is the imperative to go deep when all is as it should be at the surface? We may work to preserve what we have from the erosion of age, or we may strive to accumulate—more strength, more skills, more information—but it may be many, many years, if ever at all, before we ask "Is that all there is?"

At the extremes of experience, when the impulse is full strength, not all bodies are created equal. When the winning name is called or the winning goal is scored and the body is summoned to express the intensity of our response, we sprint, we leap, we throw our arms around whoever stands near to our joy, and we embrace. If we can yelp, leap, and sprint while embracing, so much the better. In the explosion of victory, our spirit deploys all the forces at its disposal to escape the body's containment, to throw aside our instrument and play the whole damn orchestra.

But there it is again: that house in the suburbs, the permanent fixed address that holds us back. Even the champion's body has limits to its repertoire. The *normal* body—a phrase rooted in values and suppositions that I do not personally share, but because it is widely understood, I borrow for the moment—the *normal,* non-disabled body expresses itself very much like good prose. Its sentences are correctly formed, having all the necessary components: subject, verb-in-agreement, appropriately placed modifiers, suitable articles, modestly arranged prepositions and participles, clauses linked by reason and decorum, punctuation conforming to elaborate rules of form and syntax. Like language, the body can be enormously complex but if it is constructed according to the norm, it works. It works because everyone agrees about what to expect and because, like long division, we know the steps and the sequence for working it out, extracting its meaning from the squiggled lines or bits of sound that it comes in. Like language, the grammar of the body is an arbitrary system, consisting of rules that we break at certain peril of social judgment. Bad grammar marks one; likewise the deviant body.

Some bodies break all the rules. There is nothing prosaic, for example, about writer/actor Heather Rose's body. In the opening scene of a recent television film, an actor's voice speaks the words that Heather has written to introduce herself: "My name is Heather Rose. I am thirty-two years old. I cannot walk, or talk, or wash myself, or dress myself, or even feed myself. I am completely dependent on other people for everything to do with my living."[1]

In the context of a film, where everyone's body is permitted to speak for itself, this introduction tells us what we need to know about the film's principal character. Extracted to print, however, it strips away skin from bone. The task of translation, the challenge to describe Heather in a full-bodied way that does not objectify or pathologize her may exceed the weight of my delicate stroke. But for those learned fellows who coined the endearing term "flaccid paralytic," the task of description is easy. They classify Heather as "spastic paralytic," their clinical reduction of a body that twists and curls, kinks, cowlicks, and bristles with strength and originality abundant.

I'm an insider, facing the screen. My body comes equipped with its own speaking voice and a hand that can put small pieces of food that don't weigh too much into my own mouth, but in other important respects, my daily life is more like Heather's than that of most people I know. I am watching the film for the first time, with that pointy-eared attention of a critic ready to pounce. Waiting for the filmmaker to cross the line, with a camera angle that makes Heather's wheelchair larger than her body, a voice-over that

> *commands us to marvel at her courage, a canonizing interview with*
> *one of her assistants, or a single word from among many that I*
> *abhor: "suffering," "confined," "tragic."*

Early in the film, Heather receives word that the movie that she co-wrote and starred in has been accepted for screening at Cannes. Hardly a surprise, for a documentary titled *Heather Rose Goes to Cannes*. But, for Heather in the moment, surprise is writ large. Yelp, leap, and embrace are executed with the aid of a computerized voice synthesizer, a motorized wheelchair, and a staccato sequence of halting and chaotic, yet deliberate, movements. With all of her body in full spasm, every joint taut in contortions that offer no promise of freeing her hand to spell out the words she wants to speak, or to move toward and reach out to the man who brought this news, Heather rises to the occasion. Over and over, between kicks and arches and swings at the air, she summons her limbs to the precise tasks that seem, for all the world, impossible: pressing the right keystrokes, manoeuvring the wheelchair drive-stick with requisite precision, exhaling slowly and gently into a hug.

> *I watch Heather Running-like-Nancy. And I am wrenched from*
> *my Insider Smug, tears streaming, the image of something I have*
> *never been able to see before, now alive within me.*

Feelings so large and mighty are why we must have poetry. Perfect sentences laid down end-to-end then stacked in paragraphs are woefully inadequate at the extremity of such a moment. I abandoned poetry twenty-eight years ago, when my waif-poet was rejected by the editors of a high school yearbook. But here I am at my desk, trying to describe Heather's moment of triumph, and a poet's voice returns, insistent. In the intensity of this moment, as Heather shows her true expressive force, I begin to understand the power of the not-so-normal body, the body speaking in poetry, not prose.

Full and perfect joy. A dance like fireworks in all directions, chaotic, dangerous, evanescent. Swirling concoction of the paradoxes of triumph: sacrifice and reward, pride and sorrow, loss and hope. Tender and exquisite culmination, as fingers of one hand ...... finally ...... find their way to pinch the shirt upon the shoulder of the man who shares Heather's joy. In this clutching of shirt that is Heather's embrace, I glimpse the great miracle that humans, in all of our separateness and fragility, can touch at all. And somewhere behind Heather's synthesized "Yes. Yes. Yes," I hear my own voice.

> *For as long as I can remember, the fingers of my spirit have clung to the notion that I have value. It is my mantra, the gesture of my being, this tightened hold, not second nature, but first. Locked fingers, fused with a tiny crag at the edge of the cliff of despair, trained never to reach for the helping hands of those who do not, can not, or will not believe. Fingers programmed at the level of will, leaving the rest of me free for the business of life.*
>
> *A great force has flipped this landscape on its side, and I am now suddenly—safe. Safe to let go because what has been for all time nothing more than a shard of possibility is now rock-solid beneath me. Gnarls of spirit begin to uncurl. I gulp at air, not yet skilled in the art of breathing deeply. I have value.*

Heather's body-poem is large in its phrasing, its windswept strength, its torrents of unspoken words. Mine is more like haiku, small pools and eddies and willow boughs. But we are part of the same anthology, Heather and I. *Insiders.*

> *I too have learned to Run-like-Nancy. In a studio in the woods with a picture window and a great big echo that makes my voice roar in my ears, I run each day. Running cross-country, running out loud through the woods where my head doesn't fall because, when my word-feet touch lightly, I'm not jolted by the unevenness, the roots and stones and layering of earth. I can't see where I am*

*going—it's like that in the woods—I just give over to a certain
kind of knowing, an inner compass. I take the turns in my stride,
listen to the leaves and the grass and the creatures, and just Run-
like-Nancy.*

WALKING

In 1984, my assistant, Loy, and I flew to Nairobi, where we had
arranged to meet up with Djanet, a dear friend and former assistant.
Our few weeks together were embarrassingly conventional: we
hired a driver and a Jeep, visited all the major game reserves,
and stayed at all the places tourists stay. (A disabled traveller, in my
opinion, need never apologize for following the path of least resistance.) Each morning at 3:30, we awoke with excruciating effort in
order to be on safari before sunrise. Once on the road, all eyes and
attention, we searched for the great herds that once roamed the
Kenyan plains: water buffalo, giraffe, zebra, impala, elephant.

Toward the end of one morning of dusty vigil, a darkened form
appeared at the horizon. It was I who made the first sighting. It was
far, far off, but after many days of this pursuit, my eyes and senses
were keen at spotting.

For some time I could not discern the form—was it a herd or
a single animal? We drove some distance farther. It was a solitary
creature. Ostrich perhaps, or giraffe. Unremarkable.

I cast my gaze around for something more exciting in some
other direction as we drove yet farther. But the single figure called
my eye back again and again. It moved across the open plain, slowly,
the only living being for miles.

Farther still we drove. The angles were not right for giraffe. Another mile. The shape was not ostrich. Another mile ...

Masai warrior. He took no notice of us, but just continued,
walking. One man, moving across the Kenyan plain. Answering to
no one but himself.

I cannot grasp what my eyes tell me. As he strides past, I tumble into a chaos of spiralling disbelief, senses wrestling with reason for purchase on this moment. I am numb with questions.

When I was a child, daily life presented endless and varied opportunities for wishing. Aside from those that always eluded me—I never had the strength to hold on to a wishbone or the breath to blow out more than two birthday candles at a time—there were trucks loaded with hay, trains with a caboose, words spoken at the same time as a friend, lone stars in the early night sky.

I was always ready, a wish always poised at the tip of my tongue. *I wish I could walk.* That was it. Every time. The opportunities presented themselves frequently and generally with no warning, so it was important to be ready. My wish had the resonance of correctness—a proper wish, meeting with the immediate endorsement and approval of my peers. It was uniquely mine; none of my prose-body mates could claim such a wish for themselves. If granted, it was not something I would have to share with my brother, like a gingerbread house, a telescope, or a puppy. And it could be blurted out rapidly without awkward twisting of the tongue, an important feature in the competitive dynamic that some wish invitations created.

I imagine that everyone, with a few moments' reflection, can identify the one thing that they would most like to be able to do, the one thing that they cannot, and perhaps never will be able to do. Play the piano, speak fluent French, break par, grow sleek blond hair, fly to the moon, or even just fly. In my own heart, I hold the desire to push buttons—on the telephones, tape recorders, and remote controls of this world.

For many people with disabilities like my own, the one thing they wish for is the ability to walk. Christopher Reeve, for example, the actor who leaped tall buildings in a single bound, has made it his life's work to walk again. Yet for many others, among whom I count my activist self, the seductions of medical science raise fundamentally personal, political, and ethical questions.

Only once have I walked in a dream. Careful, halting steps fuelled by such deep concentration, executed with such gravity as to bathe the act in a mystical wash of some secret art. But what if it were possible to know this secret? What if it were possible—not in the moody mist of sleep, but here and now, in the bright light of day—to revel in the effortless ordinariness of walking? Were a truck loaded with hay to pass by my window at this moment, would I still whisper that childhood wish? Do I still wish to walk?

A lot of life has been lived—and lived well—in this "folded"[2] state of never-walking. Enough life lived well to warrant careful thought about what it means not to walk, about what my disability means in the larger frame of this seated life. The simple arithmetic of it is that my disability has smartly brought me to all the things I value: my career, my friendships, my creative life, my skills, my tenacity, my intimate partner, my world view. And there is, for me, no logical reason to believe that this will not continue to be the case for as long as I remain alive and disabled.

This is not a matter of simple acceptance, of stoicism, of bravely making the best of my sorry lot. It is a matter of growing into, embracing my experience of disability. This is not to say that I embrace the exclusion, the stigma, the devalued status, the abuse, and the barriers of all descriptions that are the companions of disability. These I reject categorically. They do not build character. They are as destructive and senseless as war. I feel as impassioned about resisting these forces as others must feel in their "battle to find a cure." But let me be very clear—stigma, barriers, and exclusion are the enemy, not my disability.

In my resistance to these foes, I draw strength from the experience of oppression shared with comrades in the struggle. The loneliness, the indignities, the slings and arrows of disability have a way of galvanizing the spirit. The words of Simi Linton pump me up to a level of excitement unrivalled by something so, dare I say, pedestrian as mere walking:

We have come out not with those brown woollen lap robes over our withered legs, or dark glasses over our pale eyes but in shorts and sandles, in overalls and business suits, dressed for play and work—straightforward, unmasked, and unapologetic. We are, like Crosby, Stills, and Nash told their Woodstock audience, letting our "freak flag fly." And we are not only the high-toned wheelchair athletes seen in recent television ads but the gangly, pudgy, lumpy, and bumpy of us, declaring that shame will no longer structure our wardrobe or our discourse. We are everywhere these days, wheeling and loping down the street, tapping our canes, sucking on our breathing tubes, following our guide dogs, puffing and sipping on the mouth sticks that propel our motorized chairs. We may drool, hear voices, speak in staccato syllables, wear catheters to collect our urine, or live with a compromised immune system. We are all bound together, not by this list of our collective symptoms, but by the social and political circumstances that have forged us as a group. We have found one another and found a voice to express not despair at our fate but outrage at our social positioning. Our symptoms, though sometimes painful, scary, unpleasant, or difficult to manage, are nevertheless part of the dailiness of life. They exist and have existed in all communities throughout time. What we rail against are the strategies used to deprive us of rights, opportunity, and the pursuit of pleasure.[3]

A heady project it is to build a social movement, to come together for the express purpose of reinventing ourselves. We are forming our own counterculture. As has every civil rights struggle of the past, we sing our freedom songs:

They thought we'd keep on smiling for years to come
They thought we'd just be helpless and mild

Without our own opinion they could just cash in on
Their image of the crippled child.

(Refrain)
But Timmy and Tammy are rebelling
Their Easter seals have come unglued
They won't be apathetic; they refuse to look pathetic
They're changing their point of view.
They're poster kids no more,
Poster kids no more[4]

We decorate ourselves, our service animals, and our mobility devices with buttons, banners, and bumper stickers:

Piss on Pity[5]

Not Dead Yet[6]

Severely Normal[7]

Severely Euphemized[8]

To boldly go ... where everyone else has gone before.[9]

We craft pride, rage, and identity into emblems of impiety and resistance:

[10] [11]

In these ways we affirm ourselves as complete, complex, and *undiminished* human beings,[12] not that lesser version of humanity packaged for sale at the charity ball. We are proud of who we are, fired up with the thrill of combat, armed with radical new ideas that are a potent blend of red-hot satire and ice-cold truth. Determined to occupy the higher ground, we have been hard on Christopher Reeve and others who look like us but do not want to be like us, who seek to enter or pass in the walking world, rather than taking their place alongside us at the front line.

The politics of our disability freedom fight offer the same knots and thorns as any other mature social movement. For some, the desire to walk is a sellout, a weak-kneed succumbing to the seductions of *normalcy*. For others, it is the most intimate balm: a hope that sustains life, a bittersweet memory of home.

For me, although it's far from simple, a few things are clear. Whether as a result of political consciousness, pragmatism, or an aesthetic preference for gliding, I do not share Christopher Reeve's desire to walk. I cannot in conscience begrudge a recent immigrant to the strange and wondrous land of not-walking the wish that I once held so innocently. But I do resent the enormous investment of economic and intellectual resources demanded by quests for cures, the high-powered complex put in place to sustain Reeve's dream, a complex that takes on a life of its own and will not be diverted to address the political, environmental, and social conditions that are the primary causes of disability around the world.

I am deeply affronted by the ideological underpinnings of the cure industry. When we scratch the surface, the message that markets the cure is that reliance upon a wheelchair diminishes life, that dignity is lost whenever one is lifted into bed or onto the toilet. When such a sweeping fallacy has free roam through the valleys of popular discourse, I and my folded comrades are greatly imperilled. For lives so diminished, so bereft of dignity, what if there is no hope of cure? Does it not follow then, as some twisted ethical imperative, that such a life should not be lived? Then killing—alias "assisted death"—becomes a special kind of cure, an ultimate end to suffering deemed humanly intolerable.

Like every good activist, I have my own annoying inconsistencies and contradictions. How is my desire to push buttons on the telephone so very distinct from Mr. Reeve's desire to walk? Are these not simply two different points along the continuum between impairment and the full physical capacity deemed "*normal*" for humans—in which case, my ambitions are less sanguine than Mr. Reeve's, but of the same essential nature. If I am brutally honest I must confess to an insatiable lust for technology. I want the best motorized wheelchair that money can buy, with every state-of-the-art feature and function that I can load onto it. I am enraged by poor design, sloppy craftsmanship, and the technical bugs and glitches that are as inevitable as the common cold. A full-blown failure of my bells and whistles plunges me into such a state of passive despondency as to render my character almost unrecognizable to those who know me professionally, socially, or intimately. This said, how do I reconcile my insistence upon technically aided mobility and function with my assertions that disability is an honourable and, yes, desirable state? Do my own behaviours not suggest that I would feel differently if my disability prevented me from commanding the technology upon which my own sense of dignity and physical integrity is contingent?

These apparent conflicts and contradictions begin to dissolve when we consider walking, like running, as a mode of expression.

From a Masai warrior who spoke to me not in words but in footsteps, I begin to understand the true nature of walking. To walk as a Masai warrior is to belong, flesh, bone, and soul. It is to declare one's title. It is integral and devout. To walk as a Masai warrior is to assume one's place in the cosmos—no more, and no less.

This, I can aspire to. Perhaps this is what we all wish for, in which case the contributions of medical science and technology will be at best peripheral and at worst an impediment. For the purposes of locomotion, I am content to use the fingers of my right hand, the drive-stick of my wheelchair, the wheel, and the miracles of modern technology that link the latter two so very cleverly together. For the purposes of expression, however, of course I want to walk. Just exactly as I do. I want to walk as a Masai warrior. Just exactly as I do, when I am present and erect, confident of who I am and where I am going. I know that I have every right to be here.

The cure that propels my walk is the elixir of direction—a prescription to know but not to circumvent the dangers, to hold the path, to advance. With each step, I am more sure, more brave, more clear. I walk mindfully. I know my friends and predators, and those who may become either as I approach. I attend those who have walked ahead and have regard for those who walk behind. I am one, but not alone. I walk in full possession of self.

STANDING

April 17, 1994. My fortieth birthday. On the marsh at Point Pelee. A gentle breeze at day's end aroused in me the compulsion to capture it all in a single frame.

Only one shot remained on Patricia's roll. The sun was rapidly retreating behind the horizon, and it would take several minutes for her to climb to the top of the three-storey fire tower that I had selected as the vantage point for this self-portrait. I suppose that the chances for a successful photograph were less than fifty per cent.

Another long shot. When I was eighteen years old, I required surgery to improve respiratory function and increase my tolerance for sitting upright. My physician had informed me that chances of survival were about fifty per cent, but if I did survive, there would be no reason why I shouldn't "expect to live to be forty." I took him up on his offer, gambled, and won. Not until well into my thirty-ninth year had I begun to feel a deep unease about the bargain. A prognosis once so generous was now closing in around me, uncomfortably. Forty loomed like the runway's end, with me full throttle, not ready to lift.

Forever missing deadlines, I turned that corner of forty and carried on. Through the solstice and across the Pelee marsh. Place of transition between dry land and water, migratory resting site between the shifting hospitality of climates. Now five years since, my birthday portrait recalls a mood, an oath, a moment.

The moment fills the frame. A golden marsh extends for miles into the horizon, bleeds off the edges of the print, foreground grasses precise and crystal clear like the pane of April water that fills the image centre. A photo that rewards a closer look: solo figure, so small as almost to disappear, stands on a gentle arc of path, reflected perfectly at water's edge. The figure is me, newborn-at-forty. Standing. Four-wheel variation on a stand of pine.

> *How I love that phrase.* A stand of pine. *Magnetic. I want to be there, maybe not right inside, just far enough back to see the whole stand, still close enough—if I'm really paying attention—to catch the scent, to hear the whisper.*

Attention. A stand of pine commands the attention. It is older, stronger, wiser, richer, taller. People want to be like trees. Is it something about longevity, weathering season after season, drawing up life from an underground cosmos of footing and history? Or is it the idea of that tough protective bark all around, knots and gnarls like badges of honour? Or the possibility of cradling baby birds and chipmunks in our arms, wild and tender all at once? Perhaps it's just that thing about standing tall. Feet apart, shoulders back, ready to pounce or swing, kick or spit, draw your pistol or throw your voice. Funny things that trees wouldn't dream of doing.

At least not the trees that I know.

Almost every summer, I travel to a cottage on the Nova Scotia coast. Not the South Shore, with those beaches pretty as postcards—those beaches that choke me with a mournful longing, their invisible barbed wire forbidding my 300-pound rubber and steel footsteps from the silk of warm sand, the tickle of sea foam. My cottage sits on the Fundy Shore, rock hard and rugged like my swash-buckling on-vacation self. A small cottage on a large lot thick with spruce and pine, the generous ratio of context to element that I am perennially drawn to. And although I call it my land, my two- to three-week annual squat is but a brief inconvenience to its true pro-prietors—squirrels, chipmunks, bats, mice, skunks, and all manner of seabird and insect. They have the privilege of context, within which I am but a humble element.

Humble and awkward, as I choose my path, slaloming this way and that, never taking the full slope, gauging my traction on dewy grass and feeling my way gingerly around the bumps and stones and roots and skunk holes that wobble my rigid frame. Teetering to and fro, I do not glide with ease along nature's carpet. Machine and body wobble inelegantly, one hind wheel spinning in air as one fore wheel drops into a gulley. A strange sight I must be, six-footed animal, four that roll noisily and two that perch motionless, high above ground. Bouncing along, seated, cartoonish, like some ectopic monarch, tossed about immodestly in a throne ill-suited to this terrain.

Can I possibly belong to this landscape? To any? I bid my squeaks and rattles to stop beside a sixty-year-old black spruce. I am look-ing out toward the sea, to a line as solid and distinct as a line can be, a line not dividing ocean from shore, but a line dividing visual fields, the line where all that belched-up moss and lichen-covered rock appears to meet the sparkling windswept water, the line below which, and just out of sight, little waves thin out to dart among the pebbles in the place where tides rule and there is no line ever to be seen. I am thinking about the line below me—the machine line— its stubborn refusal to yield to the sweet invitation of Earth's soft curves, to the gentle push of my desire to ripple into them.

The sensation of fur crossing my ankle interrupts my melancholy thoughts. A quick jerk of fear gives way to recognition; a chipmunk has crossed my path, hopping across my foot as if it were a tree root along its way.

As if it were a tree root. Sweet moment of redemption. It is perhaps the highest compliment I have ever received.

Perhaps I do stand, when I am still. Perhaps I am a tree. Not a potted tree, all bound up in my steel-machine container. The steel machine does not define me, does not contain me. The steel machine is where my seed fell—and grew. It is my home, like the ship's iron hull to the barnacle. But it is not my substance. My substance is flesh and earth, root and impulse, instinct and aspiration. A healthy tree, growing not from the rock, but on it. A tree that is every bit as much of nature's plan as the grasses that grow in the watery marsh and the mountains that rise out of the velvet forest.

The wooded mountains where I have come to write.

I have so long misjudged the mountains, always thinking them cold and forbidding, all sharp edges and old stone. Ominous and obstructive. Lifeless and unmoving. Too loud, taking up their great big spaces, and absolute in that defiant standing-over-us-all kind of way.

But I had never spent time in the company of mountains. Real time. I had travelled in the mountains: cross-Canada tours with family and friends, hot springs and volcanoes in Kyushu, a Himalayan trek atop the shoulders of four sure-footed porters. But travel, for me, like running and walking, is a splendid form of doing, and doing, more often than not, is an experience quite distinct from *being*.

Strange that I in my haiku body would require lessons in the art of being still. My doing self has managed well in the world, has found ways to engage with the active chemistry of tasks and people, ideas, places, politics, and things. But my being self is a mere sapling, just five years old now, sitting on the lap of the mountain, ready at last to learn the art of simply being. Mountain changes subtle with light, season, and eon, mountain moods finding their own movement, their unique, mysterious expression.

From the mountain I see and apprehend the lesson of the marsh.

I hear the red-winged blackbird—that piercing, exquisite anthem of Canadian summer—and I return to my self-portrait. Most perfect moment, rich with paradox. Stillness teeming with life. Lithe grasses taller than me, and perennially fragile. In the silence I hear more of everything. In the click of a shutter, there is past, present, and future. As light recedes, colours emerge. The black marsh water reflects a deeply reassuring message. I have never been more alive than I am at this moment. The grace of evening. And I am part of it. In it. Of it. Still. And ever.

1999

1   *Heather Rose Goes to Cannes,* 1998. Piper Films Ltd. Director, Christopher Corin.
2   Thanks to Nancy Mairs for introducing me to this descriptive phrase, which I first encountered in her collection of essays, *Carnal Acts* (Boston: Beacon Press, 1996).
3   S. Linton, *Claiming Disability: Knowledge and Identity* (New York: New York University Press, 1998), pp. 3–4. Reprinted by permission of New York University Press.
4   "Poster Kids No More," copyright © Jane Field Socan 1994. Recorded on the cassette *The Fishing Is Free,* © 1994 Hedgehog Songs.
5   Created by Johnny Crescendo
6   Created by Bob Kafka (with thanks to Monty Python)—www.notdeadyet.org/
7   Created by Dan Wilkins—www.thenthdegree.com
8   Created by Dan Wilkins—www.thenthdegree.com
9   Created by Bill Scarborough, ADAPT of Texas
10 Logo and slogan for ADAPT—American Disabled for Attendant Programs Today. Used courtesy of ADAPT, Denver, Colorado, a grassroots disability-rights organization.

[11] Design by Anna Stonum and Designs for All, Chicago. T-shirt available from the nth degree catalog, www.thenthdegree.com/.

[12] I am grateful to Alice Walker for this insight about African Americans, which I believe applies equally to disabled persons. It can be found in her collection of essays *In Search of Our Mothers' Gardens* (San Diego: Harcourt Brace & Company, 1983), p. 85.

Salad Days

R. CHERAN

My salad days,
When I was green in judgement, cold in blood.

Shakespeare, *Antony and Cleopatra*

IT WAS A TYPICAL LAZY AFTERNOON
in Jaffna, a besieged city in the northern part of Sri Lanka and the
epicentre of Tamil resistance during the civil war. After a rice and
curry lunch, the staff of *Saturday Review,* an independent English-
language weekly, was snoozing or close to it. Ratna Raja, the typist
with the magic finger, had already slipped away for a siesta. Anton
Saverimuttu, the sub-editor, was smoking his after-lunch cigar (his
dark, locally made stogies had a reputation for driving away all manner of mosquitoes). Only Gamini Navaratne, the old Sinhalese
editor, was busy writing, his drained whisky glass beside him.

Seated on the patio of an old British colonial house that doubled as the paper's offices, I was lazily proofreading the editorial
page when I heard the unfamiliar growl of a military vehicle. I was
used to the different sounds of military vehicles, but this one was
new and far more threatening. It came straight to our gate and
stopped. For the next few minutes the silence was so complete I
thought everything in the outside world had frozen. There was no
gunfire. No thumping of military boots. Confused, I decided to stay
seated. Sitting is the best form of defence. Run and you make a
more attractive target. Suddenly they appeared inside the house,
outside the patio, everywhere—armed men in dirty green.

One of them walked straight up to me on the patio and placed his submachine gun against my head. The short barrel of the gun was firmly placed on the back of my head and it wasn't moving. He muttered something in Sinhala that I didn't understand, but I scarcely needed to, the terror in my eyes and sweat on my face were all the answer he needed. To be honest, I didn't expect him to shoot. A certain logic, the logic of assault, informed me that if he was going to do that, he'd have opened fire when he and his mates first assaulted the house.

The soldier with the submachine gun stood firm and confident. A simple provocation or the sound of a cracker is enough. He could blow my head off at any moment. I was not looking at him but I could feel his gaze, intent and fierce, on my back, on my face, on my beard, and on my trembling fingers. Then I saw old Gamini being escorted out of his room by two soldiers carrying AK-47s. One of them was obviously an officer.

"Don't harm him. He is our deputy editor," Gamini told the officer.

"We are taking him too," replied the officer.

I felt the snout of the submachine gun swing away from my head, but my guard's eyes were still locked on me. A couple more soldiers came onto the patio and began rifling through the book-shelves and the stack of back copies. I could hear a lot of noise out-side. There must be dozens of these guys out there, I thought. They've got the place surrounded. I had no idea where Ratna Raja and Anton were, but I could hear the screams of Imelda, our secretary, as still more soldiers ransacked the office.

Gamini was doing his best to communicate with the officer in Sinhala, their common language, but the officer was having none of it. He simply gestured to us to follow. We fell behind him, trailed by half a dozen soldiers. As we walked out of the gate and onto the street, I saw two South African–made Armed Personnel Carriers (APCs) called Buffels parked in front of the house. There wasn't a soul in the usually teeming street. Even the dogs had disappeared.

They stuffed us into an APC. The stench of sweat, alcohol, and cigarettes was overwhelming. Gamini was curled up between two ragged seats with heavy, soldierly meat crushing him on both sides. His frail, old body shivered as he groped for his glasses, which had fallen on the floor, where I had been forced to lie. As the APC shuddered forward, I felt the first searing stomp on my shoulder. Twenty-five stomps and about fifteen minutes later, they dragged us out. We were at Gurunagar, a dreaded military camp on the outskirts of Jaffna. The soldier with the submachine gun led me through the well-guarded entrance to a room about forty-five metres inside the camp. He shoved me inside, gave me a "you deserve this kind of treatment" look, locked the room, and vanished.

I joined the staff of the *Saturday Review* in 1984. It wasn't a big newspaper. It averaged sixteen pages a week and the print run seldom exceeded six thousand. It was crude by North American standards, typeset by hand and printed on two ancient letterpresses. Yet its reputation as a champion of press freedom, fundamental rights, and justice for minorities extended beyond the shores of Sri Lanka. In 1986 and 1987, the internationally respected journal *Index on Censorship* published articles recognizing the crucial role the *Saturday Review* was playing in the fight for democracy in Sri Lanka. The paper's mandate, in fact, was to fill the void in reporting, commentary, and analysis left by the mainstream press, which vigorously toed the government line. The *Review* could be counted on not only to reflect the Tamil perspective, but, ironically, to provide a forum for the dissident opinions of the majority Sinhalese of the south. What's more, it functioned as a reliable source for human rights monitors ranging from the UN to Amnesty International.

The government was not pleased with the *Saturday Review*. In July 1983 the security forces shut it down and sealed its offices. This was just three weeks before the government launched an ethnic pogrom against the Tamils. It was one of the worst in the history of ethnic relations in the country. Two thousand Tamils were killed and another 200,000 were forced from their homes. The *Review*'s founding editor, S. Sivanayagam, had to go underground to save his life. When the ban was lifted, the government replaced it with censorship. Significantly, the *Saturday Review* was the only paper in the country under direct government control. In those circumstances, few were prepared to take on the editorship. Only Gamini Navaratne, a fifty-six-year-old Sinhalese journalist with a deep commitment to social justice, was willing to take the risk. Thus Gamini, as he was popularly known in the Sri Lankan media circles, became the sole Sinhalese civilian to live and work in Jaffna. All of the others were soldiers. Gamini had been associated with the *Review* from its inception in 1982. His column, "Political Causerie," was one of the most-read items in the paper. As a political correspondent and senior journalist, he had come to know the country's political leaders well, including then president J. R. Jayewardene. Under Gamini's editorship the *Saturday Review* became a unique and, at times, maverick newspaper.

I had been a regular reader since my university days. After obtaining a degree in chemistry, botany, and zoology from the University of Jaffna, I decided to forgo all those fields and follow the path of political journalism. I was twenty-two years old and already writing articles and poems. Some of my work had already landed me in trouble with the government and the rebels. I wasn't a member of any of the thirty or so Tamil militant groups that were then active in Jaffna. In fact, I was critical of some of their actions and their sectarian politics. As far as my politics, poetics, and polemics went, joining the *Saturday Review* seemed the right choice for me. So it seemed at that time.

My prison cell was tiny. No windows. No marks on the walls except a few bloodstains. For four hours I shared it with my extended memories and accentuated fears. That's more than enough time for a double shower in your own sweat. Finally, the door opened and in walked a portly man wearing a T-shirt and khaki shorts. He was unarmed.

"Get up!" he barked in an unfamiliar Tamil dialect. "Take off your shirt. Walk straight. Don't look back."

He marched me to a white building about a hundred metres away. Once inside, he grabbed me by the scruff of the neck and pushed me along a labyrinth of corridors. No kicks, no blows, no words. Five steps to the right, five to the left, then another five or six steps through a double door.

"Look there." In the middle of the room, six, maybe seven, young men lay naked in a pool of blood. In the dim light, the faces were hardly visible. They lay in silence. They showed no sign of life.

"OK. That was a good beginning. Let's go."

We climbed two stairs, walked a long corridor, and ended in a room large enough for a ping-pong table and, anomalously, a loveseat. In the gloom I could just make out the faces of two officers, faces I would never forget.

"Welcome! Let's give the great journalist a decent chair," the younger one said with a cruel grin. I don't remember the older one's expression. But I did notice that he was clean-shaven.

A couple more soldiers walked in. They were heavily built and wearing only T-shirts and khaki shorts. Before I could guess why they were there, I was doubled over by three powerful punches slamming into my stomach and neck. I screamed, crumbled to the floor. It was still damp from a cleanup after the last beating. Then I sensed something approaching from my right. A heavy boot caught me on the hip. I had never, ever cried that hard in my life. I could not stop. The fifth blow landed on my head and I lost consciousness.

When I woke up, the two officers were sipping cool drinks. The pain in my stomach was unbearable. There was a steady hum in my ears, like the sound of pouring rain piped through a controlled amplifier.

"So how are you doing, courageous journalist?" The younger one said with the same cool, cruel grin. The thugs who'd beaten me up had gone and he seemed ready for a talk.

"Officer, please listen to me," I pleaded, looking alternately at each of them. "I'm not a rebel. I'm just a proofreader aspiring to become a journalist. I have nothing to hide. Don't hurt me!" At that moment I felt shame and fear simultaneously.

"Proofreader?" the older one asked with a skeptical smile. "All right, all right. I'll give you six hours and plenty of paper. You're going to write all you know about these terras, OK?"

"Officer, I've already written several articles about the history and organization of the rebels. I've also published their manifestos and political programs. You can read them in the back issues of our newspaper. I don't have anything new to write."

"I don't need that shit. I want the names and details of all the terras you know, their descriptions, and the names of all the foreign journalists visiting your newspaper office. Nothing more, nothing less."

They left me in the room. Seconds later, a pad of paper arrived with a thud. I was at the bottom of misery.

I could not write anything specific about any of the rebels I had met. There were too many of them. I didn't even know their real names. Their *noms de guerre* were easy and short. I knew a couple of Reagans, half a dozen Ghaddafis, a handful of Gandhis, and at least two Idi Amins. But none of them ever told me their secrets. Any attempts to describe them would be futile. But I had to write *something*. I could not afford to face another day as dreadful as this one. The clean-shaven officer wanted something substantial. So I had to write. I managed a few pages about two of the rebel leaders who had been living in southern India, trivia, such as where they were born, where they studied, and what happened to their girlfriends when they abandoned them. The information was not new to anyone familiar with the Tamil political scene. But it was all I knew. It was all anyone in the community knew.

I was half asleep when the officers came back the next morning. I gave them the few pages. The older one seemed uninterested. The younger one yawned.

"This is all I know. I don't know whether it's useful to you. But I am afraid I know no more."

"We will give you two more days," the older one said. "We want you to write everything, everything you know. The exact times you met with those terras, the weapons they had at that time, the type of vehicles, where their villages are ..."

I stood there in silence. Should I write fiction?

"Are you hungry?" the younger one asked.

"Yes, officer, very," I replied.

"What would you like? Chicken, pork, or beef?"

"No meat for me. I am a vegetarian. I can eat anything vegetarian, anything green."

I knew from the grapevine that this camp was called the Meat Shop. I also knew there were forms of torture peculiar to various camps and prisons. Professional torturers are creative. They have delicate names for torture. One, for example, is called *Dharma Chakra,* which normally refers to the wheel of life symbolizing the Buddha's teachings. But in this version, prisoners are stripped naked and tied in a squatting position, with their wrists bound together around their shins and their ankles tied. A pole is passed under their knees and they are suspended upside down. Then they are rotated. I knew of Sweet Shower. I knew of Joy Ride and Heli-Tour, but little did I know that Chicken, Beef, and Pork were also the names of different kinds of torture. Still, what else did I expect in a meat shop?

The officers too must have been confused since they had no torture called Vegetarian.

Finally, the younger one said, "We'll get you some vegetarian stuff."

Half an hour later, the older officer returned with two soldiers. They brought a plate of grass, dirt still on the roots, and a bunch of bitter neem leaves.

"Well, you're going to have a great salad," he said.

The moment they left, I threw up.

A strange evolution of images and names describe the country I come from.

Mango is the shape of the country if you're a tourist, pampered on the palm-fringed beaches. Serendip is what the Arab traders and travellers called it in the sixth century. Ceylon is the name the British gave it. Tear Drop is its shape as I see it. Tea and Blood are the only substances that run through its wounded veins. Lions and Tigers symbolize the majority Sinhalese and minority Tamils who have been ripping the country apart for sixteen years.

Sri Lanka gained its political independence from the British colonialists fifty-one years ago. Those years have been marked by long periods of emergency rule, ethnic pogroms, and wide-scale human rights violations. The current civil war is being waged by the Sinhalese-dominated government and the forces of militant Tamil nationalism, spearheaded by the Liberation Tigers of Tamil Eelam, popularly known as Tamil Tigers. The war is the result of brutal treatment of the minorities by the state and the minorities' violent response.

The international news media estimate that 50,000 men, women, and children have died as a direct result of the conflict. This figure does not include the 60,000 or more people formally designated as "disappeared," that is, arrested, tortured, and killed without leaving a trace. The war has cost 1 million people their homes and forced another 700,000, mainly Tamils, to seek asylum in various European countries, India, and Canada, which has been one of the largest recipients of Tamil refugees—150,000—in the past seven years. The UN Working Group on Enforced and Involuntary Removal of Persons (a euphemism for disappearances) ranks Sri Lanka number two in the world in disappearances, next only to Iraq. Yet the war is one of the forgotten wars: while international media focus on Kosovo, Sri Lanka seems too far away, both metaphorically and literally, from the strategic and "humanitarian" concerns of the West.

On the second day of my confinement, new soldiers came to my room. One who appeared to be an officer approached while I was still lying on the floor where I had slept.

"We need to test you," he said with a smile.

The officer said something in Sinhala to a tall, muscular soldier who was standing behind him. The guy looked ferocious. He pulled me up, dragged me a few metres, and flopped me on a table. I lay there helplessly on my back, waiting for another round of blows. Instead, the soldier tested my body by tapping my rib cage, chest, and neck with a curled index finger.

Instead of hearing a *thud, thud,* he must have heard a *thung, thung,* indicating how fragile my ninety-six-pound body was.

"This fellow can't withstand another round, sir," the soldier reported. I could not guess from his voice whether he was disappointed or relieved.

"OK," the officer said. "Then let's go."

The door closed. A flicker of hope ran through my mind. What if he came back and told me something completely unexpected? What if he said, you are free to go? Yet I knew that if I gave in to that hope, that's when an unexpected blow would be delivered.

The officer came back alone. "We got orders from the top," he said. "We don't want to keep you here anymore. You're released." He looked puzzled by this turn of events.

"Thanks, officer," I said.

"Are you happy?"

"Well, it is a good thing to be out of this place."

"I bet. But don't continue with your cock-and-bull stories about us. Right?"

It was my turn to smile.

"Are you a graduate?" he asked me.

"Yes. I did chemistry and zoology."

"What? Chemistry? That is even better. I was going to suggest that if you are a graduate why not get a decent job. I did history and that's why I am here, you know."

The time was 5:30. I knew the 6:00 curfew was still in effect. No way could I get to my office by six. But if I didn't, it would mean one more night here. No. That was unthinkable.

"Officer, how I can go home at this time?" I asked.

"Where do you live?"

"My home is far away, officer, and I don't want to be walking on the streets during curfew. I would appreciate it if you could drop me at my office in town."

"That's impossible. All I can do is to take you to the main gates. You can run from there. I will tell my sentries not to fire."

There was no choice. I ran and never looked back. Later I learned that Gamini had been released the same day and had pulled strings in high places to get me out. We both went back to work at the *Saturday Review.*

Before 1983 there was only a handful of Tamil rebels or Tamil terrorists, depending on your bias, in Sri Lanka. The pogroms of July 1983 and the military and political support accorded them by neighbouring India emboldened the rebels dramatically. By the end of 1984, there were thirty-five rebel groups espousing a wide spectrum of political ideologies, from nationalism and Marxism to an unholy blend of both. As ambushes and attacks on military convoys and camps increased, various Tamil rebel groups began competing for better and bigger publicity for their successful operations. A grenade-carrying rebel often accompanied press releases. We were expected to publish *or* perish!

The army wasn't far away either. A major encampment was within mortar range in an historic Dutch fort. We had already had nights of shelling, so dreadful that *Review*'s management installed bunkers beside the office. Whenever a military officer came to our office to collect a copy of our newspaper, he was always accompanied by a convoy of nine or ten military vehicles.

As if coping with censorship wasn't enough, we were also having a legal battle with the Oxford-educated minister of national security, who was hell-bent on closing our newspaper by whatever means possible.

The minister had no problem with the other three English-language papers, two of which were state owned. They were published out of Colombo, the state capital, and they all faithfully followed the official government line. In fact, a well-oiled media unit, which supported the minister, contained a bunch of popular and efficient Sinhalese and English journalists. For the minister, whom the *Review* held responsible for at least 10,000 deaths, our paper was the only threat. We were required to send all our contents, including advertisements and obituaries, to the authorities in Colombo, 400 kilometres away. The postal situation was dismal. We never got our copy back in time for the next edition, and even when we finally got it, stories would be marked "Materials have been wholly censored." We had no choice but to call ourselves "the only wholly government-censored newspaper."

We found inventive ways of coping with the censorship. Since the censor wasn't interested in stories from other countries or the headlines we put on them, we'd run an atrocity story from, say Guatemala, in which government troops had murdered hundreds of civilians, and call it "This Week's Killings." Or we'd simply leave a chunk of white space where a censorship story should have been and headline it "Who Killed Cock Robin?" We'd write about the rising cost of burials now that they were so much in demand, or the proliferation of dogs and squirrels in Jaffna with fewer and fewer people around to control them. Our readers always got it; the government never seemed to.

Dead men tell no tales. Nor dead women. Nor even dead children. It saves much explaining. This was brought home to me as never before one day in 1985. I went to the coastal village of Valvettiturai to interview two families who had lost relatives in a naval shelling the previous week. The families were poor. It was difficult to ask about the dead, two of them children. But after a slow, painful start the women began to talk. Seated near them on the floor, the men listened with occasional nods. Soon the women's tales of their sorrow came in torrents. Just as I was about to ask them for photographs of the children, an explosion shook the house.

"Army is around," said one of the older women, expressing more concern for me than for herself. "You must leave this place now." She showed me to the backyard.

"But I need my bicycle," I insisted.

One of the younger women in the family grabbed the bicycle and I left with the other men. The women stayed behind as a buffer, for it was the army's practice to round up all men under forty-five and take them to remote parts of the country from which their chances of ever returning were slim. Nobody here was taking chances. We were on our bicycles, pedalling as fast as we could. Half an hour down the road, we ran into a swarm of terror-stricken villagers.

A young man among them approached us, sweat streaming from his forehead, neck, and chest.

"It looks like they are gone now," he stammered. "They took several young men with them. They did not see me. I was hiding in the kitchen and they did not have time to search everywhere. They were in such a hurry. Then—then—we heard gunfire and explosions. We are too scared to go and find out—"

Suddenly he started crying, "*Aiyo, they took my brother.*"

It took us over an hour to pull ourselves together and set out in the direction of the explosion. By now, all of us sensed that something terrible had happened, so we decided to avoid the road. A middle-aged villager guided us along a narrow path through the bush. When we got to the village it was empty. No sign of the army. Approaching the middle of the village, I noticed a trail of blood that led to the community centre and the most ghastly sight I've ever seen: twenty-four youths, their hands tied behind their backs, had been herded into the building. Moments later, explosives had been placed inside and detonated (the blast that interrupted my interview). Most of the bodies were mutilated beyond recognition. Pieces of skull and teeth littered the rubble. On a nearby tree hung a blood-spattered sarong. About a hundred metres away, another twelve youths had been gunned down. The entire area looked like a slaughterhouse.

When I returned to the office the next day, I got a hand-delivered letter. It was from Ratna Raja, our typist. "My son was shot dead by the army yesterday," it said. "Please excuse my absence next week. I am not in a fit frame of mind to attend office."

Ratna Raja was a gentleman. After decades of service to the state, latterly as a stenographer in the Supreme Court, he was living in quiet retirement enjoying his work with the *Saturday Review,* his only major worry the marriages of his two remaining daughters. The previous week, his son, Mohan, had come to visit and was returning to his home with his eight-months' pregnant wife when he found figures in khaki barring his way. His corpse was one of those in the community centre. I knew Mohan, but I would not have recognized his body in the pile of disfigured flesh and bone. Nor would have his father.

Reporting atrocities on a regular basis began to get to me. But I couldn't avoid it. The *Saturday Review* had to keep reporting what the mainstream press wouldn't—the story from the victims' perspective. After a while, the only way I could keep my sanity was to write occasional pieces with a twist of humour, "cock-and-bull stories," as my interrogators would have it. These not only offended the military hierarchy, but also gave the newspaper a distinct voice. This one was a direct hit:

Cows have a habit of straying. It happens all over. But they should have the sense not to stray into "prohibited zones" like Harbour View Hotel in Kankesanthurai, now an army camp.

One night they strayed there, probably thinking that they could have a hearty dinner, including the leftovers of imported cheese and other goodies.

The ever alert soldiers thought that the approaching figures were terrorists crouching low. And they opened fire.

They scored a bull's eye in each case.

Finally, seven cows lay dead.

But not for long. Satisfied that the cows were not carrying grenades strapped to their udders, the lucky soldiers ended up eating them. A fine barbecue it was.

On April 24, 1987, I left our office to go to the printing plant, a few streets away. The *Saturday Review* had to be out by 2:00 P.M. that day, as usual. When I got there, I went straight to the composing room to put the finishing touches on the front page. The sturdy old Heidelberg press began to roll. I took a proof of the front page over to our printing manager's table, sat down, and started chatting with him.

Suddenly someone screamed, "Bomber!" I didn't have time to get out of my chair before a deafening blast shook the plant. Everyone ran. I bolted across the road to the grounds of a maternity hospital and jumped into a shallow open trench that served as an air-raid shelter. I huddled there for nearly an hour and a half as the bombers screamed and swooped overhead. Every few minutes we covered our ears and ducked as more bombs rained down. Pleas of "Jesu" and "Muruga" went up from the trench. I started counting the bombs. Journalist habit, I guess. After dropping ten of them, the planes disappeared as swiftly as they had come. Then the helicopter gunship appeared—it was an old nemesis. I was very familiar with that machine. Its arrival often signalled the end of the bombing raid. The old nemesis strafed the area and then vanished.

When the skies were clear, we left the trench. The printing plant was in shambles. But the damage could have been even worse; a bomb that had fallen just behind the plant hadn't gone off. The rest of the area was devastated except, ironically, for one building that escaped unscathed: the political office of the rebels. That prompted me to write a short piece for our next edition, in which I offered this advice: "If you happen to see a bomber swooping down, simply throw yourself into a rebels' camp or office. There is a one hundred per cent probability that you will never, never be hit."

With our printing plant inoperative, we postponed publication, but only for a day. With the support of other printers, we came out with a special issue: the Bomber Supplement, in which we reported that 25 people had been killed and 100 injured in the attack. In that supplement, I wished the minister of national security, the joint military operations commander, and their cohorts "sweet nightmares."

Shortly after my release from prison, the government of India mediated a truce between the Tamil rebels and the Sri Lankan government, in which the military was confined to the barracks. The negotiations failed and by the time war resumed two months later, with even greater hostility, the rebels had total control of Jaffna. Now it was their turn to control and command. They were as ruthless as the military, not only in the war they waged against the government, but in the wars they waged against one another. The power struggle among the rebel factions resulted in the death of hundreds of people, including several of my close friends. Assassinations and executions became the regular means of resolving political differences. In the *Saturday Review,* I was scathing in my criticism of the "friendly fires," as the internecine war was known. In early 1987, the Tamil Tigers, the most powerful of the rebel factions, gave me a warning: leave the country or face the consequences. I left my home in July. The *Saturday Review* survived for just three more months.

Apart from the realization that censorship is the mother of all metaphors, what did I learn from three years of writing dangerously?

The relationship between a writer and political power should always be an arm's-length one. Adversaries of each brutal power are consciously or unconsciously advocates of another. The challenge for a writer is to transcend these polarities. What better purpose for the writer than dedication to the cause of freedom? To remain honest and to maintain moral and creative integrity under any circumstances is a difficult path. But I have no other.

1999

The Boy in the Submarine

LARRY PRATT

No Poster Boy

THE BAGEL TREE IS A WELL-RUN DELI and coffee house on Whyte Avenue in Edmonton's trendy Old Strathcona district. It's owned by two sisters in their early forties, Arlene and Karen Calkins, who exercise a sunny dictatorship over their all-female staff as well as their very loyal customers. Arlene is small, energetic, and dark-haired. She greets her regulars with a knowing smile: I can already tell what you're dying to tell me. Karen, light-haired and slightly older, is one of the founders of the Bagel Tree. More detached and less attracted to crises than her sister, Karen always looks ready to head for a mountain ashram when the next pile of bills comes in. It's an expensive operation and competition for coffee drinkers is fierce. The difference at the Bagel Tree is that the staff push the right views along with the coffee and bagels. They grimace if you ask for a double hit of espresso, but reward you with a warm smile when you take a ginger tea. It's a bit like church, then, and that's because the Bagel Tree is Green, Feminist, and New Age. Everything, in fact, that is anathema to the people who have been running Alberta, and tearing it up, for the past fifty years. If I was asked to explain why Edmonton doesn't fit the conservative mould, I'd point to the Bagel Tree and its clientele.

Men are welcome at this south-side bagel matriarchy, but there's an understanding that they will check their male wildness at the door, except, of course, for Marco,★ Arlene's young son.

Marco comes flying in through the front door of the Bagel Tree, his grandfather trailing close behind in the slipstream. Arlene's dad has come to do some repairs, and Marco has come along to help. Help? Watching him in motion, I'm astounded by one seven-year-old boy's power to disorient so many adults simultaneously. The atmosphere begins to tingle, as if everyone has had one caffe latte too many. People suddenly have to check that they haven't lost their car keys. Did I miss my appointment? Marco is feeling good, manic, in fact, and he's pushing at the edge. He's bouncing into the customers, getting into everyone's space, avoiding his mother's gaze. Marco has no sense of his own territory—no ego boundary—and so he constantly intrudes into everyone else's. It's chaos wherever he goes.

Soon he has people bumping into one another and spilling their hot drinks and apologizing, "Sorry." "No, *I'm sorry*." Everyone seems perplexed by what is going on. But his mother doesn't mind Marco's antics; a born teacher, Arlene sees these visitations by Marco as reality checks for some of her New Age staff and customers, who are always going on to her about their pet remedies for the boy's mental illness. Well, here's the real thing, folks. How *about* stopping that medication? How *about* that wheat-free diet to cure paranoid schizophrenia?

"Hi, Leery," Marco greets me. I've been sitting in my favourite corner. Marco has a high, squawky voice and talks in clipped sentences using very few words. It's called poverty of speech, but mostly I can follow him.

"Hi, Marco. Did you make them close down the school today?"

He shakes his head sadly and hands me one of his teacher's worksheets, which asks the students what they will do when they grow up, and then to illustrate their choice with a sketch.

★All children's names have been changed.

"When my mother is too old to work, I will be the boss of the Bagel Tree," Marco has written. And next to this declaration, he has drawn a picture of a very large black bomb with a lighted fuse. His reputation for aggression and planned revenge has his teachers intimidated and wondering how bad will Marco be when he's *eight?*

"Good plan, Marco," I tell him. "I'm not sure I'll be drinking coffee here by then, but it's interesting."

I met Marco when he was six, and I knew that he had recently been expressing a wish to be dead. He had told his doctor he "didn't want to live, not as Marco." Somehow he could see the rest of him going on, but only if Marco were dead. He didn't like Marco. He would speak of his body or parts of it as if they belonged to some-one else, as if they had nothing to do with him. He wouldn't say "I am never happy." It was "My brain is never happy." The "I," the real self, the creative core that expresses the unified, integrated sense of ourselves, was missing. Marco can't take for granted the aliveness, the realness of his body and himself, so he hides out in his fantasy world. Some days, in the early years of the illness, he experienced himself as dead.

It was from Marco, not a psychology text, that I learned that we all live, to a degree, in two worlds—the real, available social world, and the hidden world of secrets, fantasies, and delusions. We all have, to a degree, two selves—our real or true self, that centre of association, friendship, and community, and a false self that we use to mask our fears and pain and to hide from the insults of the external world. If a child picks up from adults that it is expected to hide its feelings, it may bury its secrets, its sadness, and assume a false self. But a child who develops a serious mental illness and experiences himself as depersonalized, even dead, is in much graver danger of losing himself permanently in the inner fantasy world that we call madness. Marco is such a child.

I became interested in Marco's story while hanging out at the Bagel Tree, drinking coffee, and talking with Arlene. She encour-aged me to write about him, dictated lengthy and poignant records of her struggles with the strange illness. At that time, the boy was withdrawn, almost mute, and starting on a new medication. He'd been putting on a lot of weight, only partly because of the drug, and Arlene now was talking about—unthinkable, really—cutting back on Marco's pasta. She hauled out photo albums with pictures of Marco before his illness—a beautiful boy—and blamed the pills. But the boy's doctor and nurse thought the weight gain was evidence of Arlene's inability to say no to Marco, part of a ceaseless struggle for power between the mother and her schizophrenic son.

Some of my friends tried to talk me out of writing about Marco. Why write on a rare mental disorder like childhood schizophrenia (1 in 10,000 for children versus 1 in 100 for adolescents and adults)? Why choose a boy like Marco?

I had left the academic world in the mid-nineties and was looking for a writing project that would put some distance between that world and me. I wanted to find a story that could be written simply and without preachiness. What drew me to Marco and his illness, I suppose, was his superficial resemblance to my stepson, Shaun, who is autistic and now a young man. When I first met Shaun's mother, Trish, he was the same age as Marco was when I met him in 1996. And Arlene and Trish were both single, determined, and struggling with the authorities on their boys' behalf, and doing so with very little help. To complete the pattern, there was a third single mother raising a handicapped boy years ago—my own schoolteacher-mother raising me alone after one of the last summer polio epidemics in Ontario.

But my associations were less than helpful when it came to comprehending Marco. I was all too familiar with Shaun's autism— a condition usually involving loss of all language, lack of social relationships, aversion to close contact, mental retardation, and ritualistic, stereotypical behaviours. This, not the exceptional autistics studied by Oliver Sacks or portrayed in the film *Rain Man,* is the reality of autism, and I saw it every day. From infancy the disorder is pervasive, affecting all development.

For a long time I found myself using my experience with Shaun's disorder to comprehend Marco's. And distorting it. And getting it wrong. Marco was not autistic. He was not mentally retarded. Schizophrenia had to be understood as a distinct and complex physical brain illness, a complete syndrome of symptoms and signs, few of which are found in autism. Marco's illness could be treated.

Schizophrenia is characterized by a period of deterioration in mental functioning, followed by delusions and hallucinations, often the hearing of voices. These are the so-called positive or psychotic signs. The disorder is also characterized by thought disorder, rather than retardation, and negative symptoms such as avolition, loss of pleasure, a split between the cognitive and emotional (say, laughing when someone dies), and worsening hygiene and appearance. The most basic experience is an alteration in sensation and perception; yet another is the feeling of being "flooded" by ideas and sensations. There are also gender differences. Males develop schizophrenia earlier than females, and it is more chronic and more lethal in men. Schizophrenia with a poor prognosis and with paranoia has been linked to aggressiveness and psychopathy in some people, but there is little evidence that people with schizophrenia on medication, taken as a group, are any more violent than the rest of the population. There is, though, a small percentage of the mentally ill who *are* violent and dangerous, especially when they are off medication and abusing drugs or alcohol. The illness waxes and wanes; to borrow a lyric from Dire Straits, "It's one step forward and it's back to go."

The other part of my answer to "Why Marco?" is this: a great deal of what has been published on schizophrenia and other major mental illnesses has been written almost as if the people with the disorders did not exist. This is particularly true of children. Very few authorities bother to *listen* to what is said by psychotic people. I wanted to listen to and observe Marco. I wanted to find out why Marco—unlike most kids with the disorder—was aggressive and violent, how he was stigmatized at school, and why and how he moved between the available world and secret world. Was Marco, after all, one of us, or was he so vulnerable, so strange, so troubled that he would always be excluded from a community that was none too sympathetic to the mentally ill? Would Marco ever make a friend?

As Arlene says, Marco is no poster boy for schizophrenia. On Saturdays, his mother and Karen would take him to a mall for lunch. Without fail, something would set him off and there would be a great smash-up. Tables would fly, chairs go crashing, food and drinks would be everywhere; and Marco would be trying to punch out somebody. Then some disapproving voice would be heard remonstrating about that boy's need for discipline.

And that's when the two sisters would burst out, "Oh no, he's having a really *good* day!"

Marco's symptoms and strangeness are not the disease, merely evidence that something is wrong, something *physical,* with the brain. Underlying the signs and symptoms is a complex but quite common disease of the brain. I accept much of the so-called medical model of schizophrenia: major mental illness syndromes are biological, not psychological, in their roots, and the genetic vulnerability to acquire schizophrenia is especially strong in some families. A number of brain neurotransmitters, such as dopamine, have been strongly identified with symptoms of schizophrenia, and there is overwhelming physical evidence of structural brain abnormalities. Many researchers think the limbic system, which lies deep in the brain's centre and is the "gate" that filters incoming stimuli and organizes raw experience into coherent reality, is the source of many of schizophrenia's abnormalities and symptoms. Long ignored as a chronic, incurable mental illness, schizophrenia is now a fashionable topic for medical researchers; and now there are new anti-psychotic medications that are making it possible for sufferers to live and work outside institutions without the threat of horrible relapse. But a cure? Schizophrenia can be managed but not cured.

However, the medical model has its limits when it comes to the sufferer's relation to society. Psychiatry's image of the family and society is still in the Eisenhower era. Yet the social and family environment matters a great deal: I was intrigued by World Health Organization studies suggesting that people with schizophrenia in parts of the developing world—where the sick weren't labelled, held personally responsible, and criticized for their behaviour—do better than those in industrialized countries, where the stigma and critical emotion are strong and "Pull yourself together" passes for acceptance. Where expectations are high and sympathetic acceptance is missing, people will relapse and end up back in hospital.

I was curious to know whether there was hope for Marco. Would he be able to function in society, avoid hospitalizations, and hold a steady job? Would he be able to live independently? I distrusted the gloomy, even defeatist prognoses of the medical system. Psychiatry has a history of following intellectual fashions, and some psychiatrists have a habit of giving up on those who fail to respond to treatment. One reason the mentally ill are excluded from society and turned into pariah figures is that the professional pessimists simply write them off as chronic, degenerative cases; and then so does everyone else. Only twenty years ago, it was the practice to lump all children with autism, manic depression, schizophrenia, and other psychoses under a single rubric: childhood schizophrenia. The term was meaningless, and so a nurse would sit down with the worried parents and say, "We think little Mary is going to be a bit funny." Because of the dominance of Freudian psychoanalysis, it was also customary for psychiatrists to blame bad mothering and the family for schizophrenia or autism: "refrigerator mothers" was a typical epithet. Those who regret the pre-eminence of biological psychiatry today need to consider the alternative and the damage that it did, especially to women.

BORN VULNERABLE

Today, Marco is a nine-year-old boy who lives with his mother, his older sister, Carmen, and their collie, Merlin, in a quiet duplex not far from the Yellowhead Trail on Edmonton's north side. He is a stocky Italian-Canadian boy with large brown eyes, dark hair and complexion, and serious demeanour. He's good at math and likes card games such as King in the Corner. Marco is of average intelligence, but sometimes he seems perplexed, strange, and sad; on bad days he can be withdrawn or cold and aggressive.

Arlene tells me how it began. Five years ago, when he was just four, Marco suffered his first major psychotic disturbance. He suffered from nightmares and night terrors. He complained to Arlene that his favourite ET doll was giving him mean looks and staring at him in the dark. People were outside their house watching him. He was afraid of the bathroom, fearful of the water overflowing the toilet bowl. He was hearing noises in his head and walked around banging his ears with his fists. He was up all night, prowling around the house looking for intruders. Fearful and defensive, he began striking out at people without cause. Children would drop by their yard and Marco would drive them away with stones. He was intrusive, always in your space. He had trouble understanding his mother and sister, and his own speech was often incoherent, jumping from one topic to the next in mid-sentence.

Marco was odd and bewildered, never joyful or carefree. One night he told his mother that he had a "tight hat" on his head; he couldn't get the hat off and his head hurt all the time. There was no hat. It was impossible to reassure this small boy. He was hyper-vigilant, watchful, fearful, ready to strike out at his enemies. He was like a sentry on perpetual watch. At times he was cold, unfeeling, full of ideas for revenge. His Aunt Karen, a highly tolerant person, thought he was psychopathic and just plain bad.

Arlene got him into Edmonton's small Glenrose Hospital to have his hearing checked, but he was quickly referred to a psychologist and then a child psychiatrist. What Arlene had most feared was confirmed. Marco was severely mentally ill. At the appallingly early age of four, he had the classic signs of paranoid schizophrenia— delusions, auditory hallucinations, suspiciousness, speech and thought disorders, and lack of ego boundaries. He had lost connection with reality and was slipping into a psychotic episode. The diagnosis was a life sentence.

This cruel disease of the brain typically waxes and wanes with psychotic episodes followed by recovery periods and remissions, followed by relapses. Up to fifteen per cent of sufferers commit suicide. Schizophrenia is not curable nor preventable, but it can be treated with powerful anti-psychotic drugs (though sometimes with debilitating side effects, such as Parkinsonian-like motor disturbances) and through psychosocial therapy. Childhood schizophrenia is invariably inherited, and some researchers have argued that it is the most severe form of the disorder; that is, it has a particularly poor prognosis over time. Childhood is a time when we master the crucial cognitive, social, and psychological capacities that take us into adolescence and adulthood, and the early onset of any mental illness is bound to derail much of that process.

At five, Marco went on his first anti-psychotic drug and was off to kindergarten. But, as his mother once remarked in a gloomy moment, if Marco was going to be unwell as a child, how could he ever be well as an adult? There was hope that drug treatments would improve, but a realistic prognosis for a very young child with a devastating mental illness like schizophrenia was poor.

Marco was born genetically vulnerable. His father, who is separated from Arlene and lives in B.C., also suffers from paranoid schizophrenia and has been hospitalized during a couple of psychotic episodes. He is a big, hard-working construction worker, an Italian-Canadian with a fierce devotion to his children. In the early eighties, he married Arlene in Vancouver. They had a healthy daughter, but then he got sick. During the first psychotic episode in a Vancouver apartment several years before Marco's birth, he complained to his landlady of having a "tight hat" on his head and asked her to remove it. She called the police, he went into hospital, and he started on an anti-psychotic. After that, he was never the same person, Arlene says. At her insistence, they moved to her hometown,

Edmonton. Two things happened: he stopped his medication and again became psychotic, and Marco was conceived.

During his second episode in Edmonton, Arlene's husband thought the family house had been invaded by the creepy Addams family of network television and was obsessed by fears that people were watching their house and monitoring their conversations. He would flick his lighter in the living room, trying to drive away the Addams family. At different times and in different places, both father and son have lost connection with reality and chased the same paranoid delusions, tugged on the same invisible tight hat. Both have been psychotic and driven by voices, fears, and terrible visions. Both have lost the feeling of being real, of having a body that feels anything at all. Both have felt horribly threatened and insecure in the face of everyday life. When he was sick, Arlene's husband would stand in front of a full-length mirror for hours, trying to connect with his badly weakened self. Transfixed by his own strange reflection, he would ask his little girl, "Who am I?" "Why, you're Daddy!" she would giggle.

As Marco's case suggests, schizophrenia has a genetic component. But this needs some qualification. People inherit a predisposition to develop the disease, but other triggering events in the environment seem to be needed to activate the full-blown syndrome. Not everyone who inherits the vulnerability gets sick—not even some identical twins—and not everyone who gets schizophrenia has inherited it. Nonetheless, genetic factors may account for two-thirds of the variance in the vulnerability to the disorder. Danish studies of adopted children of schizophrenic biological mothers showed that most of the adopted children went on to develop a schizophrenic-like disorder; being raised in a different environment did not improve their chances. Still, non-genetic factors also play a role in the development and the course of schizophrenia. Viral infections during the second semester of pregnancy are suspected; so are the effects of malnutrition; stressful, compli-cated births; winter and spring births; a decrease in oxygen supply during labour; and other environmental insults to the brain.

A number of imaging studies have also demonstrated that there are neurologic and structural brain abnormalities in schizophrenics, children included. The regions of the brain affected have an influence on information-processing, recognition and the expression of emotions, memory, attention, problem-solving, and the capacity to abstract. The overall volume of the brain shrinks (by up to three per cent) in those with schizophrenia and in relatives at high risk; the shrinkage tends to be greatest in those with the most genetic loading (two or more first-degree relatives are ill). Using these measures, it may soon be possible—for better or worse—to predict which people are most likely to become psychotic in the next five to ten years.

ISLANDS, NO FERRY

It was noon and I was waiting on the third floor of the Glenrose Hospital at the children's and adolescent psychiatric units. The children—over half of whom have schizophrenia—were coming out of their day school for their break. I noticed three things. First, all were boys. Second, every one of them walked quietly down the corridor holding his right arm out so that he touched the wall as he moved along. Touching the wall is a way of compensating for a poor sense of space and distance. And, third, each child was all alone, quite cut off from any communication with the others—isolated but not autonomous. There were no gangs of small boys, no groups of two or three chattering at the same time. No leaders, no followers, no tribe. Each boy looked like "an island, entire of itself," but with no ferry connections between islands. It was preternaturally quiet, compared to an ordinary school, because no one was speaking; no one was listening to any voice besides his own inner monologue. These children don't joke or banter; they can't generalize from one context to the next, and few of them understand that they are ill or even different. To be schizophrenic is to be set apart, to be isolated from other children and the community.

Living with schizophrenia has been compared to life in a vast museum of strangeness. Time and distance collapse; a year can seem like five minutes passing, distances magnify or shrink as through a telescope. The sufferer has no filter, no way to screen out the sensations that are flooding his brain. He is terrified of change; he must stop change, immobilize life around him. Reality is flatness, sameness, a timeless present. Holding back change is a bit like holding back the water from the overflowing toilet, Marco's constant fear. When it happens, Marco panics, "Quick, Mom, call 911!" To me, he confides, "That toilet might overflow while you're in there. It goes off every Saturday."

It's Marco, not the toilet, that's always threatening to overflow. He saves his worst behaviours for home. It's a perfectly nice home, but if you go there to see him, it may feel like the countdown is already in progress. When he is doing well, Marco can usually keep it together for around two hours, but after that he can be volatile. Arlene is tense because she doesn't want her guest exposed to something outrageous, and her daughter is tense because she fully expects Marco to go off half-cocked. And the phone rings all evening—perhaps fifteen times—and each time, Arlene flinches and has the kids answer it. Marco and Carmen's dad is just having a bad day, so he is calling his children from Vancouver, and calling, and calling. Nothing awful has happened, but the illness that has afflicted Arlene's family makes everyone feel a hostage of schizophrenia.

The more I listen to Marco, the more I learn about his isolation. "I miss my dad, I want him to live with us." But Arlene has ruled that out. Marco has almost no males in his life. He has his mother, sister, aunt, nurse, doctor, babysitters, and the women at the Bagel Tree, none of whom has experienced a boy's life. Marco does know that he is different. He says, "There's something wrong in my brain," and he is aware that other boys won't be his friend. He craves friendships, but he also pushes other kids away. His sister is popular and has many good friends, and this angers him. He says he won't be happy until he has *more* friends than Carmen. For her part, Carmen is often embarrassed by Marco's behaviour, and she is reluctant to invite her friends over. Marco's rages alienate everyone, including the family, and the outcome is that he is utterly alone, a harsh fate and, for any parent, heartbreaking. It is the social isolation of the mentally ill, not their strange behaviour, that society needs to remedy.

The disease causes this isolation; stigma reinforces it. Schizophrenia impairs the ability to empathize, to understand others. Thinking is bizarre, illogical, and self-centred. Delusions, which are fixed false beliefs, are also a characteristic symptom of schizophrenia. The paranoid sufferer may believe, as Marco's father did, that he is being controlled and persecuted by forces (aliens, the CIA, the Vatican) that use the latest technologies (lasers, satellites, magnetic waves) to manipulate his behaviour. Or he may have delusions of grandeur and believe that he is both immortal and a great historical personage (Christ, Adam, Napoleon, or Gandhi) whose purpose is to redeem us. Or he may believe that he alone is receiving esoteric messages from the TV, or he may think that everyone is talking about him and making jokes or gossiping about him; that is, he imagines himself at the centre of *their* universe. In this delusional state, he gives up the idea of "otherness," of sharing common meanings with the rest of the world. Any self-world connectedness is lost. Everything that occurs in the environment relates only to *him*. And these distortions occur not because his sense of self is so powerful, but because it has been obliterated. The egocentric delusions have in common the unshakeable belief that the schizophrenic sufferer is all-important, blessed with insight into the true and secret nature of things, and extremely powerful. In psychosis, everything is connected, accidents don't happen, and only he has the key to what is happening. Many people with paranoid schizophrenia unfortunately are not free of delusional thoughts even while on medication.

MARCO IN TWO WORLDS

Schizophrenia being a waxing-and-waning mental illness, Marco has enjoyed periods of remission and relatively good health. Those who see him only when he is well are tempted to question the diagnosis altogether.

But when Marco is bad, he is *very* bad, *very* paranoid, and hard to cope with or to be around; at those times he seems (to borrow British author John Clay's metaphor) to be like a boy trapped on the ocean floor in his own submarine. Marco is ambivalent. He is hidden well out of sight, but he doesn't know whether to risk coming up or to risk sitting down there indefinitely. He fears being engulfed by other people if he comes to the surface, swallowed up in relationships, but he envies those who live in the real world and fears being lost forever if he just sits there on the bottom. Marco desperately wishes to be accepted, and he desperately wants to drive everyone away. His behaviour is compulsive and mechanical. To himself, Marco feels unreal, cut off from his body, fragmented. His mother says that every morning he has to pull his various "bits" together before he can face the day. The perception of reality is experienced in fragments rather than as a unity; say, your mother's face exists only as a series of disconnected parts, not as the whole face, or you hear and process only a bit of a conversation, then integrate it into a delusion.

When he's like that, the very last thing his mother wants to hear from her well-intentioned New Age friends or employees at the Bagel Tree is that Marco should be taken off anti-psychotic medications and put on some alternative regime—multivitamins, fish oil, homeopathy. According to these New Agers, Marco's father was not psychotic, just sensitive, when he saw the Addams family in his living room. "Maybe they *were* there, Arlene, maybe you just couldn't see them." They give her books like *Healing Yourself*. They love Arlene and think she is obsessed with Marco's troubles. They want natural solutions, not psychiatrists and anti-psychotics. Some of her staff think that Arlene should stop "managing" Marco's illness and put him under the care of alternative practicioners. But Arlene fears that could cost her the crucial support of Marco's child psychiatric team, and perhaps her own sanity as well:

> Sometimes when people suggest alternative things, I feel like saying, "Well, why don't you take him for that period." Because I've lived with Marco when he's off medication, and you feel like you're trapped in a nightmare. Even now [when he is doing well on medication], I can feel like that, because he can be quite manic. Sometimes he can get me going to where I'm spinning three feet off the ground. He'll have fifteen things going on at the same time. I'll feel like I'm trapped on a ride; you can't get off till it's over.

Marco spent the better part of his kindergarten year on Risperdal (risperidone), one of the novel "atypical" anti-psychotic drugs that became available in the 1990s. The drug worked amazingly well for several months, and Arlene thought she saw the "true personality" of her boy emerge; the real Marco, the true self behind the illness, was coming out when, as in the film *Awakenings*, the boy reacted to the drug with a rash, and all the bad symptoms reappeared. Arlene was learning about the nature of Marco's disorder. One step forward and it's back to go.

In the fall of 1996, Marco started grade one in a Catholic elementary school in north Edmonton. In itself this was absurd. That a young boy with an illness as severe as paranoid schizophrenia would be expected to integrate with healthy children into the mainstream school system—with no aide, no small special-needs class—was more a commentary on Alberta's backwardness than on Marco's abilities. He was not stabilized on medication and his thoughts were very disturbed. On Monday, 20 take away 10 would equal 10, but on Tuesday it would mean nothing at all. What he'd learn in one room he'd lose if he crossed the hall. He couldn't generalize. He was swamped by the crowds of students, the noisy hallways, and the gangs in the schoolyard. He was lost and bewildered in the big classroom. His paranoia worsened, he seldom slept, and he grew more and more agitated. He couldn't sit still at his desk, so he would pick it up and throw it. He tore up his workbooks in frustration and he violently attacked other students. Some of the attacks were impulsive and carried out in the heat of the moment, but others were coolly planned and acted on long after the moment had passed. Marco was strong, and he liked to jump on kids and attempt to beat or strangle them. After six weeks, Marco experienced a psychotic "break," spending a whole afternoon rolling up a rug on the classroom floor and refusing all communication with his worried teacher. Stressed to his limit, Marco had withdrawn into his hidden, hallucinatory world and was no longer involved in a world of self-with-others. It was at this point that his psychiatrist, Dr. Sarah Matthews of the Glenrose Hospital, intervened and removed Marco from school. For the next nine months he would be in the Glenrose's day-patient program for children with schizophrenia, spending his nights and weekends at home.

The fundamental issue concerning Marco, as his psychiatric team saw it, was his potential for aggression and his signs of psychopathy. "Even without the schizophrenia," a staff member told me, "Marco would be very difficult to handle." To the child psychiatric professionals, Marco's aggressiveness and capacity to hurt without remorse marked him from many of the ill children and adolescents on the ward. Rarely did any of them display his potential for revenge and aggression. Marco would coolly plan an attack for several days. Some of the staff thought he was already a risk to his sister and mother; by the time he reached sixteen or seventeen, he could be dangerous.

Marco was hypersensitive to criticism and teasing—he had "plate-glass feelings"—and his paranoia led him to read the activities of others egocentrically, as directed against himself. He would watch a couple of boys talking at recess and conclude, They hate me. They will hurt me. I will get them first. Full of self-dislike, he'd project his low opinion of himself onto others and end up provoking and hitting them. Projection, which is often a defence mechanism, is the process of attributing to others characteristics of our own that we prefer to deny (the philandering husband is obsessed with the fear that his wife is cheating on him). It plays a key role in paranoid thought processes.

For a long time Marco distorted or misinterpreted any gestures of friendship or interest from other children as deceptions or as hostile in intent. They were not interested in him but in the family tree house out back. Or he would drive away one potential friend because he insisted on having a dozen friends like his sister. In other ways, Marco was a controlling bully who was always isolating himself. For example, he wouldn't allow anybody to speak while he was having his meals. The noise disturbed him and he was unable to chew his food. For over a year he was obsessive about getting a dog and began to smell dog on his lunchbox, in the family car, and on his mother. "Have you had a dog in the car? Have you been driving around with a dog?" he would quiz her like a jealous husband. He wanted control more than he wanted a dog.

Lacking the capacity to empathize, Marco was often perplexed and unable to learn why others acted as they did—he usually didn't "get it." In the adult world, where so much depends on our ability to read people's cues and anticipate their preferences (for example, the receptionist who needs to know whose calls to put through to the boss), absence of empathic skills often means absence of employment as well as the absence of friends. Can you be taught empathy? At Marco's school, they worked all the time on feelings. Marco would slug some boy: "How would you feel if he did that to you?"

TAMING MARCO

It was not simply a question of finding the right drug. Marco's child psychiatrist and his psychiatric nurse at the Glenrose Hospital were not sure whether the true source of his anti-social aggressiveness was his illness or his family environment. They described him to me as "a thug," "aloof," "a spoiled brat," "a treasured Italian kid," "nasty," and "manipulative." Hypersensitive to teasing, "He spits, hits, fights, and runs away."

They blamed Arlene for failing to set limits for the boy or to subject him to the tight, low-emotions routine required by children with schizophrenia. They felt Marco exploited his mother and sister, and a home visit by one of the staff left the strong impression that the boy was not under control. He was using his tantrums and aggressive behaviour to control the family. Only a tightly organized structure, enforced consistently and, if required, in very tough, very cold language by all of his caregivers, could alter Marco's bad behaviour. They would make ample use of seclusion (or the locked "time-out" room) and a zero-tolerance approach toward his aggressiveness. Sandy Lenz, the child psychiatric nurse working with Marco, made it plain that she saw a good chance of Marco developing into a dangerous schizophrenic adolescent.

The hospital's plan could work only if the same tightly enforced routine was imposed at home. The staff wanted an unchanging, low-stress, and unemotional home environment for Marco, a rigid routine that stayed exactly as planned from week to week. Marco was terrified of change and craved sameness, repetition, and concreteness from his environment. Anything unexpected, from a change in babysitter to an alteration in the bus schedule, threatened him. In a highly impermanent world, Marco wanted certainty. Thus, the child psychiatric team told Arlene, to the extent possible, each Monday should resemble all other Mondays; Wednesday should be like every other Wednesday. Dinner at 5:30; walk the dog; play a game; take medication; two bedtime stories; lights out by 7:30, day in, day out. What most people would consider a boring, repetitive, unspontaneous daily routine was what Marco needed to feel safe. This was the only way he could learn to respect boundaries and give up his aggressive ways. He would be on medication and under supervision all day, every day of the week.

Arlene resented and resisted the hospital's advice. She didn't agree that Marco was potentially dangerous, nor did she believe that her child-rearing practices had encouraged his uncontrollable behaviour. Arlene blamed the schizophrenia, the illness, and looked to the medical team to get him under control with the right pills. Blaming the illness was expedient because it removed responsibility from herself. It also implied that he should be in the hospital and not in school. She blamed the school for placing Marco under intolerable stress; in fact, she thought he did not belong in a public school at all. She was frequently angry about being dragged away from work to sort out problems at the school. She disliked the pressures to change the structure at home.

Marco was on another of the new atypical anti-psychotics, Zyprexa (olanzapine), when he returned to elementary school in the fall of 1997. This was a promising drug that was expected to work on his negative as well as positive symptoms, and without the heavy side effects of the older neuroleptics, but it would take months to achieve its full effect. Now, in the absence of any alternative, he was in grade two but in a small "Positive Development" (behaviour-disordered) class for younger boys. Most of the boys in the class were attention-deficit, hyperactive kids who needed social skills and anger management, but the two male teachers had little knowledge of Marco's disorder. They weren't even sure that he was schizophrenic. "Was Marco abused?" they'd ask. The answer was no, he was ill. Still, they took most of their cues from the psychiatric staff at the Glenrose. Keep it simple. Make him sit in his seat. Use the time-out room. Tolerate absolutely no physical abuse and aggression. Don't give him choices.

His teachers were at first optimistic that they could modify the boy's behaviour, until one day in October when they took him down to the regular grade two classroom to meet the students. This was Marco's first exposure to a big class since his breakdown a year earlier. The teacher had them all sitting in a circle quietly. Then, with no warning, Marco reached over, put his strong hands around the neck of a seven-year-old girl, and began to strangle her with real determination. He was restrained and removed. This unprovoked violence, coming out of the blue, frightened everyone in the room. Had Marco been unsupervised, there could have been a tragedy. No one knew for certain why he had attacked. It was one of several episodes of aggression that led his teachers to conclude that Marco was unsafe to be around other kids. "Why is he here?" they asked his mother. "Marco is completely crazy," she was told. He was too paranoid, too unpredictable, too dangerous. "You never know when Marco's track is switching," they said. They took slight comfort in the fact that his illness and medication had left him rather clumsy and overweight. They told the grade two class, "God made Marco mad, but He also made him slow."

School was a place where Marco was shunned and feared, a noisy and perplexing environment that stimulated his paranoia and aggressions. It is important to listen to what Marco says and to see the school environment as he experiences it. He has complained that the other children were watching him, staring at him, and that this made him feel unhappy. The truth is that children *do* stare at those who are different, handicapped, "weird." And being stared at can make a child self-conscious, intensely aware that he is regarded as an outsider, a stranger or alien. The gaze can suggest a threat of physical danger. Aggressive staring is used to shame and intimidate, and it can be misread as the prelude to an assault.

WHOSE MARCO?

Arlene was at her lowest ebb when we talked about Marco in the last months of 1997. She shook with anger when she told me of a six-hour confrontation with Marco's doctor over the boy's future. Arlene seemed to me to have lost her power; she could see no choices but bad ones. Everyone at the Bagel Tree was indignant because Marco's school was on the point of giving up on him, and the child psychiatric unit at the Glenrose Hospital was ready to have him removed from his family and placed in a treatment facility. The anti-psychiatry New Age squad was up in arms, fully vindicated at last.

Arlene and Marco had driven to the Glenrose to see Sarah Matthews on a Saturday morning in early November 1997. It was a disaster. Marco, in his doctor's words, had gone "totally ballistic" in Matthews' office, throwing chairs and books and papers, screaming threats and insults and, once more, showing the psychiatrist that his embarrassed mother had no control over him. Dr. Matthews, rattled and fed up, had Marco removed to a locked time-out room, where he would spend much of the day. The psychiatrist "blew her stack." This is the substance of the conversation as I later heard it from both women:

> "Arlene, this is just outrageous. Marco's acting like a thug. I know you think this is the illness again. It isn't. Marco is not psychotic, and he's not coming back to the hospital again. We have too many other sick kids."
>
> "I'm sorry, Dr. Matthews, but I think he *should* be in the hospital, not at that school. I think he's out of control because he hates the school. And his medication clearly isn't working."
>
> "It's not about the medication. It's about setting limits. I'm getting calls from the school nearly every day. He's not safe. He's aggressive. What we just saw was Marco acting out. Showing me he's not under control. It's a constant power struggle. This is anti-social behaviour, not the illness."
>
> "It is the school's fault!"
>
> "Arlene, you're not in control. No one is in control of Marco. You don't listen to what we say. This has to be addressed now or he'll be dangerous in five years. He has to have limits on a twenty-four-hour basis. We need a change."
>
> "What does that mean? Change his medication?"
>
> "No. You have to give Marco up. He needs to go into a

group home—a group treatment home where someone objective can set strict limits. You have to give up custody."

"Oh no, he's too young. We need Marco at home and he needs us. I'm so shocked you would say that. I know there may come a time when I have to give him up, but it's not now."

"Think of yourself. Think of your daughter. You deserve a more normal life. This isn't good for the two of you. Marco needs to leave the family so we can make him less violent. He could be a real danger to both of you."

"I'm too upset to make any decisions now. I didn't expect this. But I'm not giving up Marco. He needs his safe base. I can still do things for Marco."

"Well, you know that I have the authority to require it, if need be. I can have him taken into custody and placed under Social Services. You have to consider this option."

Arlene came away from this meeting feeling utterly demoralized. She obsessed for weeks over Dr. Matthews' outburst. Was she just "yanking Arlene's chain," trying to get across the message that a different home environment was needed? Losing Marco would be a huge failure, and Arlene cannot tolerate failure. Nor did she have illusions about how the boy would fare in the public system. Living with a mentally ill husband and a mentally ill son for so many years had given her a certain resilience and a sense of realism about how society treats people with schizophrenia:

> There isn't public sympathy—or understanding. And I have to keep saying these things. That's my job. I guess that's why God gave me Marco, and I'm not about to keep him in the closet or be afraid to tell people about this disease. If I didn't fight for access to the Glenrose, for an aide, for schooling and everything else, none of it would be there. I have to fight for every single thing.

This was a period of real despair for Arlene. At one point, she even declared herself ready to give up the boy.

As it happened, Arlene kept Marco and was able to turn the tables and negotiate with Social Services for an aide, and she gradually implemented the changes to the home environment. But none of this mattered if it failed to address Marco's vulnerability and resistance to change. At this point, he was rigidly defiant of all authority, and his aggressions were serious ones. I believed the people at the hospital: in a few years, absent some real change, Marco might be locked up, perhaps in jail, where so many mentally ill people are ending up. His natural movement as a young boy should have been toward involvement in friendships, associations, and the community; instead, his behaviour was driving everyone away.

But Marco can switch unpredictably. Somehow the crisis over custody set the waxing-waning mechanism in motion. In the early months of 1998, Marco's submarine, trapped for many months on the ocean floor, began to move slowly to the surface. This was not a sudden remission—not an awakening—but gradually Marco opened up and became less rigid. He was more empathetic, more involved with his peers, and some of his symptoms (negative as well as positive) moderated or disappeared as the year wore on. His chronic sadness seemed to lift. Some of the paranoia remained, but he was less aggressive. Marco was developing a stronger sense of self and of his connectedness with other people. To his own great surprise, he was less isolated and he stopped driving other children away.

Marco had somehow reached a safer place. He has remained there. Why? Arlene was implementing a new regime and was seeing the advantages of a consistent routine. She herself was a bit more detached, perhaps less guilty about Marco. She was easing up and adapting to Marco's world. Perhaps most significantly, the new and potent anti-psychotic medication, olanzapine, was beginning to achieve its beneficial effect, and Marco's symptoms were subtly moderated by the influence of the drug on the brain's biochemistry.

In fact, the changes in Marco are consistent with other reports on olanzapine. It has been rated as safe and superior to the older neuroleptics such as Haldol and Mellaril in that it interacts with key receptors linked to schizophrenia and tackles negative as well as psychotic symptoms. Moreover, compared with the older class of antipsychotics, it causes far fewer side effects. Harvard psychiatrists report that a number of psychotic patients who took olanzapine regained a sense of self, a sense of connection, and a sense of purpose. All we can say is that *this* long period of instability was ending, and it's likely that the medication played a significant part in Marco's stabilization.

But there was another factor working in Marco's favour, and it had nothing to do with chemicals or behaviour management. For the first time in his life, Marco connected with another boy and made a "best friend." Daniel was newly arrived at the school and their teachers introduced them. Daniel is an attention-deficit boy who looks, next to well-fed Marco, rather fragile. Daniel was knocked down by a bus shortly after he and Marco became friends, and he was hospitalized with head injuries. After recovering in intensive care at University Hospital, he was transferred to the Glenrose, a rehabilitative hospital and a place where Marco feels secure. Arlene and Marco visited the boy regularly, and Marco, shocked by his friend's serious injuries, seemed to develop strong feelings of attachment for him. Marco gained self-confidence from his friendship with Daniel. After Daniel's return to school, the two became inseparable; Daniel's family even took Marco to church. Marco's social and emotional development received a huge boost through his relationship with the other boy. Through this friendship, Marco began to acquire a stake in a world with others. He told his greatly relieved mother he didn't need twenty friends, he simply wanted a best friend.

Some months ago, I was at Arlene's place for dinner. Marco permitted me to speak while he ate, an impressive concession. Afterwards, Marco gave me a tour of his rather crowded bedroom.

The walls had been painted a garish green to his specifications, and they glow in the dark. At the end of his bed sat ET and a large collection of stuffed animals with large eyes staring straight ahead. Marco was proud of his new stereo and his fish, and also proud of the Polaroid shots of himself and his best friend. It was growing late and my leg was getting stiff from standing in the bedroom. (I had told Marco that I had polio as a boy.) Then I heard something new.

"That's all right, Leery. Sometimes my legs hurt me, too."

1999

How Do You Carry Fire?

SANDRA SHIELDS

THE WITCH DOCTOR KILLED THE goat and read its intestines. He pulled white loops of gut out of the body cavity and spread them into a visceral mandala, seeking in their configuration both the curse and the cure. The patient was a man of about forty-five. His three wives, naked except for skirts of animal hide and thick coils of jewellery, sat behind him. Other family members and a few curious neighbours were gathered in a circle, sharing the skimpy shade of a large mopane tree.

The women glowed red-brown from the blend of butterfat and crushed ochre they rubbed over their bodies. The fat protected them from the dry climate, the ochre made them gleam the colour of the longhorn cattle that are their families' wealth. This shimmery second skin stained everything they touched. The tree trunk they leaned against, the rocks they sat on, the babies they were holding, all took on their ochre sheen. As they waited for the witch doctor to make his diagnosis, a plane passed high overhead, invisible except for the white tail, like a celestial intestine stretched across the sky.

In this part of southern Africa, the winter sky stays cloudless and pale with heat for months on end. The airplane's trail of exhaust hung in the faded blue. Below, in the arid northern reaches of Namibia, between the Skeleton Coast and the Kalahari Desert, the ten thousand people called the Himba moved their herds of goats and cows along routes worn into the hard earth by generations of bare feet.

The first ochre-stained woman I met was standing on concrete. Bare-breasted and barefoot, her eager smile was a sales tool. She motioned at me and said, "Photo?" while pointing at herself.

"Five rands," she stated, holding up one hand's worth of fingers. When I didn't produce a camera or any coins, the smile faded. She looked frustrated, a bit desperate.

Opuwo is a raw, ugly town of about four thousand people that boasts the only gas station for hundreds of kilometres, a prime location for separating tourists from their money. To one side of the gas station, in the shade of open-air market stalls, seven or eight Himba men and women sat sharing a large bottle of cheap South African wine.

In 1990, Namibia became an independent democracy, ending decades of isolation brought on by low-grade civil war. The flow of foreigners increased from a trickle to a flood when tourists and journalists arrived from South Africa, Europe, America, and Japan for the sight of unfenced land and unfettered breasts. The Himba started charging for photos in 1994, after the Discovery Channel and the BBC came through, enlisting their cooperation in turning back time. Men were asked to remove their T-shirts, digital watches, and sneakers. Women were paid to sweep villages clean of all modern refuse—the candy wrappers, pop cans, and wine bottles left lying around. Lesson well learned, the Himba began using the foreigners' desire for pictures of "untouched" tribal people as a means of leveraging themselves into the cash economy.

Set amid dry sloping hills, Opuwo was a tough place with a frontier feel. The latest 4 x 4's gassed up beside battered trucks full of goats. Peace Corps volunteers, traditional Himba, smartly dressed African bureaucrats, and busloads of tourists could all be found walking the dusty rise behind the gas station to the string of local businesses—a video rental place, a bottle store, and a big bare-bones supermarket, well stocked with South African–packaged foods, its name, PowerSave, in three-foot-high letters next to the words "Cash & Carry."

Like most travellers, we used Opuwo as a pit stop and kept going. Our destination was the Kunene River, which lies on the border between Namibia and Angola. We were going to Epupa Falls, a point about two hundred kilometres north of Opuwo, where the river widens and flows around a scattering of lush islands before crashing over a long stretch of cliffs into a dozen fingers of water.

To arrive at the Kunene River is to trade the pale dusty landscape for a rich green highway of towering palm trees where lovebirds breed and monkeys swing. Several ancient baobabs cling to rocky outcrops between the sprays of water, and on sandbars at the bottom of the falls, crocodiles sun.

The drive took us much of the day because at regular intervals we were waved down by Himba. Often there was no village in sight, just a small crowd at the side of the road. A Himba man wearing Elton John sunglasses, loafers, jeans, and a T-shirt that said "New York—Manhattan" stopped us early on. His friend wore a traditional Himba skirt with a woman's knit sweater stretched over his sexy chest and a proudly displayed digital watch on his wrist. He asked my husband, David, to reset it for him.

A young couple who needed a lift to the next village piled into the back of our truck. When they unloaded, I held their baby for them, and the solid little body left ochre stains on my hands and pants. Back in the truck, I smiled at the stains, breathed in the earthy smell of the butterfat, and felt like an initiate. We spent time with two women watering their cows at a borehole. Their male companion had a collection of shampoo bottles and kept insisting he needed some soap. A friendly young man taught us to say "me" and "you" and to count to five in Herrero (the language of the Himba) as he rode some ten kilometres, crowded in the front with us.

At Epupa Falls, we found a campground with showers and flush toilets. Most of the twenty spots were already occupied by upscale 4 x 4's. We weren't out of the truck long before a dispirited-looking young Himba woman materialized, carrying a Tetra Pak of fruit juice under her arm. She asked for a cigarette, miming desire by sticking the tip of her finger in her mouth and sucking on it. Several more women joined her, asking for sweeties once they determined we didn't have smokes.

The Himba were challenging and insistent in their begging. They asked for things as if it were their right. I was thrown off balance by these precise, in-your-face demands, so different from the downcast eyes that mark begging in North American cities. I felt that the Himba treated us as if we were spoiled children who had been given too much and needed to learn to share. It was disconcerting. A short distance upriver there were two luxury lodges, one surrounded by clipped grass and beds of marigolds, the other hidden behind a fortresslike fence. Despite myself, I felt a stab of envy at the tourists hiding behind those walls.

Our campsite at the top of the falls was exposed on all sides. The constant crash of the water was hypnotic, but it didn't drown out the generator a group of South African campers was running, nor the ATV of another camper. The next day, we headed upriver to a quieter location not far from a ramshackle Himba hut. We met the man of the hut and his young pregnant wife, asked their permission to camp, and conceded too quickly to their demands for a ten-kilogram sack of mealie meal (ground corn, a staple food in much of the African subcontinent), a smaller sack of sugar, and several pouches of black tobacco. A local headman walking past convinced David to drive his wives and him to Epupa Falls, and moments later I watched my husband and my truck head over the rocky track without me. I sat down in our quiet campsite and waited.

A few hours later the temperature slid with the sun as it dropped suddenly below the horizon. I was wearing light pants and a thin cotton shirt that did nothing to repel the growing chill. Getting stones, setting them in a circle, gathering wood kept me warm for a few minutes, but I had no matches and no sweater. Though it was often 30°C in the day, the temperature at night dropped to almost freezing. Everything was in the truck. Disoriented by travel and the novelty of this place, eager to cement new relationships, David and I had parted without thought. Now, night was falling, and I was beginning to feel a fool and afraid.

Though lonely, I wasn't alone. About three hundred metres away, up a shallow ravine, smoke swirled over the fire where three Himba boys were cooking a meal. It was my turn to beg. I stalled, feeling uncomfortable, reluctant to expose my need. It got colder. The light fell and a bat swooped past. One of the few things I had was a small Hibachi grill. Thinking, How do you carry fire? I picked it up and headed slowly toward the boys in a moment bereft of dignity but full of poetic justice.

They watched me approach. Gestured for me to join their circle. Language wasn't a problem as I pointed at their fire and then over to my cold pile of wood. They sat, blankets wrapped around their naked limbs, turning the shiny pages of a South African *House and Garden* magazine.

The oldest boy pulled a glowing stick from their fire and handed it to me, smiling. My grill hung heavy and suddenly redundant in my hand as I took my passport to warmth from him.

"That's how you carry fire," I chided myself, crossing the rocky ground back to my barren campsite. "On the end of a stick."

It is customary for Himba men to welcome travellers by visiting them at their evening fire, but later that night, after David had returned and we'd shared a supper cooked on my borrowed flames, it was the woman of the hut who came to see us. Beautiful and very pregnant, with her small daughter in tow, she settled on the ground, stretching her red limbs out, long and supple. "The men have no respect for the old ways," she said. "My husband should have stayed to greet you, but he has gone drinking at Epupa Falls, so I have come instead."

Her name was Maria. She wouldn't tell me her Himba name. "I took a better name," she said. The previous year she had travelled by train with four other Himba to Windhoek, Namibia's cosmopolitan capital. "It was good to see it," she said, "but not to stay there." The traffic lights frightened her; she confessed she didn't know when to cross.

She asked where our airplane was, and I explained that the airplane that brought us to Africa did not belong to us, that it was like the train, something you bought a ticket for and rode in with many other people.

"Why don't you have a baby?" she asked me, and I struggled to explain the birth control pill.

"How old are you?" I asked and she was embarrassed because she didn't know.

"Ask my husband," she said. "He is more clever than me." Counting is new for the Himba, something the cash economy is teaching them.

We were, it turned out, camped right beside the footpath to Epupa Falls, and the next morning we received a steady flow of Himba visitors. The day before, a trader had arrived at the falls with a truckload of alcohol, so the trail was especially busy. It was mid-morning before Maria's husband appeared, blinking at the light. He wandered over to greet us, sporting a mid-length fake leather coat over his handsome bare chest. Earlier, I had watched one of the young boys head down the path driving six goats before him, payment for the drinks Maria's husband and friends had consumed the night before.

Himba etiquette requires that they greet every person they pass, say good morning, and inquire after the other's well-being. I was learning quickly, and meeting much of the neighbourhood at the same time, welcoming an assortment of people around our fire. "You should come to Epupa Falls," several encouraged us. The truck was still there, a portable bar that had not yet run out of fuel.

A few days later, we followed the trail along the river to the falls. Maria's husband was delighted to see David and whisked him off to meet a local headman. A troop of Namibian border guards was stationed at Epupa Falls, supposedly protecting the porous border. On this day, that entailed joining the drinking party. They immediately bought me a drink, which meant getting the trader to fill up their bottle again, and included me in the circle of drinkers. The bottle passed from hand to hand in a genial fashion. Many of the faces were familiar now, men and women who had visited my campfire.

"Don't buy them alcohol, whatever you do," I'd been told before coming. It was unnerving how things that had sounded so sensible in Canada got turned inside out when I stood on that sun-baked earth. The bottle was emptied and another bought, and I knew it would soon be my turn to pay. Not paying, not entering into this age-old ritual of friendship, felt uncomfortably paternalistic. I wanted to understand as much as I could about the lives of these people, and I wasn't going to do that by standing on a soap-box. I bought the next round.

The battered old Ford was parked well away from the palm-lined shore where the tourists reclined in their lawn chairs, watching the river. There were no trees here to break the heat. The party swirled around me. David and Maria's husband came over with the local headman, who introduced himself as Karamata. "The hut you are camped beside is just a herding outpost," he said. "If you want to learn about Himba life, you should come and stay at my village."

Located several kilometres from the falls, the village lay between two hills, a short walk from the river. Four round huts, the same sun-bleached brown as the ground, sat in a wide semicircle. There was one hut for each of Karamata's three wives and an extra for visiting relatives—a regular occurrence in this tribe. The perimeter of the village was sketched in with a loose low fence of scrubby brush. Tighter, taller fences of brush surrounded two animal enclosures.

Karamata's second wife, Hypothe, patted the rock beside her and smiled broadly, inviting me to sit down. She was rocking a gourd back and forth, curdling soured milk into the yogourt-like drink that is daily fare for the Himba. Flies swarmed, landing on her and me and the baby she was holding. The butterfat on her body smelled rancid in the hot sun. Her long legs were stretched out, her ankles adorned with a thick cuff of iron beads, strung in rows. A Himba woman receives these distinctive anklets at puberty and their weight (about three pounds per leg) makes her walk slow and graceful. Of course they also make her less inclined to wander far from home.

I offered to take Hypothe's baby and was rewarded with an armful of wriggling health. Himba babies spend much of their days being held, if not by their mother, then by their father, a brother, or anyone who is around. Unable to resist, I planted a kiss on the baby's head, and Hypothe smiled approvingly. "Babies are supposed to be kissed," she said.

Life at Karamata's village unfolded at a leisurely crawl. Herding was one part physical labour to three parts killing time. His herd of goats and his prized longhorn cattle were the family's economic mainstay, a living pantry that required daily walks, food, and water interspersed with lots of waiting around. Karamata told me he didn't know how many goats he had. "Too many to count," he said. The Himba know their herds with an uncommon intimacy. They know if one animal is missing because they know each animal. My count put Karamata's herd at 116 goats and 34 cows.

Many Himba were still semi-nomadic, spending the year rotating through several village sites in order to access different grazing grounds and watering holes. It is the only way to practise successful husbandry in this marginal land. Their villages are masterpieces of simplicity. The homes Karamata and his wives had built were typical; they had tied sticks together with palm fronds and covered them with a concoction of mud and dung that dried like cement in the steady heat. Inside, the huts were dark and cool.

Tree huts served as closets, their branches performing the function of hangers. Rocks were chairs. Several rocks pulled together became the fireplace, where the family began the day, taking off the chill of the crisp hours after dawn—stove and furnace in a few motions. With minimal exertion, the family moved in a day, taking with them little but their herds.

Karamata and his family were outside, heated by the sun, blown by the wind, living with flies. They had keen senses, always heard approaching cows or cars long before I did. Like the Himba, when I wasn't asleep, I lived out in the open where the world moved through my living room freely, unannounced. I grew accustomed to other creatures sharing my space, learned which bugs could hurt me (few) and which couldn't (many). One of our two camp stools broke, so David and I took turns sitting on rocks, squatting to eat, putting our asses on the earth. The groan of our Western thighs grew quieter each time. I stopped using our little folding table and put everything on the ground. It seemed to make more sense. My fire skills improved, and I grew accustomed to the smoke of mopane, like incense, in my nose.

One day, in the cooling hour before dusk, I climbed the hill overlooking the village and watched as the cows filed home to where their calves waited, hungry and noisy. Karamata walked, a calm controlling presence, beside them. I crouched down and noticed unusual rock fragments at my feet. Nearby I located the source, a hole the diameter of a quarter, drilled down into the stony ground. With a start, I realized what it was.

If the Namibian and Angolan governments can agree on how to do it, they will build a 650-megawatt hydroelectric dam at Epupa Falls, and the palm trees, the baobabs, and Karamata's village will disappear under several hundred feet of water. The drill hole was the work of a team of geologists, currently camped at the falls and hard at work testing rock structures and mapping out potential dam sites.

Himba opinion about the project was mixed. At first, they thought it would be just another cattle dam, a place for their herds to drink. It was only when the scope of the project was finally explained to them—the level the water would reach pointed out on surrounding hills—that they understood this would be a dam of a different kind.

The Namibian government doesn't have many choices about where to create a hydroelectric dam. Most rivers in the country are seasonal, running only during the rainy season. The Kunene is one of the country's few year-round rivers. Damming it at Epupa Falls is expected to make Namibia self-sufficient in electricity. At present the country buys its energy from South Africa, but cheap and reliable domestic electricity is essential for development.

Once they understood the size of the project, many Himba opposed the dam. "It will kill us," the headmen said. Karamata wasn't so strident, but he didn't want it either. He has ancestors buried on land that would disappear under the water. The lush vegetation along the river and on the islands is excellent for grazing and has been the Himba's last resort in times of drought. The land has been theirs for centuries.

Constructing the dam will take five years and involve at least five thousand workers. The expansion of the road network, the instant city of workers and shops and bars needed to support them will dramatically alter Himba life.

"We must build the dam," a scholarly looking man who worked for a radio station in the capital told me. "Otherwise, how can we develop these people? We can't get good teachers and professionals up here without facilities. In twenty years, if the government has brought proper houses and electricity to the rest of Namibia but not here, the Himba will be angry. This area needs electricity; otherwise, how can these people have normal lives?"

Polla Brand, the president of the Namibian electrical utility, put it more crudely: "The Himbas don't want to stay like baboons. They also want televisions and lights in their homes." Brand is crass, but he's not entirely wrong.

"I want a truck," Karamata told me while he squatted by the fire, boiling water for coffee in an old army helmet, surrounded by toddlers and young people. "If our children get sick," he explained, "we don't have a truck to take them to the hospital."

Karamata's comment stayed with me. In one expression of desire, he had embraced two powerful forces for change. Motor vehicles and

Western medicine are not as dramatic as a hydroelectric dam. The changes they introduce are more subtle, yet they have been key in pulling the Himba inside the circumference of the larger economy. And just as a hydro project is not a cattle dam, so is this an economy of a different kind. Everywhere it flows, it reshapes the land and the people's lives, not as quickly as a dam, but just as surely.

We spent a week at Karamata's village and then travelled through the region for another month. On several occasions we met Himba who had been granted Karamata's wish and were piloting their own trucks. The trucks were invariably ancient beasts and the drivers were generally young men—cocky and happy. One waved us down because his truck had stalled. From what we could deduce, it was out of gas. Our jerry cans were empty, so we couldn't help, but the young man wasn't worried. He enjoyed a half hour's conversation with us and we left him patiently waiting for the next over-equipped 4 x 4 to come along.

Another truck we encountered was making a supply run to the PowerSave in Opuwo. Two goats shared the truck bed with a dozen young Himba men, a few older men, and one woman. They were camped at a bottle store, several hours short of their destination, and the older folks were having a drinking party. Sitting in the shade of two trees, they congenially passed around a Sprite tin with the top cut off. It was regularly refilled with a strong, sweet rum punch from the bottle store. When the oldest of the men passed out, a couple of the teenagers cleaned him up and made him a comfortable bed in the shade.

Later in the afternoon, the young men prepared supper using the goats in the truck. I'd never watched something I was about to eat die. The young man flipped the goat on its side and, with the calm assurance of an oft-repeated act, knelt on its windpipe with his knee. It's the way the Himba always kill their animals—quiet, bloodless, and efficient. Inside an hour, the skin was a hide, hanging to dry from a tree, and the meat was in pieces, boiling on the fire in a big metal drum. Leftovers were cut into thin strips and dried.

173

Until the flood of foreigners and their packaged foods, the Himba had a bland and simple diet. Meat was on the menu only occasionally; maize meal cooked into porridge was daily fare. Milk was drunk fresh or left to sour and rocked into the warm thick drink that I surprised myself by growing to like. Karamata said the Himba used to plant gardens and grow corn. Now, begging ground maize from tourists or finding enough money to buy it from PowerSave was easier than gardening.

That was the mission of the crowd around the truck: to reach Opuwo and to buy several fifty-kilogram sacks of mealie meal. The people spent two days camped behind the bottle store, then headed off on the final leg of their journey, a three-hour drive over the wide gravel road into Opuwo.

I was more interested in going the other direction, following the one-lane tire tracks that ran back to where they had come from, back into their village and other far-flung villages like it. For me, this bumpy track over rock and dirt and shifting sand was a path to the past, to a place where people spend time in the same fluid way others spend money.

But the thought was fanciful. Roads aren't about the past. Roads are about exchange, about the movement of people and things. They are about desire. I watched one Himba woman look over my truck with the same eyes tourists wore when they bent down to peer into Himba huts, glinting with interest and a hint of greed, another type of exotic shopper. For the Himba, these parallel ruts in the ground were an enticement, an invitation to partake in pleasures not available in dusty villages. The road was a place where money could be made, and it led to places where money could be spent. Increasingly, the Himba were choosing to walk the roads rather than the footpaths of their ancestors.

Most roads went to Opuwo. Except for students attending the big high school, the Himba did not generally live in Opuwo. Some went to shop at the PowerSave, but for most the hospital was the real draw. Until the late 1980s, Opuwo was a high-security military base from which South Africa waged war with Namibians seeking independence and with Cuba in neighbouring Angola. When the South Africans withdrew, they left behind lots of menacing razor-wire fences and a large modern hospital.

I visited the hospital for the first time while playing ambulance for a man with a knife wound. He had accidentally hacked into his right hand while cutting wood, slicing between his thumb and fore-finger, almost down to the wrist, losing sensation and mobility in that all-important opposable digit. Along with his wife and small child, he had walked the fifteen kilometres to Epupa Falls, arriving in the afternoon. The troop of border guards lacked even basic first aid supplies, so they directed him to our camp. He was calm and unperturbed while the gaping filthy wound was probed and cleaned. I had heard numerous tales of Himba stoicism in the face of pain. The European couple who ran the 700 rand per night fly-in lodge told of an old man who waited patiently outside their gate, wrapped in a blanket. When they went out, he removed the blanket to show them that his shoulder had been gored straight through by the long horn of a cow.

We delivered the man with the cut hand, along with his wife and child, to the hospital the next day. He was transferred to Windhoek, where specialists were able to mend the severed tendons and restore function to his thumb. His wife remained in Opuwo, awaiting his return.

It was normal for family members to accompany the patient to Opuwo, and the entire entourage would often stay in town for the duration of whatever treatment was required. They passed the day in the crowded African market on the edge of town, amid palm frond stalls, where freshly killed goat and beef could be bought, where women knelt over small fires, cooking bread and meat and offering it for sale. T-shirts, blouses, trousers, and shoes were sold from a tarpaulin spread on the ground. Most popular were the dingy bars where warm beer was ladled out of plastic barrels for a clientele who squatted in the dust.

Here, in the camaraderie of drink, a grave side effect of the Himba's conversion to Western medicine was developing. At the hospital, doctors had just confirmed their first local HIV case. The man was not a Himba, but the doctors I spoke with felt it was only a matter of time. The communality of the Himba extended to sex. While most adult Himba had spouses, they also had many lovers. It was ordinary courtesy for a man, if he was not home by evening, to stay away for the night so as not to surprise his wives with their boyfriends. Gonorrhea was common and young men, proud of the fact that it proclaimed them to be sexually active, wore their first gonorrhea treatment like a badge of honour.

The taboo against sex outside of the Himba community was still strong, but alcohol and the tribally mixed environment of Opuwo was helping to break it down. A thoughtful doctor, who was also a Christian missionary, voiced his concerns. He had been involved with various efforts at AIDS education in the area, but none of it was changing sexual behaviour. Worrying out loud, he spoke about the mobility of the Himba and the logistics of AIDS. "None of them stay in Opuwo," he said. "They may come here for as long as six months, but they always go back to their villages."

At a dinner party of Peace Corps volunteers, a doctor from Scotland related her efforts to educate her Himba friends about AIDS. "AIDS is a great tragedy that will affect all of you soon," she had said.

"We have had many horrors," they had responded with customary fatalism. "The war. The drought. So AIDS is next. That is normal. There is always some terrible thing about to happen."

The tourist brochures all stressed that the Himba were the "most untouched tribe in southern Africa." There were five European anthropologists in the region and one from Japan. An undergraduate class of thirty anthropology students from America had just spent a month in a Himba village. I met several journalists and drove past countless hundreds of tourists, all of us emissaries of the larger economy, bringing its merchandise to some of the last people in the world to become consumers.

The process of change from herders to customers was well underway. Witnessing it was disturbing, in part because it was harsh, and the people often looked happier and healthier in the before picture, but also because there was something hauntingly final about it. The traditional knowledge of the Himba was not written down; it was the product of hundreds of years of the intimate contact between their bare feet and this particular piece of the planet.

Opuwo and the roads radiating out from it were the contact zone. I spent several weeks on the town's dusty streets, watching the ways in which past and present were blending. Mostly I visited the busy African market at the edge of town. One day I arrived to find a group of Himba women standing in a line in a quiet corner of the market, stamping their feet into the ground, clapping their hands, raising little flurries of dust. As the afternoon picked up speed, so did the wind, grabbing the women's dust, trailing it through the stalls and open-air bars. At first there was only a handful of women, clapping and singing sporadic songs. Every few minutes, one of them would break out of the line and launch into a solo dance while the others stamped louder and whooped encouragement.

A Herrero woman came and stood beside me, laughing and pointing at the dancers. A hundred years ago, the Herrero and the Himba were one tribe. Both still speak the Herrero language, but while the Himba chose to stay in the isolation of the north, the Herrero moved south and ran into German colonials. There was a war followed by plenty of Christian missionaries, and then the Herrero put on clothes. Strikingly, they still wear the style of clothes they first donned. The woman standing beside me had on a pioneer bonnet and an orange gingham dress with a full skirt puffed out by numerous petticoats and reaching to the ground.

Her dress was dirty, her eyes spoke of mischief. She motioned me to join the Himba dancers. Laughing, I declined, challenging her to do it instead. She did, standing first in the line of clappers and stampers, then moving out in front and dancing madly for a few minutes. At the end of her dance she twirled and pointed at me.

And so I too joined the chorus line. Picked up the odd rhythm of the clapping, pounded my feet, heavy in hiking boots, into the ground. Eventually, encouraged by the women's repeated smiles and the music, I stepped out in front for a solo dance. The women whooped me on, I spun my arms, pounded my feet, felt a self-conscious flush take over my face, and returned to the safety of the chorus line.

By now, the focus of the market had shifted toward the dancing. More women joined and a large circle formed. The volume grew, the contagion spread, men joined, the circle expanded and grew another layer of clapping, stamping people. It was delicious. Laughter flowed and the whoops increased each time another person was encouraged into the centre for a solo.

The women had started the dance simply because they were happy. It was a marked contrast to the traditional dances I had watched earlier that week in the Opuwo high school auditorium, where rows of Africans sitting on chairs clapped politely at the end of each performance. A group of female students with shorn hair, wearing dresses that made them look like waitresses, did a little Himba dance. They were followed by a group of young men, gym shorts showing beneath their traditional skirts. Again, the audience sat, watched, and briefly clapped.

The evening ended with speeches from several elders, but before the last speaker began, most of the students had slipped out of the auditorium and headed for the disco down the street. "Our traditions are our life," said the speaker to an empty hall. "We must remember them."

Around the flickering light of my borrowed fire that first night I spent with Maria, she had pointed at her young daughter and said, "I will send this one to school." When I asked why, Maria replied, "Then she will learn English and can ask the tourists for things."

Growing numbers of children were leaving the family village for the confines of the classroom. Often they boarded at school, spending months away from home. They cut off their traditional braids and pulled on Western clothes. Instead of becoming expert herders, intimately acquainted with the ways of each animal and capable of finding water beneath dry riverbeds, they became literate. Well, semi-literate anyway, since rural Namibian education could be a meagre affair. I met a group of teenage boys who were in the third and fourth grades, loaded with aspirations, but bereft of any real means of reaching them.

For people whose history and traditions have been written into their jewellery and woven into their hair, a people without the written signs of language and numbers, a change in appearance is a major hole in their cultural library. The Himba have been defined by the humble everyday acts that made their lives possible. Their fathers lived in the fires that warmed them. Their herds were their pantries, their bank accounts, and part of their religion. The land has been alive for them. "Their culture is being disarmed," said a Belgian anthropologist over beers on the stoop of the Catholic mission.

Spending the day in school instead of outside, learning to read instead of to herd, Maria's daughter will know Himba culture not as the heartbeat of everyday life, but as something kept in a showcase and brought out on special evenings in the school hall. She may not call herself Himba at all, because often when Himba get dressed, they begin to refer to themselves as Herrero. Like some of the schoolchildren I met, she may look down on her parents, seeing them as dirty and stupid.

It was a one-way street. The Himba could become modern, but I could not become Himba. Their way of life was exclusive, open only to those born to it. Based on herding in a land where a delicate balance must be maintained between what the earth offers and the appetites of their animals, this way of living could not sustain expansion and did not produce material wealth.

There was so much they could ask me for and so little, beyond the all-important fire, that I could demand of them. I tried, unsuccessfully, to explain that at home I must pay for my house and my food, that back home I am poor. They didn't believe me. My car, my clothes, the tins and packets and boxes of food stored in the trunk on top of my truck, irrevocably marked me as a member of the bigger, richer world beyond. The Himba held out their hands to me everywhere I went. Their desire became the hurdle that blocked every encounter, that began most conversations.

It takes time to see. Because the Himba approached me begging, barely dressed, with few possessions, I saw them as poor. Not yet versed in the meaning of loans and overextended credit cards, they saw me as rich. But my hand was out, too. I wanted to be stained by an ochre baby, meet people who lived outside, who had time to sit beside a fire. It was a peculiar exchange. I made them want more, they made me want less.

I stayed three months in South Africa before coming home to Canada, and it cushioned my return to my customary reality. Black South Africans share with the Himba the custom of greeting everyone they pass. The streets of the small city where I stayed were alive with conversation, and squatting to chat was the norm. The habit became entrenched, and when I returned to Canada, I found myself squatting at street corners while waiting for the light to change. It took months of the quiet censure of averted eyes before the habit retreated.

In Namibia my body had begun to respond to the sun, stirring into wakefulness hours earlier than I had ever willingly risen. Five o'clock would find me and false dawn up together. I'd start a fire, put on the kettle, and hold my fingers to the flames as the sun rose and the temperature took its final just-after-dawn dip. I had never known such calm pleasure in waking. This regular contact with fire and earth would be the things I missed most when I returned to "civilization."

While it was stressful being a stranger in a strange land, observing and relentlessly being observed, I soaked up the leisurely pace of Himba life. Hurry had no meaning. Interruptions were a novelty. A whole day could blow by in the slow-motion actions of killing, cooking, and eating a goat.

I was introduced to true darkness. The phase of the moon determined the amount of light by which I cooked the evening meal. I gave up on my temperamental flashlight and learned how to organize myself on dark nights so that I could cook by the firelight, remembering where I had placed things when I put them down.

Toward the end of our stay, we turned off the wide gravel road and headed up the one-lane tire tracks that the partying shoppers had travelled down. In hours of rough driving we saw only Himba. We stopped, finally, at a tiny town consisting of a small clinic, a two-room school, and a dingy store.

Politeness required that we check in with the most senior head-man in the area. His village lay a short walk away. We crossed the sandy bottom of a dry riverbed, then headed up the rise leading to the wide plateau of the village. We walked uphill for thirty minutes over ground littered with shiny chunks of quartz. The village was over the lip of the hill, out of sight until we reached the top, and, a bit breathless from the climb, we found ourselves at centre stage. Close to fifty pairs of eyes were on us.

The headman was sitting in one of the village's two chairs, surrounded by men from miles around. Moments earlier they had killed a cow to make ready the feast that would end days of funeral ceremonies for a woman of the village. Nearby, the headman's old father sat in the other chair, a battered low-slung affair. He was ancient. His bony knees protruded from beneath a worn woollen overcoat, the kind businessmen wear in winter. His hands were long and thin and bent with years as if by a stiff wind.

In deference to age, the headman motioned for us to seek a welcome from his father. We squatted on the ground in front of the old man, introduced ourselves, gave the requisite gift of tobacco, and asked permission to stay.

The wind blew unimpeded across the flat hilltop, catching the old man's words and tossing them over the group of men sitting on the ground watching us. "The white man comes with power," the old man said. "He has more power than the black man. When the white man came, the black man lost his power. We are glad you are here with your power."

I licked my lips, dried to lizard skin by the wind. I felt, in fact, powerless, incapable of explaining that the technologies I use so casually sometimes have chilling repercussions. Beside me, David said something polite and appropriate. Thank yous were exchanged all around and the Himba got back to the matter at hand, the butchering of the cow.

The headman strode over to where the cow lay on the far side of the holy fire. Another man slit the animal from tail to throat. Its glistening insides spilled out, and the headman crouched down to discern what the guts of the cow had to say about the future fortunes of his community. Reading entrails takes time. A crowd of men gathered around the animal, pointing at the bulging membranes and discussing the twists of fate made manifest in matter.

It was just before noon when the first digital watch beeped. By quarter past the hour, the reading was done and four more watches had chimed their electronic time into the pastoral landscape.

1999

Home Movie

DON GILLMOR

WHEN I WAS AT THE UNIVERSITY OF
Calgary, I took a course in the history of film. It was the only class
I looked forward to, and in my third year I began to say that I was
going to be a filmmaker. That year, a filmmaking course was created.
There was some rudimentary classroom instruction, but eventually
we had to make a film. Mine was about the flight to Las Vegas on
Hughes Airlines. The Hughes planes, or perhaps just the ones that
went to Las Vegas, were jumbo jets that were painted canary yellow.
Gamblers and tourists returned every day, dressed for summer, richer
or poorer. This was as far as I developed the idea. At the time, I
described the film's unadorned realism as Warholian.

Reality, in that age of LSD, wasn't a valuable commodity. I had
been born while my father was in graduate school, but the thought
of having a family at the age of twenty-three was as alien to me as
joining the army. My father's generation seemed more real than my
own, their lives marked by rituals that have since decayed. Marriage
and baptism have become neglected forms, like the sonnet. They
possess a quaintness almost. My own university graduation was a
listless event. We lumbered through the alphabetical roll call toward
a vague job market. Mortgages, children, and insurance policies
were distant rumours. Youth stretched before us like a prairie horizon, endless and without obstacle. I prolonged youth, or at least its
habits, for another two decades. At forty I became a father, and

reality finally arrived in the form of a daughter. With her birth came a flood of responsibility and worry, the joyful thud of youth hitting a brick wall. I wasn't going to be a director after all.

In the birthing room at the hospital, I sleeplessly observed my wife's thirty-hour labour. Every five minutes we stood up and I held her in an improvised dance as the pain of the contractions reached its crescendo then ebbed. We staggered and glided around the ward through the day and into the night like Jane Fonda and Michael Sarrazin in *They Shoot Horses, Don't They?* It was late December and the hospital was short-staffed. At 4:00 A.M. on Christmas Day, an epidural was administered by a grumpy man appropriately named Dragan. With the pain at bay, my wife and I finally slept in the small overheated room with the sound of the baby's heartbeat broadcast over a monitor. It was womblike, the last comforting moment before the deluge. At 1:00 P.M. our daughter slid out, surprisingly pink and delicious, the true Christmas baby. All around us was the sound of false prophets being born. I changed my daughter's first diaper on the hospital scale, staring into her tar black shit as if it were tea leaves, trying to divine our future.

I toyed with the idea of videotaping her progress, a thought partly prompted by my grandfather's home movies, which an uncle had just transferred onto videotape. I had barely known my grandfather. Ralph Gillmor died at the age of eighty-six, when I was fifteen. Like me, he had had a family late; his first child was born when he was forty, the third and final child when he was fifty-four. When his youngest son was an adolescent, Ralph was seventy. This was the kind of math I had been working on lately. My grandfather and I had a kinship now, connected by this late-blooming surge toward paternity and by these films.

His films have the quality of a documentary, representing reality, though a staged reality. Onscreen we see my father playing with his brother, but they are playing for the camera. It is not family life but a re-enactment of family life. There is a sense of incompleteness: will I gradually harden into the grandfather who seemed, twenty-five years ago, generic and alien? A friend recently told me that he was turning into his father. I asked him what kind of man his father was. "The kind of guy who is standing at the edge of a party, drinking his fifth scotch, and jingling the change in his pocket." We inhabit our forebears through gesture and nuance; first we adopt the imagery.

My grandfather existed for me largely through anecdote. I knew that he had owned the first movie camera in Fort Frances, an Ontario mill town of several thousand that sits on the US border. It is separated by a bridge from International Falls, Minnesota, hometown of Tammy Faye Bakker, the celebrated evangelist and makeup artist. Fort Frances has the kind of order that company towns often have, a prim working-class alignment of tended gardens and white fences. The pulp and paper mill nourished the town and kept it in a heavy, distinct cloud that smelled of chemicals and rot. After lifting logs out of the stripping tank with a gaff for eight hours, the workers were ready to drink and fist fight with whoever was handy. With an American town of comparable size a few hundred yards away, there was always someone handy. Fort Frances was a good place to get your lights punched out. I was born there but left when I was three months old. My father and his two brothers escaped the mill, seeking refuge in American universities.

Chiefly, I had come to view my grandfather as an inventor, a native engineer. Before Lawn Boy came out with its power mower, Ralph had built one himself, using a three-quarter horsepower washing-machine motor attached to a pulley on their push mower. It was electrically powered; a 100-foot extension cord snaked over the lawn getting in the way. Ralph stood and smoked his pipe and watched happily as his sons attacked the lawn. He built a complicated Rube Goldberg receiver that allowed him to pull in American television stations, and he designed a conveyor belt that automatically transported the clinkers from their coal-burning furnace to the lane. When the Noden Causeway was constructed on Rainy Lake, he watched the project develop and offered advice, which, according to legend, was followed. He liked anything mechanical and was attracted to the movie camera because it was a gadget.

In memory, my grandfather spoke in Bing Crosbyesque noises, mellifluous sounds rather than words. He was never without a pipe in his mouth, and he wore a vest and tie and, on occasion, grey spats around the house. I remember him promising me a .22-calibre rifle when I turned thirteen. This last image probably isn't true. Had it been filmed, it might reveal an offhand remark made when I glimpsed a pair of rifles in an armoire in the room where my grandfather sometimes slept. The remark then evolved into a contract in my mind. I do know that when I turned thirteen and no rifle was forthcoming, it seemed like a betrayal.

In 1939 Ralph bought a CineKodak eight-millimetre Model 20 film camera, which was advertised with the slogan, "Push the button, and it does the rest." He recorded the development of his third child, Alan, who was born when Ralph was fifty-four and his wife, Margaret, was forty-four. In the films they look like grandparents, mimicking the baby's joy, that exaggerated pantomime that suits the medium so well. Alan sits naked on his father's lap. They are in the garden and Ralph is teaching him how to clap. There is something unsettling about the juxtaposition of the perfect infant and the middle-aged father. Partly it is the shock of self-recognition.

It was Alan who recently packaged Ralph's films, transferring them onto videotape and placing them within the framework of a commercial film. It begins with a prototypical Mickey Mouse cartoon and is followed by a Laurel and Hardy short and travelogues from the thirties that take us to Barbados and Israel ("Where Jesus Preached," the subtitle reads). Alan is a music professor and he attached a soundtrack of piano music to the images, much of it the elegiac solos that Art Tatum recorded for Capitol in the 1940s. Alan was two generations removed from his father and there wasn't much commonality between them. It is Alan's film to some degree; he is the star and the editor, and the narrative he creates is very different from my own.

The films have the canonical, repetitive movements that came to define the form. People walking self-consciously toward the camera, aimless pans. It is an instinctive rather than learned technique. It is unlikely that Ralph had ever seen a home movie at the time he made his first one. Eastman Kodak introduced the first home movie camera in 1923. Though the familiar, jerky image of the home movie has since entered our cultural vocabulary, the cameras were never a popular consumer item. They remained, essentially, a novelty for sixty years, until video cameras usurped them and the video image became a form of communication. Home movie cameras were expensive; in 1939 a CineKodak eight-millimetre Model 20 cost about fifteen dollars, almost a week's wage for a millworker. The three-minute rolls of colour film were expensive, too, and had to be sent to Rochester, New York, for developing. There was the cost of a projector, screen, and a viewer to edit with. Editing was painstaking and few people bothered, preferring to simply show whatever they had shot. This led to the last drawback: the result, which had the slightly speeded-up quality of silent films, the kinetic melancholy of a Buster Keaton short, though lacking his sense of narrative. Home movies were exclusionary. The clicking of the Bell and Howell projector eventually became one of the most dreaded sounds in the suburbs, a metronome that marked the slow march through someone else's quotidian history.

People didn't understand how movies worked, how laborious and staged the process was. So the home movie camera remained, for the most part, a curiosity. History was still made of moments rather than panoramas, of photographs rather than film. It wasn't until Zapruder and JFK's dreadful caravan that the moving image impressed upon us the burden of personal history.

After the early scenes with his new baby, Ralph isn't seen much in his films. Perhaps he was as unsettled as I was by the image. But he was more interested in the technology than the images anyway. His presence is Hitchcockian, glimpsed now and then. He is revealed more in his directorial choices and setting shots. There are random shots of locomotives, a lifelong obsession. My grandfather drove a coal-burning locomotive for a logging operation and held to the romance of that machine, or that era, for the rest of his life. The seemingly arbitrary images provide a visual framework for Ralph's life.

"Cinema attains its fullness in being the art of the real," wrote the film theorist André Bazin. My grandfather's films illustrate Bazin's theories in a literal way. Certainly there was little attempt to transform reality. Ralph posed the family on the lawn and walked back and forth in front of them, filming the static image, the smiles wilting, flies swatted at. The camera moved but the image remained stationary, a curious hybrid of still and film photography. Ralph's film technique didn't evolve much over the years, though he finally adopted a static camera, letting the actors come to him. My Uncle Don is first seen as a dead-end kid, then in his army uniform with a black eye and bandaged nose (the result of a fight with American soldiers, the most immediate enemy). The camera follows his university graduation and his wedding, and he is finally seen playing with his own baby. Don and his wife, Sophie, look incredibly glamorous, like Robert Wagner and Natalie Wood. In a series of shots, he is seen standing still, then walking toward the camera. This routine was repeated with my father, various aunts, and neighbours. There are incongruities: a peacock by the side of the house in full fan, for example. But the rest is small-town life in the 1940s. My father is first seen at the age of nine, too young for the war, wearing a flight jacket and an aviator's hat.

The earliest footage was in black and white, but within a year, my grandfather was using colour, a surprise. *The Wizard of Oz* (1939) was the first commercial film to use colour, but it was already being used in home movies. Bazin thought that technological innovations like colour, 3-D, and Cinerama reflected the underlying spirit of film, which was to reproduce reality on the screen. Oddly, the black-and-white footage of Ralph's films seems more real than the garish colour, which makes the screen look like a hand-tinted photograph. Black and white speaks to the natural state of our memories and it suits the town of Fort Frances better, with its complex grey palette, the result of billowing smokestacks.

Technically, Fort Frances is my hometown, though I lived there for only the first three months of my life, before my mother and I returned to Cambridge, Massachusetts, where my father was going to university. I have claimed several places as hometowns, the way politicians sometimes do, matching their roots to their audience. In my grandfather's films, my hometown is given a life and shape that isn't part of my memory or experience. They create a hometown for me.

After my father graduated, we settled in Winnipeg, but we returned to Fort Frances most summers to visit relatives and to swim in Rainy Lake. The local boys had a menacing quality to them, a sand-kicking bravado. This was the time of Charles Atlas, and the beach was an advertised battlefield. In the back of every comic book was the illustration of a skinny guy losing his girl to a bully. But the beach also meant seeing my glamorous Aunt Sophie in a bathing suit. I remember her picking leeches off her tanned, perfect legs and tossing them away without fear or rancour. I was terrified of leeches, but they gave me a chance to stare at her legs with impunity, and for that I was grateful. Even now, when I watch her on film as she squints into the camera in her bathing suit, my thoughts are with Burt Lancaster on that beach with Deborah Kerr in *From Here to Eternity,* the wave metaphorically washing over us.

The town is mapped in my grandfather's films. There is a homecoming parade for the returning soldiers along the main street with the town lined up cheering. There are Model T's draped in bunting, wagons drawn by horses, children on ponies, and everywhere the Canadian and American flags. *Born to Sing,* starring Leo Gorcey, is on the marquee of the Royal Theatre. Ralph's hardware store is glimpsed, a place that sold horse collars and rolls of linoleum, where everything could be bought in bulk. His interest in the hardware business was restricted to the merchandise. The customers were a persistent blight. When my Uncle Alan was a boy, he would sometimes spend Saturdays at the store with Ralph. They sat in the back room, Ralph smoking his pipe, tinkering. When the door opened and a customer came in, he said to Alan, "Be quiet, son, and maybe they'll go away."

He worked at a variety of things. He was trained as a machinist and he had a Chrysler dealership until he almost died from carbon monoxide poisoning. He drove locomotives and gave out the town's driver's licences, having the candidates drive him around Fort Frances running errands until he gave each of them, regardless of their shortcomings, a licence.

In the film there is a lingering shot of the town hospital, a surprisingly grand building with a large staircase and Corinthian columns. Ralph was one of the hospital's founders, raising money partly because he wanted to be assured a bed in the event of illness. He had a tendency to hypochondria and wanted all three of his sons to become doctors (none of them did, though my Uncle Don took a stab at it). He followed his friend Dr. O'Donnell on his rounds and developed a gastrointestinal illness most Sunday mornings so he wouldn't have to go to church.

So my grandmother went to the Presbyterian church with her sisters, their hats bobbing to the Lord's rhythms. Ralph stayed home and took a sip from the bottle of whisky he kept locked in a cabinet labelled "Special Tools" in the basement. Being a Presbyterian won't stop you from sinning, my grandmother used to say, but it will surely stop you from enjoying it. Ralph was of Irish descent and my grandmother, a Scot, referred to alcohol as the Irish disease.

In his youth Ralph had been a dandy. When he was in his twenties he squired Queenie Diplock around the Emo County Fair in a smart suit and a jaunty hat. My grandmother, then only twelve, saw this fine pair and said, perhaps apocryphally, "I'm going to marry that man someday." In later years he was insulated by his deafness. He bought an early version of the hearing aid, which had a wire running from his ear to a battery pack in his shirt pocket. When my grandmother brought home guests after church, he often turned his hearing aid off, cocooned in his thoughts, stuck in his own silent movie. She used to go to the Masonic and Order of Eastern Star dances with Dr. Neely, the local veterinarian, because Ralph wouldn't take her. After twenty-six years of marriage, my grandfather finally took her out to dinner. They went to the Husky station on the highway.

The last time I saw my grandfather, I was fourteen, on a train from Winnipeg to Atikokan. I was with a group of boys from Camp Stevens; we were going to Turtle River to begin a two-week canoe trip, to become voyageurs, in the camp's lofty historical parlance. The train stopped in Fort Frances and I saw my grandfather on the platform, watching the train come in as he did every day.

He didn't recognize me when I approached him. It is commonplace but still odd to re-introduce yourself to an ailing grandfather. I outlined all the necessary connections and he nodded and smiled and we shook hands. There were three other boys waiting for me on the platform, so I left my grandfather to his trains. As an adolescent I had few opportunities to feel worldly, but here was a town I knew. I suggested that we shoot a few games of pool while we were waiting. As we walked toward the pool hall, the train pulled out of the station. There wasn't another train until the next day. The Greyhound bus went that afternoon, but we didn't have enough money for the fare and I didn't want to ask my grandfather for money. Instead we lied to the driver of the bus and told him we lived in Atikokan and our parents would be waiting at the bus station with the fare. They weren't, of course, and the bus driver offered to beat us up, which he said would do us a world of good.

My grandfather died a few months later. My father and his brother Don were at his bedside as he lay in a coma in the hospital he had helped found. His lips were puckering in a regular rhythm. My father asked his brother what Ralph was doing. "Smoking his pipe," Don said.

My own life wasn't conducted on film. We didn't have a film camera. My life was documented within the white borders of photographs, a static image with a smile that was engineered for the camera. It is a fair, if limited, representation of a shy boy. I hated having my picture taken, and still do. Photographs of me always have a pained, staged quality, as if the camera was interrupting a much cozier reality, the one I carried in my head. Which it was. That clenched gaze is a reminder that I wasn't the wild youth that my memory has preserved, that some unwanted streak of conservatism and self-consciousness inhabited me like a parasite, eating away at the version of myself I held so dear.

But my life was conducted on film in the broad, commercial sense. *The Wild One,* seen at about the age of twelve, was mesmerizing. I would be Brando, sullen and beautiful. Half of this prophecy came true during adolescence. Later I would pine for Redford's hair or Newman's steely isolation. Jane Fonda and I would meet and hit it off during the filming of *Barbarella.* "A member of a film audience tends to identify himself with the film's hero by a psychological process," André Bazin wrote, "the result of which is to turn the audience into a 'mass' and to render emotion uniform." Bazin didn't live to see how his theories flowered. He died in 1958 at the age of forty.

I saw Walt Disney's *Darby O'Gill and the Little People* at the Royal Theatre in Fort Frances when I was six and was terrified by those sinister leprechauns. I had nightmares and my grandmother came in, to soothe me, I thought, but she was annoyed at the frivolous source of my fear. It was only a movie, she said. The leprechauns weren't real. Some years later, I was again at the Royal, watching one of those cheesy foreign action films that padded double bills and occupied drive-ins during those years. It was crudely dubbed, and men with black beards were chasing one another through the Italian Alps. I was sitting with my younger brother and my cousin, who was my age. Behind us, a row of locals tormented us. Milk Duds bounced off our heads, popcorn sailed past our ears.

I turned to see several pale, thin-lipped boys, porridge-eating northern Ontario hillbillies. It was a quick, furtive glance, an unreliable snapshot of those sons of the mill, waiting to pound us.

Home movies reside somewhere between the discerning honesty of the still camera and the necessary falsehoods of commercial film. The home movie shows what a still photographer sees before he orders the world into a pose. There is a recognizable shorthand: children playing games with a muted spontaneity, splashing one another, husbands playfully goosing their wives, vaudevillian grins. Each family is reduced to a sunny, uncomplicated unit. Home movies of the white middle class have an interchangeable quality, a theme that various artists and filmmakers have explored. The lawns, props, technique, and jug-eared children possess a uniformity.

To the uninitiated—those outside the family—the images offer dull, comforting proof that the family exists, that it is well provided for. They have a '53 Pontiac and a birthday cake. They have an adequate water supply. But those who are steeped in the family mythologies can create a story from the images. We know that the child building the sandcastle is now a Nobel laureate, or a drug addict. He died at Vimy Ridge, or of heartbreak. We become both the spectator and author of the film. The power (and boredom) of home movies comes from the vast space that exists between the pictures and the viewer, a space that we fill with our own narratives, with history, sentiment, and dread.

Most of all, home movies are about mortality. We know how the story ends. They are invested with what Roland Barthes described as "that rather terrible thing which is there in every photograph: the return of the dead."

The undeniable pathos of home movies, that quality that is exploited when they are inserted into commercial or documentary films, comes partly from their sheer ordinariness. When I watch my grandfather's films, it is not Rosebud and some lost youth I see, but the vanishing possibilities of adulthood. Home movies present both

our limitations (I won't be a director after all) and renewed possibilities (my daughter will become prime minister). I am placed
within an historical framework that has nothing to do with the
sweeping scope of world events, a framework made of banal incre-
ments: a new Chrysler, the summer garden, an unexpected child.
Within my grandfather's films lies a theme of simple procreation, of
embracing life at its most fundamental level, and this animal reality
provides a certain comfort. Home movies offer a collectivity; I am
bound at least by the narrow line of my family history.

In the end, I chose not to videotape my daughter's development, a decision I could easily come to regret. I was a reluctant subject for the camera and now I'm a reluctant director. I want to live
within the frame. Having come late to reality, I don't want to retreat
into the artifice of videotape, coaxing my daughter to "Say something for the camera," though this is a selfish decision, given the
enjoyment I have gotten from my grandfather's films. I want the
filmed evidence of the past and the immediacy of the present; I
want to be at the centre, a generational flaw. But the footage would
probably appeal to my daughter forty years from now, when it,
along with music videos and most of our popular culture, will seem
naive. She would have seen images similar to those I saw in my
grandfather's films. The impression would be one of stability, though
this is a trick of perspective, the becalmed past viewed from the tur-
bulent present. Every previous generation seems more anchored
than the present one, whether by war, peace, the Depression, religion, or vanishing rural values. Every generation witnesses the Birth
of the Modern.

My grandfather's life and my own both proceeded in ragged
bursts, rather than the sustained line of my father and his brothers.
They came out of the 1950s, driven forward to education, families,
and prosperity. The lives of my father and uncles are suited to
the narrative form, to long linear films. My grandfather's life and
mine are closer to montage, which the great Russian film director and theorist Sergei Eisenstein described as the most powerful

compositional means of telling a story. It is the best way to tell a story where gaps in logic and chronology appear. And what is my grandfather's story? A middle-aged man with a family. A compelling story if you happen to be one, too. It is only as we enter the dilemmas of our ancestors that they become complicated to us. Eventually we come to inhabit the home movie.

1997

Ticket to Fiction:
Art & War in Belgrade

DRAGAN TODOROVIC

IT IS THE SUMMER OF 1989, AND three of us are standing on the promenade in Split, one of the biggest seaports in Croatia. Zvone is editor-in-chief of *Omladinska iskra,* an alternative pan-Yugoslav magazine with an excellent reputation. He is also a first-class rock photographer and our friend. The magazine offices are in the penthouse of an old building, and he has invited us to stay there as long as we wish. In return, we're to do an article on Split, the way two inland guys see it. The way we saw it was, we loved it, but thought that Split needed more laughter, more subversion. The city was too serious. So we decided to pose nude in the heart of the city's tourist area, five metres from some expensive restaurants and a few steps from the sea.

Right now, while we smoke, Zvone is doing something like push-ups on the pavement. Stefan Lupino is a big European name in photography and he always does push-ups before he starts a session. The parody is obvious: Lupino is a bodybuilder; Zvone is tall and thin. Lupino has this dark look of a Balkan man; Zvone is blond. Lupino's models are these gorgeous Paris women; Mica the Turk and I are two skinny Serbian guys.

"Look, Zvopino," says Turk, "I want my dick to look awesome in the picture. My grandchildren will see it one day and I don't want them to think that I was a schmuck. No, my shmok has to look like a shmok, but not me. Got it?"

"Don't even think of taking the business into your hands here," says Zvone. "They will arrest us. What am I saying—they will arrest us anyway."

"Correction: they will arrest you. We have train tickets for tonight, remember?" says Turk.

Here we are, discovering that it's not so easy to be nude models, especially on the street. In the meantime, attracted by Zvone's athletics, kids start gathering. "This is not good," says Turk. "You better call some of your girlfriends, Zvopino, and get rid of these children."

The children leave, but the parents gather, dangerously close. Zvone says, "It's now or never," we take our trunks off, and he clicks several times. While getting dressed, we can hear the mumble of disapproval from the crowd.

Later that evening we leave Split. I have a week of my holiday left, so I don't go back to Belgrade to my job as an editor of the magazine *Rock!* until later, but when I arrive at work, the editorial secretary has already hung my nude posters all over the place. Colleagues cheer loudly when I appear and gather in front of one of the posters, pretending to analyze the art.

"You look, well, not quite respectable, if you know what I mean," says one.

"That's because the Croats have these special photo-filters to make us Serbs look smaller, I've heard," says another.

"But you showed your dick to the Croats, and that's what counts," somebody commends me.

I join the cheerful laughter, but I can't get rid of this feeling in my stomach that something is wrong. I've had it for more than a week now. Two days before we left Split, Turk and I met this beautiful girl on a lonely stretch of path by the coast and invited her for a drink. She turned around and looked carefully to make sure no one was watching before she said, "Guys, I'd gladly go, but I must not be seen with you, understand?"

"Why?" I was confused. "Because we're tourists?"

"No, because you are Serbs."

This is an important pre-war memory for me. That turned out to be my last visit to Split—the war started a year and a half later.

The voice on the radio, an excited, breathless male voice, keeps repeating, "If you hear this, please come and join us. There are only two hundred of us, and strong police forces have been seen in the surrounding streets. I repeat: we are students who do a peaceful protest against police brutality. Please join us. Only if there are enough of us they won't attack ..."

It is 2:30 in the morning, March 10, 1991. The army tanks are on the streets of Belgrade, protecting the regime of Slobodan Milosevic from hundreds of thousands of angry protesters. I have already spent the whole day on the streets, amidst clouds of tear gas, flying stones, broken glass, water cannons. My friends confirm over the phone my worst fears: thousands are being arrested under the mantle of darkness and under threat of the tanks. There's been some shooting and two men are reported dead. I can't sleep.

I take my balaclava, an old scarf, a bottle of water, and the thickest jacket I have. That day I had learned my first lesson about confronting the police: they are trained to hit either on the head or in the kidney area of your back. A thick balaclava and a good jacket can prolong your life on the streets. A soaked scarf offers some protection against tear gas, enough to get you to the closest building entrance. The place where the students are gathered is just around the corner from where I live.

From my sixth-floor apartment, I tiptoe down to the sidewalk and stick to the shadows of my narrow street, waiting for my eyes to get accustomed to the darkness. Through the open window of an apartment on the first floor, I hear the same radio station and see the silhouette of a man nervously walking in circles. I move slowly, from shadow to shadow. Fifty metres behind me, around the other corner, is a tank. Although I can't hear it, I know it, because earlier that night I almost drove straight into it.

I am a professional journalist, but not this time. I don't carry any of the tools of my profession. No camera, no recorder in my pocket. This is not about glory, not about publicity, not about recording facts; this is a game of numbers, and I want to be another number where it counts.

Finally, I'm there. What I see around the corner is a group of about a hundred young people sitting on the cold asphalt of a March night around the fountain on the Terazije. Somebody is up there, speaking to them, and although I can't see him, I recognize his voice: Leka, one of the leading Yugoslav actors, and a friend from my army service. I can also see other shapes slipping from passages and side streets and joining the crowd.

I come out into the light.

I have never learned any martial arts, I am not tall, and I've had only three or four good fights in my life, but the reasoning in my head is turned off. What takes me out is the pure adrenaline of a street fighter and just one thought: you can't use tanks against your own people!

This is also a pre-war memory.

Only four months later, a patrol of Croatian police was caught in a Serbian ambush in Borovo Selo, and that was the start of the war that Serbia never officially declared. That was the day I declared my war.

When did the State start to interfere with my life? Was it at the age of sixteen, when I was recommended for and, without being asked, made a member of the Communist Party because I was a good student in high school? Was it at the age of seven, when I was received into the Pioneers organization? Or was it even earlier, when I was five, and some cousin bought me a small book printed in Cyrillic with legends of Tito as a reward for learning to read so early? Finally, was it when I was zero, and my mother got one room, without a bathroom, kitchen, or anything else, for being a member of the Communist Party, and she brought me to those four square metres from the hospital in September of 1958?

The first lessons in morality that I remember were simple: do not steal, do not display your parents' condoms when guests are around, and do not forget that the partisans were good and the Germans were bad. This last lesson was particularly important in Kragujevac, where I was born: on October 21, 1941, in retaliation for the killing of some German soldiers, the German troops shot more than seven thousand men in one day, among them a classroom of high school students and their professor. Later I attended the same high school and had some classes in the memorial classroom. I still remember those black-and-white pictures, the faces in the cheap wooden frames, pale faces, smart faces, stupid faces, interesting genetic material never to be realized. Yet, in a strange twist, Serbian history does not have the term "holocaust." Why? I guess because every forty years or so, we have a war with someone.

In World War I, almost the whole Serbian population had to leave the country and cross Albania in search of refuge from the Austro-Hungarian troops. Then the Serbs returned, beat the shit out of the Austrian Army, and formed Yugoslavia. In World War II, almost 650,000 people—Jews and Serbs and Gypsies—died in the Croatian concentration camp at Jasenovac. Over 350,000 Serbs died in that one place alone. I don't know anyone whose family did not have at least one dead in that war. Then the Red Army came and the Serbs joined and beat the shit out of Hitler's army. Before World War I, we had Balkan wars, and before that we had … wars. So, we don't take war too seriously. First they kill us a little bit, and then we kill them. And that's OK. Next?

Interesting, but I swear I don't remember anyone, ever, telling me not to kill. That lesson in morals is just too dangerous where I come from.

In 1991, after the war had started and the border between Serbia and Croatia was already closed, Branimir Johnny Stulic came to Belgrade. His parents still lived in Zagreb, but he wanted to tell his Belgrade friends that they were not isolated.

At that time, my friends had already started leaving Serbia. Nobody talked about it, neither the ones who travelled, nor the ones who stayed. Gangsters of all kinds were out on the streets of Serbia, hoping to scare the opponents of the regime and to organize paramilitary forces (because Serbia officially never was at war with Croatia). Arkan's Tigers were the worst of them, bloodthirsty killers on the fields of Croatia and Bosnia, thugs and extortionists at home in Belgrade. The right-wing political parties also had started demanding that those who left be treated as traitors, with all their possessions nationalized.

It was no wonder friends who were leaving would call only one or two nights before departure. A few I didn't have the chance to say goodbye to at all. Three days or a week later, someone would say, "Oh, they just called from London." Their tone was always offhand, as if mentioning the weather.

Johnny Stulic was born in Croatia, of mixed Serbian-Croatian parents. In 1981 he brought out the first album with his band, Azra, and, by putting out a new record every six months or so, he quickly became a leading name in the rock scene of ex-Yugoslavia. Because his songs were strongly politicized, they received an unprecedented response from several generations and provided a kind of underground code. He was the first musician to abandon the golden rule of the uninformed silence, of "I don't know, therefore I exist." At a time when the Yugoslav Communist Party still had a strong hold on media and culture, he wrote in support of the anti-Communist Solidarnosc movement in Poland. He ridiculed communist hardliners, the working class, the failed revolution of 1968, and, yes, he wrote some of the most amazing songs about love. Absurdly as it happens—we became friends after 1985, when Johnny left Yugoslavia to live in Holland.

When he reappeared in Belgrade in 1991, he had just finished making a superb record in Sarajevo and was looking for a publisher, since his original company was Croatian. We were both slightly crazy at the time, for different reasons. His fans, who belonged to both the nations at war, had been cut in two. I still believed that understanding could halt the war, and that the understanding could be achieved by talk. He told me he wanted to create a party that he intended to name the Party of Work (Naked Dick), and insisted this was to be the full name, including brackets and what was between them. "If you believe that the working class really rules in this country, all you will have in the end is a naked dick," he said. I thought that this might go well with an old idea I had of doing live interviews in front of an audience, but not for any recording or broadcasting media. So we travelled through the Serbian province for two weeks, to the places where God had said goodbye a long time ago, and we did our strange show. He would sing a little, accompanied by his acoustic guitar, then I would come out and we'd talk about the Naked Dick Party, then he'd sing again, and we'd leave. He didn't want any money, and I took only enough to cover expenses. Pure fiction, or pure absurd, whatever you want. We were promoting two things that didn't exist: his party didn't have a headquarters, money, or even membership cards, and his Sarajevan album wouldn't be published until five years later. A madly beautiful woman was our driver. She was a painter, and her drunken boyfriend was always with us. Johnny would tell us funny stories from his past, and we would all laugh, and something was desperate in all that.

"When I was in the Yugoslav Army," he said while we were driving along the Ibar River, "I did this impression of an incredibly stupid and ugly Nazi officer. Someone had tipped off the security officer, and he calls me one day and says, 'Stulic, do your impression for me.' So I did, I thought they wanted it for some army show or something. And then he says, 'Stulic, this is the People's Army with great tradition in fighting the Nazis, and we won't allow something like that here. If you want to do an impression, do an impression of an officer of the Yugoslav Army'!"

One night, in between our hopeless travels, we sit in my apartment in Belgrade and drink.

"Why did you leave?" I ask him.

"Because they would have killed me if I hadn't," he says. "Lennon, Marley, Hendrix, Che, all the people of the Revolution are dead. I am one of them; it would be the same."

"You can't be serious."

"I am. I know it sounds like paranoia, but I guess that all those dead heroes just didn't want to sound paranoid."

We fall silent for some time. Then I say, "Why are we doing this?"

"Our tour?" he asks. "We have to do something, I guess."

About that time several hundred young mothers had organized an action called "All the President's Babies." They brought their numbered babies to the front porch of Milosevic's villa, symbolically giving them to him, because they were no longer able to take care of them. "Babies of the nation to the Father of the nation," was one of the slogans. Someone else had collected all the court songs, or odes written through the ages for the rulers of Serbia by leading Serbian poets, and published them in an anthology called *The Anthology of Boot-licking Serbian Poetry*. It sold out in less than a month.

Peace culture versus war culture?

In South Slavic languages, the common word for war is "rat" (rhymes with "strut") and, oddly, it is the anagram of "art," a common international word in all the South Slavic languages. Art is perceived in the Balkans the way war is perceived, both by the notion of fight: war means destructive fight, while art is constructive fight; war is about enslaving a territory, art about liberating it; war is based on the primitive, animal characteristics of the human mind, art is about bringing out the best in the mind. The artists through the centuries have either celebrated or denounced war. A long list of books, paintings, poems, and songs deals with the.

experience of war, mostly in a celebratory way. There is no neutral position in the history of arts in ex-Yugoslav countries in regards to this phenomenon.

During the war, all connections including mail and telephone between Croatia and Serbia were cut off, and the rare foreign correspondents I met in Belgrade were unable to tell me anything about Zvone.

In 1991 Mica the Turk went to the front to write a story about the battle for Vukovar. There he heard Zvone's name for the first time since the war had started. On a bus full of Croatian POWs waiting to be exchanged for Serbian prisoners, he met a Croat who told him that he had run into Zvone right there in Vukovar, where he was taking pictures for some Croatian magazine.

As it turned out, Turk and Zvone must have been no more than a few hundred metres away from each other one night. Both Serbian and Croatian governments were forcibly mobilizing their citizens in those months, so it was just a touch of luck that neither had to shoot at the other.

"I can't sleep anymore," says Turk while we talk about this.

"Yes, I understand."

"No, you don't," says Turk. "I can't sleep because of the silence. In the night there, you hear grenades, bullets, explosions, screams, and then you get used to it. Here, I hear only this unbearable silence."

Centuries ago in the late fall of 1991, my brother and I were driving along the Ibar River, where I had driven only a few months before with Johnny Stulic. My brother had just come out of the hospital, with a shell fragment in his neck and two fingers missing on his right hand. He had got it in the battle of Vukovar.

Close to the place called the Valley of Lilacs, across the river, the ruins of a medieval palace stand on the top of a steep hill. Among the blocks of local Kopaonik stone, ten centuries ago piled into real estate for some Serbian feudal lord, among those rocks shaped into metaphors of power, today only crickets, snakes, and long lizards live.

I have never learned for certain to whom that once-powerful castle belonged. One time I saw a TV documentary about some ruins on the Ibar, but it was filmed from a helicopter, so I couldn't be sure it was this castle. Power seen from above does not look like power seen from below. When I was a boy, my father told me it was Jerina's castle. She was the wife of a very powerful medieval Serbian lord, and famous for building many, many castles. People hated her because they had to work on those buildings for years. They named her the Damned Jerina, and over time she became the Dark Shadow of Doom.

Even today Serbian peasants tend to blame Jerina as soon as they see the ominous traces of power. Wherever there is stone on top of stone and a snake below, it belonged to Jerina.

We stopped the car in front of a motel in the Valley of Lilacs. There was the sound of a mountain creek somewhere in the surrounding bushes. It was a sunny day. My brother and I got out and looked up, toward Jerina's castle. These rotten, broken teeth of a once-powerful jaw woke up my appetite for dinner. My brother saw something else.

He was at Vukovar. He had met Jerina.

A macho man from Montenegro who calls himself Rambo Amadeus sits across from me at the studio table. He is an eclectic musician who combines rock, rap, folk, and jazz into a mixture that targets kitsch culture and strongly criticizes societal hypocrisy. Rambo is usually very provocative, and I'm looking forward to this talk show with him. A few weeks ago, parliamentary elections were held in Serbia. In the last minutes before pre-electoral silence, Rambo appeared on TV, addressing voters in general: "Listen, you monkeys! In forty-eight hours you'll have the chance to change our lives, to get rid of this criminal, Milosevic. Think carefully how you vote; otherwise I'll find where you live!" Milosevic's Socialist Party won a majority again.

We are in the studio of Art Channel, the alternative, private TV station in Belgrade where I now work. A transmitter of very limited power covers only parts of Belgrade; politics is taboo. Nonetheless, it is one of the few remaining shelters for journalists who want to stay independent. Or, rather, this is one of the few remaining illusions of independent journalism.

When I come into the studio two hours before the show, I find just one camera, and the cameraman is playing some shooting game on the editing computer. "We are taping a wedding ceremony," he tells me. "You'll have only this camera, but don't worry; I'll change the shot every now and then."

So Macho Rambo and I start talking. We warm up by beginning with his career in general, before I question his artistic standards, and then steer him to his political beliefs. But something is wrong: this artist, this very engaged intellectual, is mild tonight. No matter how hard I try, he stays distanced.

During the second break, I ask him if he is having problems with the interview.

"No," he says laconically. "But is there any sense in talking to the cattle?"

We start the third and last part of the show; we are already into the sign-off courtesies when I suddenly have an urge to do something absurd. And I do: in the middle of his sentence, I lift the microphone from the table between us, take the tablecloth, and put it around my shoulders. Silence. We are still on the air. And then it's over.

After the show, Rambo the Cop-out asks, "What was it? You were trying to save the show?"

I respond truthfully, "No, I don't know what it was. I just had to do it."

What a beautiful interview I would give! My dignified face of a world traveller, my mild, yet so decisive manners, my shining intelligence, and my experience of an Atlantis survivor ... Several cameras around me and I take my time, maybe I even drink wine ... it has to be a 1993 red wine because I believe in a balance of pleasure: that was a bad year where I was, so it must have been a sunny year somewhere else. I might tell the audience how to recognize the slow coming of darkness, how condensed sadness can grip your chest and halt your breathing. I might instruct how to withdraw from life, how to pick friends in times of war. I would even know how to keep meat fresh out of the fridge in the summer, and how to recognize your time for leaving.

And I would tell them, "I can't explain how I know how to treat a wound, though I never learned it in school, I just know. I know how to avoid the first hit, how to use keys as a self-defence weapon, how to kill with only one blow. Some of this maybe comes from my experience, but some, even the majority, comes from my, from our, genes. Every generation in my family had at least one war. The fact that I am here says we all learned fast."

I would say that one orgasm in war counts as five in peace, that weather gets worse when the war starts, that fear is the only universal language we have, and that despair is the mother of courage. I would tell them how to keep warm without heating, how to listen to the messages of the night, what to hear when one hears words, how to cut the meat for your brother who lost his fingers on the front and joke about it.

Nobody asks me for an interview. So I write. I am a sower of this seed that doesn't grow into anything we need.

I know Dubravka from many years ago. She is a teaching assistant at Belgrade's University of Arts and a playwright. She is a born activist, a natural guerrilla. In 1992, during the war in Croatia, we worked together on the *Pacifik,* an anti-war magazine privately published several times a year under very difficult circumstances.

In January 1993 Dubravka tells me she has been invited to join a small group of people in Austria who are working to establish AIM (Alternativna Informativna Mreza—Alternative Informative

Network), a network among intellectuals of ex-Yugoslavia. It would be a way of exchanging truth instead of various government propaganda. The project was initiated several months earlier in Ukraine, at a meeting of the association of free radio stations of Europe. Dubravka tells me that the talks were sponsored by a strange group of people, a sort of free-love commune called Longo Mai based in France. She has been asked to go to Austria and to bring one reliable co-worker with her. Milica, who was in Ukraine at that meeting, is not able to go; and Dubravka proposes me. We are to travel at the end of January.

For the first time I will be able to watch international diplomacy at work. Though it is impossible for a citizen of Serbia to get an Austrian visa, with a fax from Longo Mai, I send my passport to the Austrian Embassy, and back it comes with a visa.

Everything is under a veil of secrecy. I am not supposed to talk too much about this trip. Instead of travelling through Croatia, which would shorten the trip to twelve hours maximum, we will have to take the bus to Hungary, then to Slovenia, then the train to Austria, more than thirty-six hours altogether.

I am looking at my Yugoslav passport. It has a red cover with "SFR Jugoslavija" inscribed in front, as in "Socialist Federal Republic of Yugoslavia." That country—my country—does not exist anymore. The passport was issued in 1991. Even at that time, such a Yugoslavia did not exist.

So, what is this red booklet?

A membership card of the League of Expatriates. An ID from Atlantis. A one-way ticket to fiction.

Bleiburg is on the Austrian border with Slovenia. Not even a village, just a group of houses in search of a post office. The local train carries noisy schoolchildren and tired, bored commuters. It stops at every other house, taking a couple of hours to travel the short distance from the border. It is almost dark when we arrive. There is nothing around, no cab, no public transportation, no driver we could ask for a ride. Dubravka asks a woman behind the station's counter about the *gesthaus* where we are supposed to wait. It turns out to be in the centre of the village. We start walking and Dubravka tells me that we are supposed to sit and wait in there until someone comes to pick us up. I have a feeling of something creepy; I don't know what it is. Bleiburg has no landmarks and, except for an occasional car, no signs of life. The air is fresh; subalpine night is falling and that is never a traveller's friend, but there is something else. I ask Dubravka if she feels what I feel, and she does. "There is something historical about this place," she says. "I can't remember what it was. Maybe some famous Nazi was born here, or something." Maybe. Not impossible for a village named "Lead Town."

We arrive at a small guesthouse with a Gothic inscription in front. We are the only customers. Behind the bar is an older man with a young woman who looks like him; they don't answer our salutes. We sit in the corner. They stand behind the bar and watch us. After fifteen minutes or so, the woman takes our order. We come from a country where the level of inflation is over 10 million per cent and we each have a monthly income of about ten German marks, so we order just some coffee. And we wait. There is nothing to read, no TV around, only some yodelling on the radio. The owner and his daughter do not talk, neither to us nor between themselves. After two hours, Dubravka makes a call. At the other end, in the commune in the mountains, some woman instructs us to continue to wait.

Finally, after four hours, during which nobody else comes into this place and we drink maybe seven or eight glasses of water each, two men appear at the door. We didn't hear the sound of their engine; they have parked cautiously up the road. They wear dark coats and black hats with wide brims. In not many words, they say something in German to the owner and the woman. These two finally give us a friendly look. We go out and get into the van. It is an hour's drive up the mountains. As the vehicle slowly winds up the narrow mountain road and the lights in the small valley become dim, I finally remember the story about Lead Town.

For a long time after World War II, it was a secret. Not until the eighties did the first articles appear in Yugoslav print about the massacre in this village in 1945. When the Red Army started defeating Nazi troops in the last months of war, all the German sympathizers—Chetniks from Serbia, equally with the Croatian Ustashas—started withdrawing toward the northwest, toward the Austrian border. They believed that anything was better than facing the Russian communists. There they would meet British and American troops and surrender themselves happily. The Allies made a concentration camp for the POWs and waited to see what to do with these people, who all thought they would end up in court and later continue to live in the West. We are talking about small fish here; the big majority of these "enemies" had been forcefully mobilized and had committed no war crime. The articles said that according to the prisoners' lists found later, there were maybe 15,000 people in the Bleiburg concentration camp.

Then the Russians and Tito's partisans came and asked to take over the prisoners. The Allies had enough difficulties finding food for all these POWs, so they hesitantly agreed. The communists went through the lists of names, taking off to prison a few-score prisoners under suspicion for committing war crimes, and closed the camp. Closed? In less than three days, thousands of helpless prisoners were shot to death in the darkness of the woods surrounding Bleiburg. Big mass tombs in the woods still hide the bones.

My uncle disappeared in World War II. When we searched for him in 1964, the trace led to Bosnia, then somewhere toward the northwest, toward the Austrian border. Bleiburg?

The first story my grandmother told me about my grandfather was that he was imprisoned by Germans and spent some time in a concentration camp. He learned German there, in self-defence, I guess, and returned to his village after the war, the only person who spoke a foreign language. A learned man of the world, who had been all the way to Germany. My father, a poor mountaineer in the fifties, was enrolled in military school and later served three years as Tito's guardian. During those eight years with the army, he learned the basic skills that later fed us. For many generations, the culture came into my family either through the war or the things related to it. War culture versus peace culture?

The first pictures I remember from childhood were from the poetry of the Kosovo cycle: Serbian knights in shining armour riding their big white horses against the Turkish hordes on their dark Arab studs in 1389. The sound of the Novi Trg sword hitting Damascus sabre, the adrenaline of a fighter who forks three Turks at once with his shaft and throws them over his shoulder into the river, as described in one of the poems. The Serbian minstrels (gus-lari) kept this cycle alive for six centuries. Later it became fashionable in Europe when Goethe translated the cycle into German. The mere fact that these poems were that old remained an important lesson in the tradition of my nation.

The war kept coming through culture at all times, even later. In those years when I started learning about the cultures of the Far East, one of the first books I read was Sun Tzu Wu's The Art of War. *When I started taking Dylan seriously, it was "The Hard Rain." Vietnam got me really interested in the world of politics. I was ten or eleven at the time, but Yugoslav TV was full of stories about this imperialist country taking on a small nation. We all identified. The best comedy was* MASH.

The Longo Mai commune turns out to be a big ranch in the Austrian Alps. The place where our driver turns left doesn't have any sign and the road looks like a definition of dead end. We pass two no-trespassing signs on the narrow stretch that leads us to the first curve behind the hill. Then, suddenly, the road is much wider as it sweeps through the woods. They are expecting us; in the yard several men and women, dogs, chickens, horses, and some cattle are all freely wandering around at this late hour. It looks very much like the Grateful Dead preparing for a world tour. The men and women take us into the big four-storey house, and there we meet the delegate journalists from the other republics of ex-Yugoslavia: Vesna Kesic and someone else from Zagreb, Borut and a woman from Slovenia, Zeljko from Montenegro. During dinner, in the warm and hospitable atmosphere, sitting on the benches around the long table, we learn more about our hosts. The original Longo Mai commune was founded in the sixties in France by an old millionaire. Later it established separate families in Austria and a few other European countries. The majority of the Austrian family is highly educated. Among them are two doctors, one lawyer, several professors. Two of the women and one man stay on the ranch all the time. One of the women is beautiful, like a Swedish model. Children (about fifteen of them) are a collective responsibility, and the members of the commune teach the preschool kids. When they grow up, I have been told, it will be up to them to decide if they will stay in the commune or leave. It is not laid out, but there is an obvious power structure; a man who looks like Klaus Kinski is silent and self-confident, and nothing starts before he is asked.

The next morning we start talking about the project. "Kinski" tells us Longo Mai is in a position to finance the purchase and installation of a network of computers in the capitals of all the ex-Yugoslav republics, which means the fastest available modems and PCs and special software custom-designed by a German company. Each workstation is to be a local information-gathering centre. I am to be the workstation operator in Belgrade. The raison d'être of the project is to create more understanding among the intelligentsia of different nationalities, and also to offer independent information to the world media, because the network we create will be available to subscribers.

"Who is financing the whole thing?" I ask. The answer never comes.

"What do we publish, what kind of information?" someone else asks.

"It doesn't have to be an article ready for publishing. Almost anything will do: the price of bread, the percentage of inflation, public opinion on certain politicians, anything," explains a Longo Mai communist who is missing a finger.

"This news is for sale? Will we get paid for it?" asks the Montenegrin.

"Yes. We will serve as a reliable source for the world media."

"The original idea was different," protests Dubravka. "We wanted to communicate privately, and for humanitarian reasons, to keep the old connections alive, to build confidence between us, and thus help overcome our local nationalisms."

"For that idea we were not able to find the money," No-Finger answers. "But if we can sell the information, we can still keep everything else on the network. The software developed for us allows us to create separate channels, unavailable for the public," continues No-Finger, who turns out to be one of the engineers who will install and maintain the network, but at the same time stay on the ranch all the time. Interesting. I remembered reading somewhere that the intelligence services have research centres where they process exactly such information. It helps in doing the political analyses and creating strategic decisions based on them.

So, is this whole thing to be considered a career move for me? A journalist who came in from the cold?

We spend the entire day discussing the project. At lunchtime I sit next to Ms. Vesna Kesic, a well-known Croatian journalist and feminist, named after the Slav goddess of spring. She starts discussing the hot issue of the day. A special commission led by the Polish politician Tadeus Mazowiecky has just published the results of its inquiry into organized rape by Serbian troops in Bosnia. The number published is terrifying—over 50,000 women. The world media reported on it. And this discussion leads to our first international conflict that day.

Vesna argues that because the number of raped women was so great, we have to talk about a genocide against Muslims.

"Genocide is defined by extermination, not by rape," I say.

"So you are not disturbed by this number?" asks Vesna.

"I would be if I trusted that report. But there are two big problems with it: one, you won't find the single name of a victim in the whole report and, two, the numbers. The war in Bosnia is going on for how long? Nine months? Ten? Make it ten. Three hundred days. If you believe Mazowiecky, every single day, some hundred and fifty to two hundred new women were raped. Was there any fighting with all that sex?"

By this time, only Vesna and I can be heard around the table. Someone is translating to the Austrians in the background. People are sipping soup as if their lives depend on it.

Vesna puts down her spoon and turns to me. "As a man, I don't think you can understand how a woman who has been raped can feel about it. It is probable they wouldn't let their names be known because of shame."

I put down my spoon, too. "As an intellectual, you should know that Mazowiecky does not have a case. No court in the world would take it seriously without, at least, one name. No one except in Croatia. Or Serbia."

The love of the others for the soup reaches unbelievable proportions.

"The mathematics does not help explain war. I still think it's possible, even probable, the number is right," continues Vesna.

"Sure," I hear myself saying, "that's because it is well known that the Serbs are the best fuckers in the world."

I guess the Austrians don't have the word for "fucking," because the translator stops translating.

"What did you say?" asks Vesna quietly.

"It was mythology. Like the stuff you're saying."

I go out for a smoke. She goes upstairs. Inside, I think somebody has just drowned in his soup.

It was never this bad, although I've always had the problem. Names disappear from my memory. It does not seem to be linked with affection. I have to ask again and again for names, even of the women I am attracted to, even the men I think will make good comrades.

I can still remember high school chemistry lessons, the knowledge never put to practical use; I can still recite the poems I learned by heart to impress the girls. The pictures of the cornfields by the road to Belgrade are still fresh in my memory from twenty years ago, and the image of my uncle, who got out of bed one day, still in pyjamas, to drive me on his new red motorcycle to see the cherry trees in blossom. I still see the bluish stripes of his washed-out pyjamas, smell the gasoline, hear the voice of his wife telling him his flu was not over yet. Everything is with me still. Everything but the names.

I never decided to forget anyone's name, I swear. The control tower of my brain did. The no-fly zone over the territory where the feelings are sheltered. This will sound strange, but I do believe that I don't have any influence on that: when all other emotional mechanisms reopen, the names will come back.

After lunch, the session continues. By sheer coincidence, some Longo Maians sit between Vesna and me. Narrow windows and the big fireplace of the old mountain house somehow take us two centuries backwards. Exactly where we all belong.

There are more incidents, this time between Montenegrin and Slovenian delegates, then between Croats and Slovenians, then between Dubravka and the Austrians, then we're all arguing in our own languages and the Austrians stare at us, trying to decode from our faces. Kinski begins to look shaken and wounded. He has turned into Fitzkaraldo trying to take the ship across the mountain, even though the locals don't share his dream. "You see why the war on Balkans was inevitable?" I say. He replies with something that might be a smile. Or the result of a really fast early-morning shave.

Fortunately, the goodness of the world community is unshakeable, it seems. No-Finger, Kinski, and the rest serve drinks, talk mild, and we slowly gather that in this fucked-up world it is wise to take glass beads when offered. So, deep in the night, when everyone is either drunk or broken, we eat domestic smoked ham and cheese, and someone brings in a guitar. Dubravka starts playing and in self-defence we decide to sing together. Then we realize there is no song that everyone knows. We don't yodel. Croatian songs demand several well-trained voices. Slovenian songs can't be sung without an accordion, and Serbian songs are so sad nobody dares to start one of them. It turns out that we all know international communist songs. We start with "The Internationale," move on to the Italian "Bandiera Rossa," continue with the Russian "Podmoskovnie Vecera," and end with a Yugoslav partisan's song, "Konjuh Planinom."

Montenegrin Zeljko sits next to me. A tall, sexy-looking woman—I don't remember her name—who belongs to the commune, brings some more wine, and he whispers to me, "She's good, eh?"

"Who?" I ask, staring at her legs.

"Her. The tall one. The only good-looking communist."

"We're all communists here, man. Besides, comrades don't fuck each other."

Someone in the meantime must have remained sober and made all the plans, because the next morning I am given a modem and a bunch of floppy disks. Some other guys get notebooks and some other stuff I don't recognize. And in no time we are on the road home, whatever home is. Warriors of peace. Knights of benevolence. Undertakers of seclusion.

Ladies and gentlemen, please allow me to poison you tonight. To pour the sad songs of my people into your dreams, to spill the ghosts of a destroyed country into your air. Let me introduce you to my dead friends, and to those dispersed all over the world trying so hard to learn new customs, trying to say what hurts them, may it be a thin dust of memories, a fine ash of hopes, a golden powder of lost loves, may it even be unsayable. We have no other means than to sing our sad songs to you, my dears. Everything is so slow, intolerably slow in this life, so let me show you the Speed of Pain, the only speed known to humans greater than the speed of light. Let me say thank you for all you did and even more for what you didn't do, my lovely ones. Because we all did it together, didn't we? We were all there, we saw it all happening, but we didn't do enough to stop it. So let's take off our skins tonight, let's mix our blood, let's clench our fists into a never-ending cramp of impotence, let's shit on this civilization by singing. Have you seen that Herzog's film? The one where an Australian Aborigine goes to court, and the judge asks who can translate what the man says, and there's no one in the courtroom who can do it, and finally someone says that this man is the last of his tribe, and no one else in the universe speaks his language anymore, that one, did you see it? Did you feel it in your bones, did you feel how it must be to be the last one, the one who closes the doors of Heaven when every-one else is already left? Did you?

I admit: I am a poisoner. Sometimes, in the summer nights, I open my window and play the sad songs of my youth with all the power I can get from that Japanese box. I hope that this will not hurt anyone. Sad songs can kill only those who sing them.

I know it's too late. Who cares? My mutiny is impossible to con-trol, but very killable: close the window and I'm gone. My teepee is a safe prison: there's no solid thing I could hang myself on. There is no solid thing, I say.

My language you won't understand. Once I kissed a German girl on the sand of an Adriatic beach. The night was hot and the world was mine, and, not knowing German, I started whispering the softest words of my language. I thought that if I said šuma, ljubav, proleće, jesen, djeva, kiša, milovanje, she would not understand the meaning, but would hear the whisper of centuries.

She left. She got up and left.

This tobacco I keep lighting, all my relations. All my relations. You know what? This idea about soft words is not mine. I think I stole it from somebody. We all do it. All the time. It's a Byzantine thing, they say. I'll cut a piece of a virgin lamb to trick my god into the sacrifice of a virgin. A virgin is a virgin is a virgin is a rose.

I cheat. I steal. I kill. The Ten Commandments were never written in my language. Enlighten me, please! If somebody kills my brother, what should I do? If someone destroys my country ... What was that with bread? Did you ever feed ten thousand refugees with two fish? Wow! And the sea opened, you say ... If all seas open, shall we ever learn to swim?

Leave it. It's over, we can all go to sleep now. History. Nada. Nichts.

On the way back, I stay with my wife Silvija's distant cousins in Maribor, a Slovenian town close to the Austrian border. They drive me around on the weekend, but on Monday I am left alone and I go downtown. I enter a café at lunchtime, a line of people already there. I understand Slovenian and can speak some version of it, but I decide to use Serbian language and loudly ask someone what the time is. The woman behind the counter turns to me, leaving all her customers in line, and asks if I come from Belgrade. When I confirm, her eyes become shiny and she says, "Sir, tell your friends over there that we miss you so much. We miss our Yugoslavia."

Has our war culture defined me?

Here is what it did for me: When Slobodan Milosevic brought his mixture of communism and nationalism, his offer didn't work for me. I was well steeped in my religion, my culture, and a millennium of Serbian history, so I didn't have to hate the Croats to define myself. The differences between us were exactly what made my generation love our unity and the idea of Yugoslavia.

Was I aggressive?

> *Oh yes, fighting for this idea that was not profitable for politi-*
> *cians anymore, but was the only roof my generation had.*
>
> *My war culture gave me a will to fight against the regime in all*
> *possible ways, to stay on the streets when the clouds of tear gas were*
> *rolling, when people with their faces smashed by police batons were*
> *passing by me, when water cannons were spraying us.*
>
> *Was I a hero?*
>
> *Never. Silvija was with me all the time. Did she feel like a hero-*
> *ine? No. But we both felt it was the only normal thing to do when*
> *you don't agree with angels that plan your life without asking.*

I travel again the night roads that take me back to my country under heavy darkness. In the morning I discover that the public transportation in Belgrade is on strike, and I have to take a cab that charges thirty dollars for what normally would cost five. The driver has judged me by my heavy bag, which in Serbia at the time means you come from or will travel abroad, in both cases having hard currency with you. And my bag was heavy with the things bought in an Austrian supermarket—food, cosmetics, medicine. Glass beads for the wild shores.

A couple of months pass. I don't have any news from Longo Mai. When I develop the film I shot in Austria, a strange thing happens: the only faces I can see on the pictures are the faces of ex-Yugoslav delegates. The Longo Maians were there, but they either turned their backs to the camera or covered their faces with their hands.

Dubravka calls in June to say that the two engineers from the commune are in Belgrade and waiting for me in her apartment. I take my secret weapons, the modem and the software, from the drawer, but I decide not to carry them with me. Again that feeling, or that logic: why haven't they called to say they were coming?

Dubravka lets me in and I see two familiar faces, No-Finger and another one with dirty hair, the second engineer, waiting for me. After very brief formalities, they get down to business. Did I bring the modem and the software with me?

"No," I say. "I thought that you might want to install it in my apartment, since I am to be the operator in Belgrade."

They exchange looks. "Well, not really. We will install it in Milica's apartment. It has been decided that she will be the operator."

Milica was the original delegate in Ukraine, on the first meeting.

"And what will be my role in the project?"

"None. It has been decided that you shouldn't be part of it."

"What do you mean by that? Who has decided?"

"Well, it is not important. Please tell us when you can bring the modem and the software. We would prefer it to be this afternoon since we are in a hurry."

"Oh yes? Because there has been a rumour that the Serbian borders will be closed for travel, so you're in a hurry, eh? Too bad, because I suddenly remembered that I need to clean the modem. It's been dusty, you know, and it will probably take a couple of days, during which time I would like Kinski to call me and explain the whole decision. Understood?"

Dirty Hair stood up threateningly. "What did you say?"

I continue to sit, bringing my right foot closer in case I need to jump. "Listen, monkey, better sit down, and be very careful what you do. I might think you're attacking me, and that wouldn't be good for your commune. They'd have lost a prominent shampoo-saver."

No-Finger gives a sign and Dirty Hair sits down, very pale. Dubravka turns to me. "I told them, I am out of the project, too. Too much is muddy. Regarding the modem and the stuff, you decide."

"I have already decided. They won't get the things until Kinski gives me a satisfactory explanation."

No-Finger is the good cop today. "Listen, I know how you feel now, but we need to finish this and go. Yes, it is about closing borders. My child is sick and is afraid to go to the hospital without me. I just want to finish it and go. Please?"

I stare at him, then at Dubravka, then at Dirty Hair. I could swear that they shimmer one foot above the ground. They all must be part of a mirage on this dry horizon. "Come with me," I finally say to No-Finger, "and I'll give you the stuff."

The Alternative Informative Network is still in operation, though as a news agency rather than an anti-war hotline. Its customers are local media outlets. The centres are in Zagreb, Belgrade, Podgorica, Skopje, Sarajevo, and Ljubljana. The original Slovenian team from Maribor fell out of the project immediately after the conference in Austria. The delegates claimed that on the way back, the equipment (two notebooks, one server, and several modems) was found and confiscated by customs. Later I discovered that Radio Student in Maribor, the station the Slovenian delegates came from, had very similar equipment. No-Finger and Dirty Hair, who travelled around setting up the network, charged sixty-five Deutsche marks per hour, six times more than an average monthly salary in Belgrade. In Zagreb alone they charged for more than 180 working hours. A rumour says that out of some 75,000 Deutsche marks for the whole project, more than 50,000 stayed with the Longo Mai for installation expenses. Milica, who took over the Belgrade centre, used the position to obtain a grant sufficient to emigrate to London. Vesna Kesic continued to travel to different peace conferences as an authentic victim from long-suffering Croatia. Mazowiecky's report was never proved, but it was not forgotten either. Dubravka emigrated to the United States. And someone from Slovenia called me one day to say that the big, old mountain house of Longo Mai burned to the ground a year after our secret meeting.

In June of 1993, Serbia is in its second year under sanctions. One day I see a long line of women, men, and children in what used to be the beautiful downtown, on Knez Mihailova Street, waiting for their daily loaf of bread. People are smuggling gasoline, food, medicine. It's difficult to find cigarettes and, even if you do, they are ridiculously expensive. For weeks now I have been buying shag tobacco on the Zeleni Venac market, in the heart of Belgrade, from a man who had to run away from Zadar, on the Croatian coast, where he had a café and his own business. But he was married to a

Croat woman. One night his neighbour called him and said that he had seen a blacklist with the man's family on it. They had to leave everything behind and drive away that same night. Now the family, five of them, lives in a studio on the outskirts of Belgrade, and he is smuggling tobacco from Macedonia to feed his family. I am buying his tobacco because it is the only gold I can afford.

One day the police started checking the market. The State does not give up its monopoly that easily. I find my dealer in the crowd and he thrusts a handful of his own tobacco at me and tells me to find him in the morning in a small café close to the market. Since then, we meet secretly. I feed his kids; he services my nerves. Sometimes we roll that Macedonian tobacco together, pretending to try it. There's nothing to try, we both know how it is—bitter as poverty, strong as anger, and yellow as the skin of a prisoner. It grows well where illusions don't.

At the end of 1993 Laura Silberman, an American journalist who travelled to Split, agreed to take my letter for Zvone with her. I didn't know his address; I didn't even know if he was still living in Split, so on the envelope I wrote, "For Zvone Krstulovic, wherever he might be." When Laura returned she called to say that she had given the letter to some journalist from Split. He said that Zvone was not there anymore, but he would try to reach him. By this time I had already changed jobs three times and apartments four times and didn't have much hope.

In the next few months, however, mail between the two countries started passing again, and one day I found a big yellow envelope in my mailbox. To my surprise the stamp was Croatian, but there was no return address. Inside I found only a glossy magazine called *Start (of the new generation)*. I flipped through its pages. Nothing in there. No message. Still, I was very happy; to get a Croatian magazine at that time felt like meeting an old friend again. I went upstairs, fixed a coffee, and started reading. The first thing I discovered was that Zvone was the editor-in-chief of this magazine, published in Zagreb. The second thing was that not only had he received my letter, he had published it on pages 4 and 5:

… The friends that have stayed here change in slow motion. I can't notice any big difference from day to day or week to week, but if I remember the way they talked a year ago, it seems that their language is shifting towards something I don't want to speak. Chauvinism slowly enters our culture, I guess for several reasons: those who are afraid to emigrate have subconsciously decided to become closer to the masses, to return to "the Family." Some of my friends got really fed up with CNN and Amanpour and western media in general. They are reacting to the kind of reporting that puts all Serbs under a big black hat, but the reaction to that means accepting the embrace of the herd. There's no other way. Except out of this country.

I don't know if you've heard, but I lost my job because of those nude pictures. Officially. Unofficially I can see the reasons more clearly now. It happened at the end of that year; the president of the company didn't even talk to me; he had just sent a message that the editors-in-chief of *Politika* do not pose nude. But, fuck, I'm glad we did it! It was the last subversion without bombs!

I don't know if you'll get this letter, but it's so refreshing to be able to tell you that you're a dirty Croat again. If I say it here, some of them will kiss me. Some will leave. No jokes anymore…

With the letter, Zvone published a single photo: a street corner with a mailbox. The only thing that was intact in the picture was the mailbox, everything else was destroyed, the houses, the lamp-posts, all the windows. I recognized Vukovar. The photographer was Zvone. What I've got from him was a code: I've read your letter, I've seen that you're the same. I am the same; we fight shoulder to shoulder in the same cause.

If anyone had asked me on that day how I felt, I'd probably have answered that everything was OK, wonderful. I had heard from my friend Zvone. But this letter hit me right between the eyes. I turned around and saw that all the objects around me were found objects, that all the people I called friends in Belgrade now were found friends. Duchamp would have loved it. My life had turned into a Dada exhibition.

How do we know when something is not a fiction?

One afternoon in 1994, in Belgrade, I started flipping through the pages of my small telephone book. I was looking for a guest for my TV talk show. Croatian artists: not available. Slovenian and Bosnian artists: not available. Tarot Barney: killed in combat in Bosnia. Cira: killed in Croatia. Marjan: in New Zealand and Sanja with him. Black: joined Arkan's Tigers in Bosnia. Johnny Stulic: back in Amsterdam. Mica the Turk: in Kragujevac, had a mild heart attack. Dubravka: in the States. Bole and Bojana: in Canada. Bachus: San Francisco. Bottle: London. Dejan: in Belgrade, but was my guest last time. Jazzer: Amsterdam. Lisa: in Milan. Teša: suicide by Russian roulette. Slobodan: dead. Snezana: in Bonn. Spasa …

What happened? Sure I have pictures, but I also have Photoshop software, capable of making anything possible on a photo, and pre-invented by J. V. Stalin. Otherwise: no tattoos, no bites, no Kama Sutran half moons on my skin. No condoms under my bed, no lipstick on my glasses, no forgotten umbrellas on my shelf.

Did I have them, did they have me? Was it a dream? Did we really play bridge? Did we love each other? Our past is a pastel in the rain. Ask not what your country can do for you, but what you can do to hide away from your country.

Spasa is an artist. I meet him one day in the summer of 1994 in the pedestrian zone in the centre of Belgrade. We know each other from our hometown, Kragujevac, and, although we don't meet often, we spend some time together whenever we bump into each other on the street. The day is from a brewer's dream. The girls are half naked and there's that vibration of insanity that comes with the summer into all big cities. We pick some small café on a shadowy sidewalk and take our beers outside to drink.

"So, how are things?" I ask.

"Good," he says, "I'm going to war."

"When?"

"Now," he says.

I drink my beer, then pull some smokes, and keep looking at him. He likes to joke and I expect a smile to loosen his face, the bearded face of a Serbian Che. But his eyes stay narrow and serious and that smile, it seems, won't come.

"You were drafted?" I ask.

"No, I'm going to volunteer. I was just on my way when I met you."

"Volunteer? With whom do you want to go to Bosnia?" At that time, even minor political parties in Serbia had their mini-armies there, not to mention major parties and the army of Bosnian Serbs, not to mention Arkan's Tigers.

"Doesn't matter," he responds. "I'm just fed up with this waiting. We just sit and wait for the war to end, and there's no real life, everything is just waiting. I did my part, now I'm going to fight."

Last night, Belgrade TV showed a story about Bosnian Serbs being massacred by Muslims in some distant village. I thought that maybe he had reacted to it.

"But that's exactly what they want," I say. "You watch too much television. Can't you see they're doing that on purpose: whenever they need new volunteers, they come up with some massacre by the Muslims. How do you know it's true? How do we know these are not corpses from a few months ago?"

"Does it really matter?"

"Of course it does. Remember how, at the beginning of Bosnia, Muslim TV showed some massacred bodies and accused the Serbs, and two weeks later it was proved that those actually were the bodies of Serbs, massacred by Muslims?"

Spasa looks into my eyes carefully. "Corpses are corpses. It might go on for years. There is no critical mass of soldiers in there to end the fighting one way or the other. What I mean is it doesn't matter anymore, at least not to me, who will win this war. All that matters is for it to be over. *Finito,* you understand? We don't really live while the war is going on. What do we do? You write for your drawer, right? He paints for his attic. I do my thing for my cellar. Is that what we wanted? Is that what we planned? We get no attention, and people don't have the money to buy what we do. Even when the war is over, it will take some time for this country to recover, so, the sooner, the better."

"But, man, you could easily be killed there. Is that the attention you want, to be another corpse on the screen? If this is too slow for you, why not just go and live somewhere else? You don't have kids, it wouldn't be that hard for you."

Spasa has this laughter that cuts you in two. The Inquisition would have burned him for it. "Live where? Go to the States and do my macramé? They think it's for housewives, not for serious artists. Italy? I wouldn't know how to order a beer. France? To work in a café on Champs Elysées washing the dishes? You know, if this was the 1930s, it would be much easier. A person could go to Berlin to become a Nazi, or to Moscow to be a commie, or to America to join Capone. But now? I don't believe in capitalism, and I've seen what socialism does. Where do we go? Where?"

I don't have a clue, but I don't want him to go to war. I look covertly at my watch. It is almost 5:00 on Friday. If we sit here long enough there is a good chance the volunteers offices will be closed. So I order another round.

"Spasa, we're all centaurs, half men, half horses. The brains are up there, but sometimes we just don't think fast enough for these strong, fast legs. They just take us somewhere and then the brain's no use to us. Brains do not work where grenades fly. Don't let your legs take you into the living mud. Is this your war, is this my war? Did you make any decision, no matter how small, that led to this war? Did you vote for Milosevic? Did we vote for Muslim leaders? What's the biggest difference between before the war and now? We live much worse, they live much better. Milosevic has a son, so let him send his son to war. There, that's one volunteer that will make the critical mass, so you can stay here and drink with me."

"But I'm an anarchist. I have this woman, I have these hands, and I have this ugly head. There's nothing anywhere else in the world, no system, no power, no idea that I'm attracted to. I didn't even know I was an anarchist before this war. Now I do. And where do the anarchists fit? Nowhere. Even the idea of anarchy is dead. So, you know, at least I'm going to fight until I come up with something I can believe in."

It is difficult to beat him when you agree with him and I go for the lowest level of persuasion: material stuff. It's 5:20.

"When the war started, in Croatia, I said to myself, OK, this is the same old thing. But the serious shit would be Bosnia. Jesus, people of different religions and nationalities are living side by side there. If it starts, I'm out, I'm definitely out of the country the same day! But, look, here I am. How did it happen? Because I looked around, like now: beautiful women, good friends, nice cafés on the sidewalk. Sometimes we can live on air. I think that's how the prisoners in concentration camps survived. Read Salamov: you start enjoying the breadcrumbs when there's no more bread."

"That's for mice, not men."

"Possible. But mice live to tell about it; heroes don't. I've never thought you'd like to have a street named after you."

"Fuck you."

"No, fuck you. Besides, I really did. Look at your watch. It's 5:45, and it's Friday. You won't find any office open now."

So we sit and drink slowly. When I get home after 10:00, Silvija says, "You're drunk. What did you do?"

"I just saved my own life," I say.

Spasa never went to war. But he never said thanks, either.

Silvija and I are packing. This is not an ordinary trip, this is the Final Trip. We are emigrating tomorrow.

Lufthansa allows two bags, thirty-two kilograms each. So, the only persons we can bring with us are the dead. The only books allowed are small books. It means dictionaries. No history books, no cookbooks, no encyclopedias. No reputation. No old shoes. No heavy feelings either. No food, no drinks, no records. No reputation. No family, no friends, no success, no failure.

What's the name for this? Ethical cleansing? We will arrive in Canada as what, as whom? Will our memories pass customs?

I transfer all the files from my computer in Belgrade to floppy disks. Extra memory for the road. When we arrive, I discover that the airport magnetic frames irrevocably destroyed one-third of the disks.

I don't need the disk to remember the day.

It was the beginning of summer, a few months after the big demonstration, and we rented some video to watch in the afternoon while waiting for Dejan and Milica. It turned out to be an extremely depressing film, *Awakenings*. Our friends came in the evening and asked why we were so sombre. We told them and they asked to borrow the cassette for the night. Our warnings didn't stop them.

The next day, around three in the afternoon, Dejan brought the cassette back. He told me he was in a hurry, so I went downstairs and waited for him in front of the building. When he opened the window of his Opel, I saw that he was sombre, too. "It is terrible," he said.

"Film? I told you," I said.

"The news," he said, "haven't you heard the news? It started."

"What started?"

"The war," he said, and left.

And I remember standing there, on the hot asphalt in front of Building Number Six in Milorada Sapcanina Street in Belgrade,

Anno Domini 1991, and I remember that it was somehow solemn and the music that I always hear in my head was suddenly strong and godlike, Bach of my inner cathedral, and I remember that only one thought kept coming back over and over, no matter how hard I tried to chase it away: This is my war. It is my turn.

And everybody in my family, for centuries, had at least one war. And everybody learned how to kill, and how to live, and I saw that it was good. And all my life was hedonistic until now, because that is the way our men lived, and it was so. And I fucked left and right, and I thought up and down, and I lived, and I saw that it was good. And the big cloud was coming on the horizon, and I had a dream, and no children stayed alive in my dream. And I saw two dark pillars coming toward me, and I thought, Oh, these must be my tornadoes, and it was so. And I looked to the left, and I looked to the right, and I was calm because behind me, to my right, there stood a temple of no particular god, and I knew that that temple, without walls, without anything but Ionic pillars and the roof, was my shelter, and I saw that it was good. And I am opening the umbrella of my skin over the people I love, because the Western rain has already started and the first bullets are knocking on our windows. And for thirty years you've been teaching me how to hate, you, black seed of the lepers, you, dark stinking jaws of an open wound, and now you're coming to take me with you, in vain, in vain, beasts, for my heart belongs to my love. And, oh, Zeus, give the thunder to my hands, and, Sofia, give the wisdom to my heart, and, Perun, you long-forgotten god of Slavs, let your lightning strike them in the eye, and Vesna, goddess of spring, let thy love be my ruler forever. Because my time has come, and I'm scared shitless, and I don't want to die, and I don't have kids, and I didn't publish enough books, and I haven't told the best stories of my guts, and many good women would like to fuck me, and there's no point in disappointing them, because we are all your seed, Vesna, goddess of spring, goddess of love, my goddess. Amen.

1998

Wankers and Widows and Chancers and Saints

MARK ANTHONY JARMAN

Travel is the ruin of all happiness! There's no looking at a building here after seeing Italy.

Fanny Burney, 1782

The truth is often a terrible weapon of aggression.

Alfred Adler, 1929

RECRUITS STRAPPED INSIDE THE AMAZING MACHINE

FROM THE GET-GO ON THE painted 747 we drink hooch madly, privately, foppishly, British Airways headphones on the so-called rock channel with some cockney DJ nattering and spinning hit singles from 1966, from my ancient grade-school history. Eight miles high and 800 mph with the Yardbirds and Kinks; Ike & Tina giving me shivers with "River Deep," "Mountain High," and Pet Clark's voice booming past her white lipstick.

Some of us are bored, blasé about travel. Some of us should be pistol-whipped. My drowned Irish grandfather was never flung through air at 800 mph with "Shapes of Things to Come" crashing the hairs of his inner ear.

Shoehorned into blue seats zooming over Rocky Mountain House, Hudson Bay, Baffin Island, Greenland, it's impossible to escape the TV screens placed overhead every few rows. You can't *not* see Madonna's large mouth or the special-effects volcano punctuating the mindless in-flight disaster movie.

We're zooming over Iceland. We're on the polar route, but inside this finely engineered aluminum tube it's hot and stuffy. We wipe our brows with British Airways "Refreshing Tissue," moist towelettes in tiny packs resembling condom wrappers.

It's hot and stuffy but crowhop out on that big wing one inch past this pane of Plexi and you'd freeze to death. You'd freeze-dry and blow off like a shrivelled maple leaf, but that's okay, that's part of the buzz, the commodity. We are manic tourists, we are hick-yokel appetite personified, party-hardy hayseed consumers with shy eyes and backteeth floating. We're happy, *special*.

The British pilots, Reginald and Nigel, have such beautiful, decent accents. "Thanks to our cabin crew."

"Long night flights are difficult, of course."

The British Airways cabin crews are dedicated, are days from a strike.

Our dedicated British stewardess, trying to cut back our impending jet lag and inebriation, ferries us round after round of water, orange juice, tomato juice, and then she hands out free bananas to go with the rivers of booze.

Soon we'll be dancing on Carnaby Street with Twiggy and the corpse of Sid Vicious, marching for a larf with Ulster's kick-the-Pope brigades! Yes! I'll be knocking back black garrulous pints with James Joyce and Martin Amis and Maggie Thatcher and forgetting why I came, forgetting my murky family legends and Irish errands, because Britain is a seductive stewardess and Europe is a giant theme park: granite gargoyles and short skirts and ivory beerpulls and flying buttresses a construct just for me!

But then—then arrives that half-drunk epiphany.

My eyes clear and I see I'm a fool, fallen from suave *jet-set* infallibility into a Freudian pop-art installation, *product*.

My eyes clear and I see myself riding an assembly line that fills Europe. Row upon row of inebriated tourists clutching erect bananas and waiting to be serviced.

RIDING ON THE NORTHERN LINE

My father was born in Oxford. My mother is from Dublin. I feel the pull of rival kingdoms. This trip, I'm visiting the two kingdoms. My parents, both in the Royal Navy, met during the war. The Oxford side of the family did not approve of my father's secret wartime marriage to an Irish woman while on a thirty-six-hour leave in London. My English father is dead now. My Irish mother, at this moment, is not talking to me over one thing or another, even though I am going to prowl her old neighbourhoods. In fact, she's not talking to me *because* I like to prowl her old neighbourhoods. She'd rather I didn't pry, name names, use her or the family as raw material. She'd rather I wrote nice Hallmark cards or chased ambulances. Maybe I am chasing ambulances.

In my bedroom at my aunt and uncle's house in north London is an "Irish mug," with its handle inside the mug instead of outside. An Irish joke. Ha ha. Very good.

"What do you think of the IRA?" my English aunt asks me down in a crowded tube station. Before I can answer she says, "Well, what could anyone think of the IRA. They're *monsters.*"

My English relatives hate the IRA and don't know that my Irish uncles were in the IRA circa 1916. I keep my mouth shut, as my English father would have.

My English relatives are kind and generous; they are not villains—they give me anything I want, spoil me. My English relatives look down on the Irish as a gunnysack of curs and wildcats.

THE KITCHEN TABLE IN THE CITY

In Dublin I'm staying with my Aunt Rose. Rose married my mother's favourite brother, Brendan. Brendan died not long after my trip here in 1981. Rose has a bad chest cough, a pleasing face, and still golfs as much as she can. Her sons, Padraic and Sharkey, my cousins, used to joke that she golfed so much they felt like orphans.

Rose and I sit for hours in her semi-detached house talking about the family. Rose says my Aunt Bess hardly came to see her husband, Danny, when he was dying. Danny was my uncle, my mother's older brother.

"Unconscious in the hospital, sure Brendan'd go and stay most of the night (he got off work at half past four then). One time, now Bridie told me this, she said, Bridie she said Bess arrived, she said, and Danny *hooshed* her hand away, she said, and held on to Bridie's hand. *Hooshed* it away and he's unconscious and aren't his eyes closed, but *hooshed* her hand away.

"Brendan he said to me, he said Bess ought to have married a docker, he said, you know dockers they're all big and strong and they'd put a boot up your backside, he said. That woman! No man'd put up with what Danny did. Danny had a hard life."

My Uncle Danny worked as a cooper and cut peat in the country for extra money. Danny was only fifty-two when he died. Hardening of the arteries, we were told. Danny had to help raise the family after his father, my grandfather, drowned; Danny had to take over as the oldest male in the family. My mother looked up to him like a father. He'd been in the IRA when he was young, was dragged out of bed by the Black & Tans and taken to jail for interrogation.

Always thin, Rose says to me, poor Danny worked and worked and worked and didn't have time to put flesh on his bones.

Jurassic Park in Dublin's Oldest Gay Club

Padraic, my favourite cousin, came out of the closet just after my 1981 trip. He didn't tell me. No one told me. No Irish relatives wanted to phone Canada to say did you know your man is a little light in the loafers?

The entrance to the club, down a lane, seems clandestine. A curly haired man in a black suitcoat pounds and kicks at the club's big door: "I'LL HAVE YOU BY THE BOLLOCKS!" he bellows. I assume he's just been turfed.

A big, buzzcut doorman leans out the entrance, glowers, but seems willing to wait the man out rather than lay him out. My cousin and I sneak past the scene, through the disputed portal, pretending not to notice, and pay our covers at a wicket.

Bad disco plays inside (is there good disco?). My cousin takes me to the "traditional" Irish pub side of the club. The male bartenders are dressed in Margaret Thatcher drag. It looks like the joke gets old after a few hours of adjusting your sweaty nylon wig and being run off your feet behind the bar.

I guess now I know he's gay. The place appears to be several smoky clubs smashed together: oak panels in the first room, tortured black steel in another, a gyrating dance floor through a passageway, and above it psychedelic light shows on a screen. Stairs climb up to different territories and colours and preferences. Older patrons prefer the trad side: Jurassic Park it's nicknamed, because of their age, our age, because we're dinosaurs now.

Padraic gives me a tour of all the different nooks and crannies and explains who likes which parts. A friend asks if he's giving me a tour of the club or of all his ex-boyfriends. I realize I don't know him anymore.

Years ago he spent a summer with us in Canada, working construction for my brother-in-law, buying doughnuts on the way to work at six in the morning, rolling a huge packer on a steep hill, hanging out with my friends, hiking in the Rockies of Montana and Alberta, drinking beer and driving gravel roads to the lake in pickup trucks. He drove on the wrong side of the road, wanted to go to California, thinking it minutes away. He had a goofy, open quality about him, a hollow leg when it came to eating potatoes, was fun, great crack.

I also spent a lot of time with him in Ireland in 1981. We double-dated, walked around Dublin, took fast trains to the west. That history seems gone now, wiped clean. He seems to date his life from after those years. He shows me his club, a happy swagger to his walk, his head high and looking all about, greeting everyone, eager to take life in.

Padraic's companion of fourteen years is dead. I don't ask but assume AIDS. I don't ask if Padraic's HIV positive.

A young man with pointy Star Trek sideburns says brightly to another man, "Tell your lover to shave his balls. It's great." He waves his hands down toward his lap and we all dutifully look at his lap. "A little bristly when it grows back in, but still, it's great." He says he marks "Shave Pubes" regularly on his calendar.

I try to remain open-minded but involuntarily cringe, thinking of a razor down there. Perhaps a touch of castration anxiety. I want to ask if he uses shaving cream, but I refrain. What if you cut yourself? I hope they don't notice another cringe. They might not. Much of the club's pierced and buffed clientele is on various controlled substances, including heroin, Special K, crystal meth, cocaine, Ecstasy, and, of course, Guinness Stout.

Up north it's the infamous marching season for the Orangemen, time for the petrol bombs and rubber bullets and flaming lorries, but you'd never know it here in Dublin, here in Jurassic Park. History means little to the antsy guy who strips his shirt on the dance floor. Here they do not discuss Armalite rifles versus the ballot box.

A drunk man roots madly at our feet, cursing, pushing us aside.

"What are you doing?" we ask.

"I'm asking you to move!" he shouts. He's lost a backpack or package.

One of our party quips lightly, "Well, can you look farther down the bar?"

"That some kind of joke?!" His voice is very threatening. Some in our party drift away from trouble (the troubles). "That some kind of joke?!"

I'm irritated, almost want a fight.

Like me he's digging for something from earlier, from the past. He's digging at our feet. I'm tempted to boot him in the head.

Later he finds his pack farther down the bar, where we jokingly told him to look.

"SEE!" he exclaims, swollen with indignation. "It wasn't *fiction!*"

"American?"

"Canadian."

"Same thing."

In Jurassic Park there is no uniform look. I see solitary men who remind me of my Tory uncle in England: bald, portly, not working out or watching their figure, not into gay gym culture, not into dancing the night away with no shirt. What Prufrock thoughts lurk behind those impassive, jowly masks?

Cousin Padraic: his grandfather is my grandfather. I forget. Padraic thinks one old bachelor uncle, our favourite, now deceased, was secretly gay. "I'm as sure *he* was gay as I'm sure *I'm* gay." I remember reading John Rechy's *City of Night* two decades ago in my uncle's cramped apartment. He always called me son. This is probably not what the older members of our families want to hear, to *out* someone after his death.

The funny thing is that even if he was gay, my grumpy uncle would have hated this place: bartenders in frumpy Margaret Thatcher drag and a disco-inferno herd jumping around like a right bunch of eejits at a Village People revival (or the Chemical Brothers or retro jungle or Nine Inch Nails) and guys chatting merrily of the many clear advantages of taking a razor to their balls. Jurassic Park would not be a haven for my dear old uncle.

A tall man leaving kisses me quickly on the mouth. This surprises me.

Padraic says he thinks he wants a son. He has seen what having a son has done for his brother, Sharkey. "Changed him completely. A new man," Padraic says.

Cousin Sharkey's Redneck Section

Padraic's younger brother, Sharkey, drives me anywhere I want, Sharkey finds the time. He's a good guy. He's an Irish policeman.

Sharkey says he heard a joke. "A teacher asks her schoolkids to use the word 'beautiful' in a sentence. A girl says, 'Last night the

sunset was beautiful.' Very good. Teacher asks, 'Now then, can anyone use it twice in one sentence?' Boy puts his hand up, says, 'Me
sister said she's pregnant and me father says, Beautiful, just fucking
beautiful.'"

"SHARKEY!" protests his mother, Rose, from the backseat.
"You never heard such language in *our* house. Where did you pick
it up? You use it and don't even *know!*" (There is some irony here
since Rose uses the word "thing" in almost every sentence and
doesn't know. How was the movie? Oh it was *thing*. My mother
does the same: *Mrs. Thing called.*)

Both my Irish cousins are funny, with the gift of the gab. Padraic
is a single nomad, globetrotting to Miami, San Francisco, Spain,
Brussels, Bath, Bristol. He likes art and books, works in architecture,
is fixing up a Victorian rowhouse in Dublin's city core, near the
James Joyce Centre. His long-time partner is dead.

Sharkey has a pretty wife and small boy and another baby on
the way. He is rooted in the suburbs, a house on the same street as
his mother, the street he grew up on. He has no books, likes golf
with his boss, TV, a pint at the local. Sharkey is more conservative
but is also more irreverent.

Two Irish brothers, same womb, same parents and grandparents,
same city, but living on different planets.

SHITE AND ONIONS IN THE NATIONAL LIBRARY

My Aunt Rose and I hunch inside Dublin's National Library, tor-
turing our eyes, poring over myopic rolls of microfilm, searching for
Michael, my drowned Irish grandfather. Cacophony of drills, buzz
saws, and jackhammers from renovations; men in the hallway,
men on the roof. Bright summer sunlight makes it almost impossible to read the murky screen. Both our heads are bent inside an
ancient low-tech microfilm projector, a big black box with one
side open and a white surface on the bottom. Rose drapes her black
coat over us to block the sunlight. We resemble nineteenth-century
photographers.

I have just one photo of my lost grandfather, Michael, a turn-of-the-century family portrait, when Michael and Mary had only two children, not the ten he left when he drowned. They look young and happy and well dressed; they look good in their clothes. Michael's eyes are playful. I can see his face without looking at the picture. His head tilts slightly, a calm half-smile on his face, the confidence of a physical man, comfortable with the camera, with his rough suit and vest, comfortable with himself, or deft at hiding his doubts. His hair is cropped close and a hawknose juts over a big moustache. His collars are high and Edwardian and under his coat is a fancy waistcoat. He's a hard worker in good shape: no fat at his neck or stomach. His dark, tough hand rests on his wife's shoulder.

My grandmother Mary Doyle looks pretty and buxom in her high-necked blouse with a tight waist, her thick hair tied up loosely in a chignon. The two young children must be Kathleen, who died young, and Danny, a smiling baby who became the man of the family after Michael drowned, who worked and worked and died at fifty-two. At the time of the photo they might have still been living on Malachi Road, not moved yet to Usher's Island.

I sense Michael can be a funny man—he doesn't take the event of the portrait seriously—but I assume he can be serious, has light and dark, has the family temper when crossed, has a hand hard as oak.

I know his hand is tough because he was a Master Cooper with the St. James's Gate Guinness Brewery, once the largest brewery in the world. Working for *Uncle Arthur,* he termed it, after Arthur Guinness, who founded it in 1759.

My grandfather Michael made oak barrels with his bare hands and a blade, like a machete, to carve heavy planks of English oak and Quebec oak into perfectly curved staves, measuring those precise cuts with his eye, using no nails, no screws, and slicing those oak pieces into a watertight fit. A steam bell makes the oak pliable, iron hoops hold the staves together, and a windlass tightens the ends, gives the barrel its shape. Michael collects and burns the oak's shavings to char or *blaze* the inside of the new cask.

Dark wood, different sizes, some barrels taller than a man: Ale Puncheons, Union Butts, Porter Butts, Barm Hogsheads, London Hogsheads, or Bosnia Export Hogsheads. The stave yards, the Coopers' Dressing Shed, the Branding Room, the Broken Cask Yard, the Cask Cleaning Shed: *We clean about twelve thousand casks daily by washing, scrubbing, and steaming.* Shipping barrels full of stout down the River Liffey, barges and schooners rolling to the ends of the earth from his hard hands.

My grandfather Michael belonged to the Regular Dublin Operative Coopers' Society, 5 Blackhall Street, Dublin. Coopering—building and repairing barrels, from Middle English (*cowper*) or Latin (*cupa*) for "cask or cup"—has been a profession since shipbuilding or before. How many oak casks did Michael create? All his precise work gone, history now, lost with their stiff leather aprons. Metal kegs doomed this society, this craft, drowned it.

In Dublin's National Library, the 1922 newspapers are full of raids and ambushes, snipers at the window, shots from the hedge, shots in the head, dragged from the bed (as my IRA uncles were in those years), dragged to fields, killed in a dark cinema, or shot four times but survived to tell the tale.

Why am I so interested in Michael the drowned man? No one else is. I suppose I seek something official instead of the shifting murky family versions of his death. Rose and other relatives in Dublin heard he drowned in the Liffey, while my mother had always said a canal in the country. Some said a whirlpool in the water pulled him down. Some suggested alcohol had to be a factor, that they must have been stopping at pubs out in the country and been paloothered, paralytic.

Because of my grandfather's death by drowning, my eye is drawn to tales of water: swimmers, ships sinking, bathtubs, drownings. It seems so easy to drown, to just disappear in the weeds and wake, the unuttered words, the lungs going to gills.

Scrolling the old Dublin newspapers takes forever. Digging up the past is harder than I expected, more tedious than I expected.

Drowning is so much faster, maybe ninety seconds. My aunt and I struggle to make the big balky machine focus its lens, struggle to thread and scroll old metal reels, scanning torn pages of newsprint converted to film, tiny articles and headlines and banns and ads, blurred print and photos, weird fonts swimming, miles of pages, looking for that one name, looking for that one entry that means something to me or the family.

King's County Burnings—Fine Mansions Given to Flames
Woman Directs Ambush
Saved from Drowning Fishing for Crabs Fell in Strong Current
Prompt and Plucky Action
Gored by a Bull
Ten Rules for Longer Life

An older man bellows, two projectors to our right. "SHITE AND ONIONS, CAN SOMEONE HELP ME WITH THIS BLOODY FILM?!"

A librarian shows up, tries to soothe him.

"IF YOU SEND ME DOWN THOSE BLOODY STAIRS ONE MORE TIME!"

Drills, grinders, hammers, and white-haired researchers shouting shite and onions: this is the wildest, most raucous library I've ever been in. Ireland seems inherently noisy, lively, crazed; more so since I've come here directly after seeing rather (*rawther*) reserved relatives in England. I try to keep reading, searching.

Michael Collins Lying in State in General's Uniform
Hands Hold Crucifix & Beads of Rosary
"Aren't the Boys Great," He'd Say

I am seeing the same articles and headlines reporting Michael Collins's assassination that my Irish grandfather read at his home on Usher's Island, at his leisure after work at the Coopers' Shed. He's the same age I am. I wonder if he has a favourite chair. They have a grand piano. I see Michael Lyons sitting by a lace curtain window, smoking his pipe, popping open a corked bottle of black porter or hop-bitters, reading the buff-coloured newspaper after work, as I do. The kids are noisy playing on the stairs. He hasn't had supper yet, looks forward to a good meal with strong tea and sugar, and after supper a slice of pungent farm cheese in the drawing room.

He hasn't drowned yet, but it's getting close. I'm the future coming back to travel in the past, the wild colonial boy who wants a pint with his dead grandfather.

Many who passed through the chamber of death deeply moved by the scene which met their gaze. 5000 per Hour at City Hall
  Uniformed Guards and Six Tall Candles
  Bridges Black with People, Windows and Curbs Filled as Far as Eye Can See
    All Hotels Closed NOTICE: "Cessation of Work"

This last detail intrigues me. I realize this "Cessation of Work" is what kills my grandfather: the holiday. Michael Collins's official day of mourning kills my grandparent. If he'd been at work at the Guinness Coopers' Shed that Monday he'd have lived, had another ten kids with Mary.

Women and Girls Gave Way to Their Sorrow
Sad Relics: General Collins' Bloodstained Coat & Cap
Austrian Fails Channel Swim
Child's Strange Death—Scalded by Water from a Motor Radiator
Had Piles 40 Years Now Cured
Weissmuller The Human Hydroplane

I almost give up, but then I find him, find a tiny article, find my grandfather and his smaller, less celebrated death.

IRISH TIMES
Tuesday August 29, 1922
DUBLIN AND THE PROVINCES
News From All Parts

Drowned While Bathing
Michael Lyons, aged 42 of 11 Usher's Island, an employé of
Messrs. Guinness and Co., was drowned while bathing in The
Grand Canal, Dublin, yesterday. He was unable to swim, and
went beyond his depth, and the efforts of two others to rescue him
failed.

Three lines. That's all she wrote, as they say. Here is my drowned grandfather, Michael. Same age as I am. This is what I came for, why I flew the polar route, got paloothered, held a free banana.

Why did their efforts to rescue him fail? Those who could tell me are dead.

My mother believes her father's heart stopped from the shock of the cold water. My mother wants me to see a doctor to get my heart looked at, just in case. Nearly everyone agreed Michael couldn't swim, yet Aunt Bridie tells me later she believed him a good swimmer. No one knows exactly where he drowned. No one in the family has ever been to the spot in the country or even knew which canal.

I want to chase the place down, possess it somehow, a tourist believing he has the right to a souvenir.

Another reason for my morbid interest: my grandfather drowned the very day of the huge funeral procession for Michael Collins, the famous Irish revolutionary and commander-in-chief of the provisional government's War Council of 1922, a time of horrific bloody anarchy and arson, torture, mutilation, and murder, a time of roving gangs and gangsters and punks and flying squads, when the Irish maimed and castrated and used a hammer to get information, hunting one another down, a price on your head no matter which side you took, those wanting the peace treaty with the English versus those who refused it, families torn apart, a time where the Irish killed more Irish than their old enemy the Brits ever managed.

My mother says she hates politics now because she had so much of it in the house as a child.

Rose and I decide we've had enough. I'll come back another day to wade through more papers (cities could have ten daily newspapers then). With some relief I exit the crazy library and the men on the rooftops. Nice to get outside into the 1990s, to relax and stretch and move and breathe fresh air. My aunt has an errand, so we wave goodbye outside the Kildare Hotel.

I need food and drink after my Irish death trip, and I need silence after the raucous library. The Kildare pub is quiet, but thirty seconds after I order a pint, the pub fills with a shouting after-work crowd, tilts from empty to full, alters animus, and a crowing happy crowd drives me out.

Trendy parts of Dublin like Grafton Street and Temple Bar are similarly packed and hot. People hear Temple Bar is cool (and hot), so they go sit on the curbs with backpacks just to be in Temple Bar, even though other streets are more interesting. I have pleasant memories of Grafton Street, but I hate it this trip. It's become a street of well-heeled shoppers rubbernecking and bumping one another with pastel-perfect sweaters and name-brand bags with string handles. I wish to avoid the fleshy shopping tourists, even though I know I am one of them. I find on this trip I have a pathological aversion to the mob, an aversion that is worsening as I get older.

I flee past the bustling Tara Street Station, following the river to the spectral City Quay across the Liffey from the Customs House and the Royal Canal, tall masted clippers gone like ghosts, but the soft sea air noticeably cooler, fresher. I see a Guinness sign in the distance, stumble on an empty pub up this way, run by artists and no television blaring. Like my phantom grandfather, I move away from the blathering crowds and packed bridges, find my own private refuges.

In the Funnel Bar I drink in peace and stare at the river where the schooners used to dock, think about the frustrating search, the fractious blood relations, the drowned man who eludes me.

I catch up on my journal, eat an oyster sandwich, guide pints of ale to my mouth and write postcards to Sharon and my three young boys. I hope that Visa bills I run up here may not find me in Canada, and I stare at the Liffey's murky moving water and the mouth of the Royal Canal.

AUNT BRIDIE IN COUNTY LAOIS

My cousin James picks me up at Rose's early on a Sunday morning in Dublin. We drive southwest to a coal miners' church, to meet Bridie at mass.

Rose is my city aunt and Bridie is my country aunt. I want to visit with Bridie and any relatives she can introduce me to, see the family farms, see the lay of the land, because my grandfather and grandmother both came from the landlocked country around Kilkenny City, Athy, Wolfhill, Shanrath, Johnswell, Muine Bheag, a quiet area where three counties, Carlow, Kilkenny, and Laois, bump into one another.

A coal mine nearby at Castlecomer once employed a number of locals: good anthracite burns very cleanly with no smoke. The mine is closed now, played out. The coal miners built this big stone church on a hill in the fields and trees.

Bridie's husband, Uncle Willie, used to drive a coal truck around the narrow local lanes, delivering coal to steady customers: businesses and convents. It's nice country, but not striking, not a tourist destination. Cattle moaning and roaming stony pastures, and little in the way of crops or drama.

Like Rose in Dublin, the country priest has a bad cough; we wonder if he'll get through mass.

Aunt Bridie's farm is just down the hill from the church. She is in her late seventies but is still my mother's baby sister. Bridie is both funny and stern. She has a no-nonsense face, thick glasses, and strong opinions, a trait she shares with my mother and grandmother and most of the clan.

Her daughter and son-in-law live in another house in the same farmyard. Years ago I had a big meal at this farm—but I can hardly remember it. Maybe it was after the rock fest I went to at Macroom. I remember the two farmhouses close to each other, mother and daughter and grandchildren. I know it was a sunny day and a startling white cloth draped a long table and Mary the daughter, my cousin, sang old ballads with a lovely voice and I talked with Willie, an uncle by marriage, talked with Willie about my grandfather's drowning and learned little.

Willie is now a dead man in a grave beside this church, the grave we stand at after church in a light misty rain. He's down there in the ground and we shift from foot to foot. Where does a man's memory go, that information, opinions, that big white Irish head that took in so many jokes and pints and potatoes and drove so many trucks of coal? Lowered into the stony earth, into Ireland and its endless seasons of rainwater.

Another widow in a world of widows. I visit widow after widow with the knowledge that I'll leave a widow someday; the question is *when?*

"Ah, this rain!" exclaims Bridie in Kilkenny. "My hair'll be a *boosh!*"

You would think she'd lived in Ireland for seventy-five years and never encountered rain.

"A squib coming! It's spilling out of the high heavens! We'll be drowned!"

Sometimes I feel I'm in a melodramatic Synge play or Flann O'Brien's comic masterpiece *The Poor Mouth.*

"I'll be drowned. Don't want to get wet today. If I get wet, it'll dry into me and I'll catch a cold. Won't be able to go up to Dublin with youse."

I hadn't thought of it that way (and our family does have bad luck with water).

My aunt stays in her dry car while I walk alone through Kilkenny, a beautiful medieval city and Ireland's centre of power in the Middle Ages, until Cromwell showed up. She sits in her car or shops at Dunne's while I cut through tiny winding streets and black limestone passages to Irishtown and St. Canice's Cathedral, where the hated Oliver Cromwell stabled his army's horses (Cromwell did the same to St. Patrick's Cathedral in Dublin), Kilkenny streets where my grandfather walked to hurling matches as a country boy in a cloth cap, in a light rain, where Jonathan Swift walked and meditated as a student.

Bridie's driving is comical. She comes to a stop in fourth gear and then tries to start up again while still in fourth. The car stalls.

"It's been doing that."

She tries third gear and attempts to start up again. No dice. She tries reverse instead of first gear. We start hopping backwards like a demented frog.

"Now would my driving be making you nervous?"

"Ah, not at all," I lie. I'm glad for a lift.

"Well, some say it does."

In the centre of Kilkenny she finds the traffic a bit much and starts hitting curbs and medians and missing driveways. She pulls over to recover in front of the castle on the river. "When I get nervous, I get het up."

We drive sunny backroads to Johnswell and an ancient mortar cottage with blue window frames and a tin roof that was once thatched, the tiny white cottage in a glen where my grandfather was born, now empty and damp, though still solid looking. Tiny windows to avoid an old tax on windows. One relative wants to bulldoze the old cottage. Another wants to keep it. I think it's beautiful.

For exercise I wander uphill to some deserted farms where the mortar on a house is falling off to reveal mismatched stones used like bricks and slate tiles broken and falling from the rooftop and the roof with giant holes and trees growing through these holes. Birds rush out and scare me. The stonework is overtaken by plant life, half drowning. These would have been thriving farms with real people when my grandfather was a boy.

"Here looking for your roots, are ya?"
"Uh, no. Yes. No."

I have a good sleep in my aunt's spare bedroom. No rooster on the farm; a cow mooing outside my window at ten is my alarm clock. Nice. Feel a long way from leafless, noisy SoHo or Padraic's crowded nightclub scene. At night my aunt pokes her head in, saying, Here's a drop of holy water, flinging some drops into my bedroom. Thanks, I say, see you in the morning. Please God, she answers.

My aunts Bridie and Rose at times remind me of my mother and also of my aunts Josie and May in Philly. I forget who is who, who I'm talking to. The rolling countryside reminds me of where our family went to the lake, the same rocky penury and big clouds of my childhood.

Time seems fluid, plays tricks, is out of joint, and I get dislodged, forget where I am, who I'm with, what year it is. The smell of peat burning, pictures of Jesus and Mary, an old stove with white enamel and iron legs, I'm clearly in the old world, far in the past, and then on Bridie's old radio a song by Guided By Voices from Ohio via New York's trendy Matador label, a song from the future confusing me. How did they do that? How did they send that song back in time to me?

I chop wood for Bridie, happy to get some exercise after constant meals with different relatives, the back bacon and eggs and fried bread and blood sausage and roast beef and potatoes and gravy and Guinness Stout.

The axe's wooden handle is broken and the remnant is sharp, so I wear pink plastic dishwashing gloves and feel ridiculous.

I chop stumps, and clouds move over the stone stables, the cows and the white Charolais calf and the two dogs, then Bridie's son-in-law, Mee-haul (Michael), finds his big bull dead on a gate. A ripe heifer in the next enclosure. The prize bull tried to get over the steel gate and got hung up, its own huge weight pressing down until it suffocated. The steel gate too sturdy. Desire killed the bull. It died alone. Michael found it, his face red.

Bridie is sad about the bull. "A big beautiful bull. It was fine with its own cows, but someone else's—go through fences and ditches to get at it."

She's sad about the dead bull but happy I've cut her some "sticks."

My Aunt Bridie takes me to a crossroads pub that night: money is evident in its outside lights and sign. Several televisions in its bright and spiffy rooms. It would not have looked like this in my grandfather's day. My grandfather survived without TV.

Nirvana plays on a jukebox and a young woman sings along drunkenly in another room. Not all Irish are blessed with a natural voice, not all sing like a lark.

Bartender looks in the direction of her voice, says, "Kurt Cobain'd die *again* if he heard that."

The affable bartender tilts his head to show me a scar in his short hair.

"Hit on the head with a bottle and then five lads beat me. I'd kicked out one or two from the bar and then refused to give up my newspaper. One: reading it. Two: they were acting smart."

He kept reading his newspaper and a lad smashed a bottle on his bent head. Then kicked him when he was down bleeding into the rug. Lucky it wasn't worse. Could've died. Courts gave one and two years and changed that to nothing and six months on appeal. One guy was convicted later in England for stealing £1500.

We have a few drinks. My aunt drinks vodka and Seven. The conversation moves to Gypsies or *travellers* in the area.

They are refused service and jobs. They are accused of stealing anything not nailed down and of drinking too much and not being able to handle alcohol. There are rumours in the pub of a fight with a Gypsy in another town and then a shotgun being used in the public market.

The young bartender says, "I don't serve travellers. They drink and then fight. Steal and wreck the place. I know they're human but they're different. They're terrible. Steal and fight. Time'll come we'll have to serve them. I give them takeout."

A friend, Tamas Dobozy, asked relatives in Hungary why they hated the Gypsies. *Because they steal.* Tamas asked a Gypsy why they stole. *Because they hate us.*

A young fox does odd circles, confused, spinning in our headlights. Beautiful tail. Huge ears. Rabbits cross the country road. Hedgerows grow into the road, making it narrower. Man dead who used to cut them back.

After the pub with the bright lights, my Aunt Bridie takes me to a more primitive country pub out in the fields, a few miles uphill, closer to her farm and the coal miners' church. No big lights or signs, not spiffy. No televisions. A large local family is drinking there for Month's Mind, a month after the death of their father (another widow). All ages. I can tell Bridie feels bad that she missed their mass (her mass yesterday was dedicated to Willie, a year after his death). Margaret the bartender has the same chest cough as the priest and Rose in Dublin.

In the country pub on the hill, there is a man who looks dead. I can't take my eyes off him but I don't want to be caught staring. He looks driven from another century, risen from the stony earth, from the potato fields, dirt still like fine powder on his clothes and hollow cheeks, like dusting on a vegetable. Black hair and eyebrows and large ears, a compelling wastrel face more Mediterranean or Slavic Gypsy than Irish. His coal black eyes glitter but don't quite focus, are not quite with us. I keep staring. He moves carefully, slowly drifts a glass to his mouth, a pipe lifted *slow-mo,* nods or looks up at the group surrounding him only occasionally, peers only occasionally into our puzzling world. Maybe I'm related to him.

My aunt nods, says, "Your man over there, in and out of the hospital, he gets right and then kills himself with drink."

I get the notion he passed out from poteen in the corner of a forgotten field, passed out in the weeds and crowfoot herbs of another century and woke up and wandered in here for a drink, for a smart drop to warm his chilled, puckered innards. Staring at the past is like staring at an accident. I can't stop staring at this wrinkled wanderer, get confused, and that night have a clear dream about my high school girlfriend, that she had suitors and I was jealous. Again I feel I'm being whipsawed back and forth through time.

TRAIN IN VAIN

Larry, a family friend, gives us a ride to the train station.

"Hope this'll get you there," he says of his little car.

"Anything wrong?"

"Ah now, the wheels turn all ra—"

Like my aunt, Larry loves fourth gear, even at five miles per hour. They want to get to fourth as soon as they can, even when hardly moving. Larry comes almost to a stop and tries to take a corner still in fourth. Gear down! I want to scream.

The train is late. We stand on the narrow platform and stare along the narrow tracks as if we can will the train into being. I wonder if my grandparents, leaving for the big city, looked at these same sleepers and iron rails. Iron filings and Dublin our magnet. A group of teenage girls have clearly modelled their look on Alanis Morissette, a dash of Spice Girls. The ugly seventies look is big. Many kids wear black Adidas track suits. I feel like an extra in *Trainspotting*. The town was founded in the twelfth century. Once there were monasteries, kings, oak forests.

"Let. Eejit train always bloody LET!" complains a rumpled local.

His skinhead son mentions needing money for some school project.

"Ah jaysus, kids today come home from school, need a pound for this a pound for that. I was lucky to get 1 p. 1 p! I had to walk to school barefoot!"

"Ya didn't," says a woman.

"I did."

"Ya didn't."

"There was no money and no waste. No tins of meat for a gob-shite cat. We would've skinned and eaten the bloody cat and been happy for it."

The night before, I got depressed looking at old family pictures. My dead English father looks so dashing and happy and young before they had kids. Both my mother and father look so young and happy. There are no pictures of my grandparents in the box. Photos mustn't have been common then. I've taken about seven rolls with Sharon's camera and just found out it's on the wrong setting. In 1981 my big backpack with rolls of film and journals from England, Ireland, and France was stolen in Spain. I view that trip as a phantom trip because I lost any record of it.

The train is crowded, so my Aunt Bridie and I can't sit together. Bridie, in a seat across the aisle, smiles happily at me, excited that we're heading to the big city.

I sit with three older men; I look at a paper and listen to them surreptitiously. Much more public banter in Ireland than in England. On my first visit to London, I noticed a typically English tendency: as you sit down on the tube you raise your newspaper as a silent barrier. You go down and paper comes up in one smooth move.

That summer of 1981 I rode the night boat across to Ireland and caught a doubledecker bus at the port of Dun Laoghaire at about six in the morning. I climbed to the top with two young New Zealand women. A man uncorked a big bottle of rye and passed it around the passengers. A man in uniform, a conductor or a guard, I don't know, took a swig and handed the bottle along. Boy howdy, is this a different country from England, I thought. No one hiding behind their papers.

My father liked his paper. I have English blood and Irish blood. I love London, and London in the late nineties is vibrant, on a roll, but something in my divided genes *connects* with Ireland. Ireland is repressed, but Ireland is also wilder, looser, less worried about what the next person thinks.

A man on the train says, "I never took a drink in my life, but my three sons are making up for it." I think of my three young boys home in Canada, wonder what they'll be up to in a few years.

"Must be desperate for a sober man to listen to three or four drunks."

"Ah sure Kilkenny used have some good hurlers. Gave everything and that's a lot! No longer."

I see another fox in a field. Cattle, Dorset sheep, Romneys, sleek silky horses, stud farms, villages. There would have been more sheep a century ago. Pleasant landscapes zip by. Like my father I hide behind my paper.

Lady Di on Yacht with Dodi
Portadown Woman Loses Eye to Rubber Bullet
Abba Musical Set for 1999
Sampras Wins Wimbledon
Few Mourn Pedophile Priest

I see a strangely compelling article about an East German man who was dead for four years before he was discovered in the attic of a house, mummified and watching television. There's something perfect about a dead person watching TV.

"I got a hip replacement. Worked on my feet all my life so I'm out to grass, out to grass. Got the new hip in and played my first eighteen and moya wasn't I hitting the ball grand! Hitting it grand."

The train stops and we are ordered off by men in army surplus jackets and ski masks. They must have pulled the emergency cord. They run up the aisles yelling Off! Off! Not all have weapons, but

I see one handgun. I don't know who they represent. They could be IRA provos or a splinter group like the RIRA (Real IRA) or the UDA (Ulster Defence Association) or UVF (Ulster Volunteer Force) or UFF (Ulster Freedom Fighters) or another splinter group, the LVF (Loyalist Volunteer Force), or the Apprentice Boys or maybe it's the Women's Coalition or the Catholic Women's League or the local Chamber of Commerce.

Glass breaks in another car, windows breaking. No one knows what's going on. The golfers are quiet. I carry my small knapsack, one I carried in 1981, and we jostle calmly in the aisle, push to the doors, and have to jump down to the ground. It's grassy below, but it's a good jump. I help my aunt, her skirt out like a parachute, pull something in my back, feel a mix of adrenaline and fear in my stomach.

When all the passengers are off and walking toward some warehouses, the masked men start burning the train, including the engine. You wouldn't think that metal and plastic would burn but they do. They use something, and the plaid seats where we sat darken, then flame. Much smoke and the smell is sickening.

What a waste, I think. This demonstration brings out the Puritan cheapskate in me. Why are they burning a train? Just to do it? What's the fecking point? Who on earth is going to learn anything from this lesson? Who is going to be better off?

"*Let,*" I recall for some reason, "train is always *let.*"

"What's that?"

"Nothing."

I suppose it's to show that they can do it if they want, that they run the show, punish the joyriders and dealers, administer six-packs, burn the odd train.

No one is hurt. I didn't get six-packed, didn't get bullets in the elbows, wrists, knees. This is just like a movie, someone says. Modern blue buses take my aunt and me the rest of the way to Dublin. People seem excited, then tired. My aunt's brothers, my uncles, used to be masked men, used to be in the IRA around 1916.

No longer. My dead uncles grew to hate the modern IRA, thinking it rotten with Libyans and Marxists. I think of my aunt in England: *Well, what could anyone think of the IRA.*

In the newspapers, a burning train rates, like my grandfather, a tiny paragraph. In Canada it would be the event of a lifetime, a hijacked, burning VIA train would be front page news for days, would attract a Royal Commission. Here my charred train is part of "another day of violence over Protestant marches," not as important as the holiday swimwear Di wears before she heads up to Paris for dinner with Dodi.

7000 Orangemen in Dark Suits Defy Ban
Blair Condemns 'Orchestrated Violence'
'Terrorist' Explosion Caused by Meteorite
Di Gives Jiggle Show in Bikini
No Justice No Train
Boy Saved up to Neck in Mud

LADIES WATCH YOUR PURSES

We drive to look for the canal where our grandfather drowned and we drive to the graveyard to see how many bodies are in the narrow grave on Finglas Road. No one is sure how many bodies are there and the others are curious now that I bring it up. Five bodies in the German car: Sharkey is our obliging chauffeur, driving Rose, Bridie, myself to our history lessons, and Sharkey's little boy has come along for the ride.

While driving to Glasnevin Cemetery, Sharkey points into a dim stretch of row housing. "Used to be a nice little valley. Some bad parts in that neighbourhood. Batons always out when we're in Finglas. Riots every weekend. No time for community work. They just march us in, expect us to solve everything. Can't get to the root of the bloody problem that way. They just send us in with batons to crack a few heads of the local boyos. Solves nothing."

"*Still,*" Sharkey says, in a lighter voice, "*they enjoy it and we enjoy it.*" A hint of a grin as he drives.

I can't imagine Padraic bopping shitrats on the head.

Rose and Bridie decide our generation is much worse than their era, swearing and naughty jokes and drinking and carrying on. "Why, nowadays everything's *thing.*"

Sharkey disagrees. "It's not *thing.* Remember Dad's friend Ginger Smith? Drove a lorry for Guinness and he was a thirty-pint man. Ginger Smith drank a skinful at every pub where he delivered stout. We'd be sacked now. If we did that on the job now, we'd be sacked."

We stop at a police checkpoint. The men stare in. It's Marching Season in Drumacree and the Bog, and they're expecting trouble. Bombs are going off again, trains hijacked and burned. I noticed airports in England and Ireland were tense: Please Do Not Leave Luggage Unattended. Bank machines say to report any untended package.

Sharkey the policeman nods at the policemen and they wave us through. Sharkey is wearing a bright red golf shirt, jeans, and work-boots. I wonder if policemen have some secret signal.

Two of Sharkey's cars have been stolen: one car burned, one car stripped.

"Because you're a garda?" I ask.

Sharkey shrugs, noncommital.

He drives a luxurious moulded German car. My cousins are like pilots in a wraparound cockpit now, better cars than mine. When we park, Sharkey winds a big blue bike chain around the steering wheel and steering column. Lots of crime in the new improved Ireland.

"That chain stop anything?"

"Feck no, just looks like it does."

This is another change in Ireland: fewer cars or apartments were available when I was here almost two decades ago. Padraic and Sharkey had to borrow their dad's tiny Toyota. First they'd say to me, Mark, we're going to Howth for a pint, care to come along? Sure,

I'd say. Then they'd yell, Mom! Mark wants to go out (blaming me, their foreign cousin). Can we borrow the car? Ordinarily they might not get it. A car then was more of a rare luxury.

Now we drive wide, elevated highways, Celtic autobahns, and I see fewer shady lanes and hedgerows. EU money for roads, infrastructure, marketing (*to market, to market, to fetch us a pig*). More money, more freedoms, and more problems. But would they go back to how it was, to the good old days before it was *thing*? Doubtful.

Unbelievable amounts of crime from just a few addicts, Sharkey tells me. It's grown though, whole areas now stunned on heroin. Kids grow up with it, with no parents basically, porch light on but nobody home, no fecking rules, and neighbours down the row all the same. He says they don't even get high after a while but have to keep shooting or be sick. Some junkies quit just so they can crank up again later and have the high once more. I'd rather hang out with lepers. No offence.

Perhaps this is the price (*no money down!*) of jumping into the new world, of racing from thatched roofs and peat to real estate scandals, cow chips to silicon chips, rolling from rosaries to cell phones (*easy payments!*).

Everyone in Dublin asks proudly, Hasn't it changed?! I hear the phrase "Celtic Tiger" more times than I care to remember. The boom has people sounding like Texans, although they still have the lovely Dublin accent. Hasn't it changed?

Utterly, I say, but no one gets the 1916 Yeats allusion. Bespectacled W. B. Yeats seems quaint and innocent and myopic against this backdrop of pharmaceuticals and disco dreck and monster house renovations. How would Willie tell the dancer from *this* particular dance?

Sharkey tells me addicts picked up for questioning are allowed a solicitor and a doctor. "If it's a good doctor he gives me their methadone to hold while I'm asking them questions. Pour out a bit of their meth," he says, holding up his thumb and fingers to tilt an imaginary vial, "and they start to talk, they start *grassing,* they'll tell you anything. Of course you can't believe most of what they say. They'll say anything."

Sharkey works at the airport now, intercepting illegal aliens, who are arriving in larger and larger numbers. He's had several free trips escorting aliens back to Amsterdam, Paris, and other cities, which sounds like a bit of all right. Most aliens are black, from countries like Somalia, Mauritania, Senegal, or Zaire. Some illegals are from eastern Europe, say Romania, or maybe Czech or Slovak Gypsies or Roma. Sharkey complains they are lured by agents (like Mexico's *coyotes)* and Internet stories of free hotel rooms, generous dole payments, and Ireland's booming economy (there's that Celtic Tiger again!).

Of course there is a public uproar and backlash over this. There are less-than-charitable letters to the editor about nig-nogs taking Irish money. Sharkey the policeman complains about the aliens pouring in, while Padraic the liberal is embarrassed and enraged at the open prejudice in Dublin.

This hatred of immigrants seems almost humorous to me in light of history, the diaspora; there must be some irony in a country sending out millions of starving immigrants in coffin ships, and then hating the ones turning up at its own door.

Some migrants pay a fortune to get ferried here, only to get turned about and shoved back. One crooked agent plunked a group of African refugees on a boat from England to Ireland but told them they were sailing to Canada (talk about your basic journey without maps).

Sharkey is also against *travellers,* Irish Gypsies, and bleeding hearts who want to serve them.

Sharkey says with a bit of a whistle in his sentence, "You serve one traveller and, *swoo-it,* you get a swarm of them and they steal from you and they fight and wreck the place. You can't serve them. You can't."

We drive in the narrow stone entrance. I like graveyards, these upside-down cities, and Glasnevin is an impressive graveyard. All the rebels and patriots who are anyone are buried here. This is where the martyrs meet: Charles Parnell, the Chief, the Uncrowned King of Ireland hounded to an early grave after being named in an 1890 divorce suit; Daniel O'Connell the Great Liberator; also Michael Collins, The General, The Big Man with a big hole in his head he needed like a hole in the head. Flowers and statues and pictures fall all over the pale slab of Michael Collins's grave, as if it's a Hollywood sidewalk. Because of Neil Jordan's movie, Collins is a media star, a *personality*.

Stone walls, stone lintels, stone everywhere in a miniature Connemara. No golden bough or elk moving through a sunlit mountain meadow, no pine needle paths, no spiderwebs shaking in golden light. Black-and-grey stone as far as you can see.

A high Norman tower with a pointed cap dominates the spooky marble crypts and mondo grey crucifixes with Jesus (slightly cross-eyed) hanging sadly on them, the lichen-crowded crosses and aloof stone archbishops lying on their backs, staring with regret at the roods and roof of their monument. The bishops wear the same rueful expression as the Prufrock men in jowly Jurassic Park.

Sharkey's little boy climbs gleefully over these giant prone bishops. Their arms are folded; at feet and head they are tended by wincing stone angels. My aunts, sharing a bright umbrella, stroll past lime-stone sarcophagi.

It takes some searching but we find the narrow grave. My aunts place flowers: tiger lilies and daisies. The modest tombstone contains Michael Lyons, Mary Lyons, and their children Cathleen, Michael, and Jean. Five relatives hidden in this tiny plot. The Glasnevin paperwork spells their names Kathleen and Jane. This reminds me of Irish clocks: I've yet to see two that agree. The gravestone says "JESUS MERCY MARY HELP" and under that "IHS," a Greek abbreviation for Jesus that I remember seeing on church crosses when I was an altar boy.

The gravestone is from Thomas Street, close to Guinness, my mother's old neighbourhood by the river.

Many Glasnevin tombstones are kicked over. I see a loser peeking in the iron fence rails and a sign: "Ladies Watch Your Purses." A Dublin man was murdered here in a recent robbery and he died sprawled over his wife's grave.

The 1922 newspaper says the Grand Canal, and an old funeral card says Ashtown, but we can't find it, lost and irritated driving around lush rainy countryside outside of Dublin, finally asking in at a canoe and kayak club on the pretty River Liffey.

A man holding up a kayak says, "Ashtown is on the *Royal* Canal."

"Can't be," I say.

"I know north Dublin like the back of my hand," Kayak Man says, "especially the water. It's on the Royal."

Kayak Man finds a map and shows us. Sharkey says he knows the way. It's very frustrating to be looking along the wrong canal, on a wild goose chase.

"Most drownings at the lock," Kayak Man says.

I'm pissed off, can't get over the newspaper saying the Grand Canal, the wrong canal, feeling foolish, pissed off at driving in circles and looking in the wrong place, and so I neglect to ask Kayak Man why most drownings are at the lock.

The Angler's Rest in the afternoon: a lovely country pub where we stop for a break while looking for Ashtown. Fishing gear and gorgeous Paul Henry prints on the pub's walls, similar to a Henry painting my mother has. I assume it's a print because the originals are worth a fortune. A grateful or smitten patient gave it to my mother, a striking wartime nurse.

At first we drink outside on a narrow porch because Sharkey's little boy is asleep in the car and we can see him from there. When the child wakes up, Sharkey runs to grab him so he doesn't think we've deserted him, and then, to my surprise, we all troop inside the bar, sit by the fire. Laws on children and pubs are more relaxed than what I'm used to in Canada.

The bartender had cousins emigrate to Toronto in the 1950s; he never heard from them again.

I tell him my mother went to western Canada in 1952.

"Ah then, she'll know them," he decides.

We zigzag pleasant leafy backroads, double back the way we came earlier, bearing north by northwest. There is a misty rain but a fair bit of light bouncing off the cloud cover. We cross a small bridge and beside us there is a lockhouse and forbidding black gates held in stone walls that drop down into the water. Dried seaweed or rushes on the black gates. We've found Lock #11 on the Royal Canal.

Later that evening we stop at a seaside pub, then walk to an upstairs pasta place for dinner. Sharkey knows all the locals and all the owners from when he walked the beat in this area. Says they used to come in and throw their police hats on the table and drink until four in the morning with the doors locked.

"Horse walks into an Irish pub. Your man says, Why the long face?"

"What's the difference between a redhead and a terrorist? You can negotiate with a terrorist."

After a few drinks my aunts are in stitches and staggering. They're hilarious, like giggling schoolgirls. It takes very little to set them off, for them to have a grand evening. I admire this. Leaving the pasta place they take some time negotiating a narrow rickety stairway. Some young thing waits irritably at the bottom of the stairs with her eyes to the side and up, world-weary at seventeen, disgusted with anyone who is not seventeen.

Sharkey complains that the guards in the Gaeltacht, Gaelic-speaking areas in the west, are paid twelve per cent more and have far less trouble than their counterparts in the cities, who deal with knives and needles and bottles and bombs.

"The whole Gaelic thing is a racket," he says. "Farmers in the west get grants for sheep up a mountain; they borrow neighbours' herds and get paid by the head."

"Not anymore," protests his mother, Rose.

"They did."

"They got on to them now."

"They get grants to keep up their stone walls. Eligible every three years, so they kick them over every three years."

"Sharkey, they don't!"

"They do!"

"You're a terror."

On a Dublin wall I saw spraypainted graffiti that said "NIGGERS OUT!"

Sprayed over top of that was a new message: "RACIST WANKERS OUT!"

I thought, That could be my two cousins at work.

Bridie complains to me about loud foreign students dominating our suburban train. "They come here to learn English and all yabbering in Spanish."

Somehow the O. J. Simpson trial comes up and Bridie says to me smiling, "Your man must've been hungry to bite an ear off."

"Uh, I think that's Mike Tyson."

She looks at me through her thick glasses as if I'm always splitting hairs.

A SECRET GUNMAN

In the middle of my visit, Padraic leaves for Spain with plans to rent a red convertible and seduce an acquaintance, claiming he didn't know when I was going to be here.

I return to the National Library and notice that Michael Collins was shot dead in an ambush at Beal na Blath, in the hills near Macroom. This is where I went with Padraic to a rock fest in 1981: Elvis Costello (good Irish name that) and the Undertones, from Derry, and some other bands. Collins's armoured car and machine gun didn't help him outside Macroom. I slept in a tent with an Irish woman, no idea where I was.

At the outdoor concert I posed as a music journalist from Canada and was admitted to a muddy pen right in front of the stage, where I took fast pictures of Costello and the Attractions while studying the sky above for beer cans lobbed high by ersatz punks in the audience behind us. The ersatz Irish punks didn't care for rock writers, didn't know I was faking it. They were talented at lobbing the cans up so they arced down like shells onto our heads. It hurt if you got beaned. I'd look up, take a picture with my old Russian camera, look up again for incoming, take another picture. A phony war with beer cans. They had rage, had the range.

In the real 1922 war a secret gunman has the range, pulls a trigger, kills Michael Collins, leading to the death of my grandfather the day of Collins's funeral. I associate the two deaths. I believe it was a .303 shell. The exit wound huge, part of Collins's head gone, the convoy lost for hours, the convoy driving in circles in enemy territory (though Collins was from that part of Ireland), while Michael bleeds in their arms (*their efforts to rescue him failed*), dies in their arms (now my mind flashes on poor Jackie and JFK's smashed head in her lap and their confused motorcade).

Some accounts say the triggerman was sorry when he heard who he killed. Others insist it was an English secret-service sniper who nailed him. After all, hadn't Collins killed any number of English intelligence men?

The mysterious triggerman hit more than the Big Man's brain, more than the commander-in-chief, hit more than Hollywood fame and Irish hagiography. The triggerman left my grandmother a widow with ten children to raise on her own. Kathleen with a lovely oval face who died young; Daniel, the oldest son, who smiled as a baby and played violin and worked hard and was a lovely singer but *hooshed* away his wife's hand on his deathbed; Martin, my favourite uncle, who in family lore slept through the Black & Tans dragging Danny out of the same bed; Michael, who fell in the Dog Pond in Phoenix Park, was in his good clothes and afraid to come home and got pneumonia and died young; Josephine, who's in a nursing home in Philly and met her husband, George, in her mother's boarding house; Mary, who had a lovely voice and played piano and died in Philly; Kay, my spitfire mother named after the dead eldest daughter; James, her favourite brother, who was athletic and sang and may also have been IRA, who married Rose and is dead; Jean, who died young, perhaps of rheumatic fever, serious doctors and nurses stomping up and down the many stairs; and Bridget, my funny, feisty aunt in the country who step-danced and also met her husband in her mother's tall, narrow boarding house over the river.

After her husband's drowning, my grandmother had to convert their Victorian tenement into a boarding house, Island Hotel (*Board & Residence. Every Comfort. Terms Moderate*), just two doors down from the house in James Joyce's story *The Dead,* the same house used to film John Huston's movie version of *The Dead.*

One morning I take a long walk down the quays, past the many bridges, to see the old places. The Joyce house is boarded up, corrugated metal over what was a beautiful Georgian entrance, fanlight still visible, second floor shutters broken open by squatters, trash heaped out front. In a car you pass without a glance. It's ugly, and giant lorries and trailers shake the sidewalk and foundations. It's unpleasant to walk in the trucks' constant roar and acrid wind.

James Joyce's aunts had the same last name, Lyons, as my mother's family. I like to amuse myself with the possibility of being related to "Sunny Jim." My favourite uncle, who may or may not have been gay, may have taken music lessons at James Joyce's aunts' house, but he made a face at the teacher and was kicked out.

The houses, sadly close to falling down, are on Usher's Island, not an island but a block lining the River Liffey, close to the train station and close to the giant Guinness Brewery, which employed my grandfather and several uncles and one cousin. Guinness with its old chimneys and walls and tunnels and whiskey towers and plumes of steam and the smell of malt in the neighbourhood. Guinness the ruthless modern corporation that kills small breweries in Ireland and exports fake Irish culture as *product* around the world despite NEVER being owned by the Irish. My Aunt Bridie says a job with Guinness was thought of as *money, dead or alive,* because of their pensions for widows.

Guinness Brewery was British, but the house on Usher's Island was a safe house for rebels during the Troubles around 1916 and into the 1920s. Lorries of uniformed men in the street, Black & Tans banging at the door, and my grandmother putting on her act (*Ah, you're waking all my poor babies and me a poor widow*), wondering who had informed on the safe house, who was in the pay of the Castle.

My Irish side of the family has racetrack luck with dates: my mother born right in the middle of the doomed 1916 Easter Uprising, British artillery crashing Georgian slate, bullets lodging in stone walls and bodies, Sackville Street and the post office destroyed, the martyrs shot, and my mother's head pushing out of the womb, peeking around, criticizing, my grandmother putting on the poor mouth to buy time for her friends and sons and strangers to climb the big wooden chair upstairs and out the skylight and running over the row-house roofs.

First they run from the Brits and Black & Tans, then after Collins signed the Anglo-Irish treaty they run from the Irish, run from their own, run from Michael Collins, the Big Man.

My family split, as Ireland did. Some relatives in the country liked Michael Collins and the treaty, but my grandfather and grand-mother's family in the city followed de Valera, who was anti-treaty, who was a bit of an ass, though he eventually rose to *Taoiseach* or prime minister. My grandfather didn't live long enough to see this, but he did know that Collins was shot dead in the hills and brought by steamer from Cork to Dublin, brought across the water.

Half of Ireland swarming Dublin for the parade for the famous corpse, downtown statues black with people climbing for a vantage point, and my grandfather Michael Lyons moves the opposite way (as I would), travels out into the country for a tram ride, a good long walk, and a swim. The two Michaels. The famous death and the obscure death.

THE CANAL

In Sharkey's German car we have tracked down the obscure death, found the canal and Lock #11, where my grandfather drowned, such a beautiful spot, lush, verdant, its danger masked, like Ireland: much beauty and a chance of danger.

At the canal I take several photos of the water and the lock-house and gates and clogged weeds and rushes. We walk the banks, stand thinking in the mist and light's diffuse lens. The sky white and the banks green. This stretch of canal is so peaceful, quiet, innocent. I look in and see my reflection.

On the other bank, trees hang over the calm water. It reminds me of pre-Raphaelite renditions of Ophelia drowning: soft rushes, mist-muted greens, ethereal and unearthly, shadows of birds on leaves and water like small hands passing.

At the side of the canal, I imagine Michael leaving his bowler hat on the shore, his shoes dusty from walking the roads, sweat at the small of his back, a hot sunny day and cooling down a grand idea, laughing at the cold water shock.

All the way in, boys! Last one in buys the next round!

His moustache wet in the cool murky water, perhaps a wide barge barging from the lock, a barge heaped with peat for Dublin hearths or a Guinness barge stacked with his barrels, splitting the group, a high tarry hull at his face and its wake rises over his scalp, the boat pushing past, and his friends on the other side can't see. And blast it all to hell, where's Michael?

Or the black gates under the lockhouse creak open and pour out water, the fast current stirring the rushes (*drownings always by the lock*), a surge of water changing the depth and Michael my grandfather goes under, slick footing gone and fine kettle of fish he can't swim, arms out, keep his mouth up and failing, realizing he is in trouble and his sputtering grief at the thought of their grief if he can't get out of this balls-up, thinking of his wife in a long swaying skirt, moving room to room, past the piano, beeswax polish on the hardwood, kettle on the gas glimmer, her stiff lace curtains she's so careful with, his toughened cooper's hand on her, the children reading or drawing together on the big landing on the stairs where the light is good, then one girl, the six-year-old, my mother, coming down the stairs of #11 Usher's Island toward the River Liffey, and my grandfather underwater below Lock #11 thinking, This is a mess, bloody stupid, not a good time for this, not at all. They'll expect him at work tomorrow, ten kids, he is not ready for this. *Is this how it is then?* Is there time to think, to be embarrassed, disgusted, sorry?

The funeral procession for Collins marches in the sun, passes the ruined GPO, the post office where Collins was wounded and captured six years earlier, lines of priests shuffling past in long black cassocks, dirges playing, Ireland in mourning, ninety slow minutes to snake past any point, the body carried, the holy water, uniformed soldiers burnt by the sun.

In the water under the sun, the body carried, puzzled, ninety slow seconds to drown, no oxygen, pain, brain giving order after order, reflexes and ritual, songbirds swooping the canal, strange underwater murmurs, pops and cracks, cymbals, pressure on the heart.

Michael's brain remembers his father swimming outside Kilkenny, the rushes and ruined castles, fish and insects, sunlight refracting in the cold water, a white dory skimming past the black castle walls, Jesus Mercy Mary Help, can't go now, I just want to walk home, in that big door, the children reading, the dark piano in a safe world, world's sky shutting down darker as if going under trees, light shrinking around a kerosene lantern.

His head aims down, body falling away from the tall people on the narrow shore, under their feet, shore stretching overhead like a middle sky, his pocket watch on shore ticking in a pocket, hands moving, spooky eels slinking away and back, blood in your loud heart, noise in your ears like wild steam shooting through the Cask Cleaning Shed, keep your mouth closed, watch-works ticking, feet kicking, arms pushing mud, finally forced to pry open your mouth for air, for something, to shout, protest, to climb out laughing with your muscles and smash that tiny ticking pocket watch and walk home singing, but air bursts out of your mouth, exploding bubbles and light in a halo and heavy canal water flows to fill your lungs like sacks and no more singing the old rebel songs in the drawing room and never again in your mouth a dry piece of Mary's tasty home-made soda bread and never again a seaside tram trip to the Eye of Ireland.

Barrels float, barges float, but my grandfather drifts two or three feet under the water, head down in a slow dive with eels in the green distances and canal shadows, moving with the current, water-logged, a vigorous boy from the inland farm in landlocked County Laois, a physical man good with an adze and a hammer, muscles gone, exhausted, hypercarbic, muscles dying in agony in a place of beauty, thirty seconds on the watch, a minute, pain lessening, and his eyes open to the new green world, staring out.

His face staring out of the few photos, a good-natured man with mischievous eyes, our family face, my face at a 747 window, a man my age, like me a man who enjoyed walking with his young sons and became a man walking the bottom of the Royal Canal by Lock #11, alone, a man swimming in green microfilm (*their efforts to rescue him failed*).

I feel *my* efforts have failed. I haven't found anything. I'm wasting my time with this. A kind of melancholy descends on me like a dengue sweat. I have, however, seen my grandfather's birthplace on the hillside farm, and I've seen Kilkenny; I've walked his Dublin neighbourhood, and stood at the Royal Canal looking into the green depths. I have seen what I think of as the four corners of my grandfather's shortened life.

In the farming country near Kilkenny, I studied a group of relatives gathered to eat Sunday dinner and I mused about the odd genetic zigzags of family and the *range* of what makes you. I didn't feel these people passing me platters were family; I didn't see familiar faces. The family name and land and photos handed to strangers over centuries: related but not really linked. Too many traits are fluke: culture, accent, eye colour; too many traits are conditioned by your era and your birthplace, your brick home, and witty wintry upbringing.

How quickly a family branch can veer off into different galaxies. My mother and father had three blond children in Oxford after the war. I was the first child born after they emigrated to western Canada, after they crossed the water. We're strangers now to our relatives. What if I had been born crying under the golden spires of Oxford? How different would I be? How much of my blood is Irish? How much is Norman or Viking raider, a ruddy snake in the woodpile? How much is the random green breast of the new world that weaned me, that nourished my private version of the family face?

The family house in Dublin is now a scooter shop: the Island Hotel (*Every Comfort. Terms Moderate*) has become Scooter Island with pictures of the Jam, Quadrophenia, and other mod icons and a roof like an airplane hangar and the smell of Guinness malt still hanging in the neighbourhood air. In the late seventies in Canada, I listened to the Jam and wondered what England was like. The Mod and ska scene was huge in Ireland and England when I was last over in 1981, but it now seems quaint. The owner's son is friendly and shows me what he can there and in the next house, a car-upholstery business.

My mother's house gutted and converted to a big garage. The Joyce house boarded up, trashed, patrolled by squatters and ghosts from *The Dead*.

WHITE HORSES, BLUE LIGHT

The pretty woman from the Guinness Corporation is extremely polite but insists they have no record of my grandfather or my uncles.

I protest, "But my aunt is on a Guinness pension this moment!"

"Well, I can't be explaining everything now, can I?"

At Rose's kitchen table over black tea, my city aunt and my country aunt complain that kids today watch too much TV and get no exercise.

"Ah sure the next generation won't need legs, Brendan always said. Driven here and there and sit around. We cycled and walked everywhere."

"I ran miles to the Model School to save the streetcar fare!"

"Didn't I cycle from Dublin to the farm?"

"Didn't Marty and Danny and Brendan walk for miles in the country with father?"

"He'd give them a penny and they filled their caps with apples at the orchard."

"Marty was a great one for walking. Next generation won't need legs."

"That's what Brendan said."

"Driving everywhere now or watching the silly telly! Too much TV—kids get *thing*."

So after another huge supper I ask my aunts if they feel like a walk.

"Ah no. A show coming up on the telly." The tasty scandal of the summer: former prime minister Charles Haughey is being investigated. On a civil servant's salary he has somehow bought an island in the west, a yacht, lush houses, a stud farm, and several downtown highrises. It's scoundrel time.

"That Charley, he's a *chancer*," says Bridie, laughing at the television. "Look at those fools breaking an ankle to shake hands with Charley! Oh, he's a chancer," she says. "If he gets out of this one he's Houdini."

"You go out if you like," my aunts say.

I go out, cross the tracks. The local is a dump, a kip. A man with red hair is complaining about rich Americans buying up authentic Irish pubs and shipping them piece by bloody piece overseas. Sure didn't they send one lock, stock, and barrel to Budapest? And another one to Siberia?

I think, No one is going to buy this crapola pub and ship it across the globe. Ireland is not going to lose this pub.

This is my last night in Ireland. Tomorrow I fly back to England for another stay, then back home to Canada, zooming the polar route once more with the other passive passengers. I can't relax, don't want to be blasé about travel. I don't know when I'll be back in Ireland. We used to tease my mother, calling out, Mom, there's a special on Ireland, and she'd come running everytime. I don't want to watch this country like a special. My last night in this crazy theme park and I want to be out doing something, anything, but I can't bear to stay in a kip by myself just for the sake of staying in a pub.

The light is blue. White horses thunder past in the lane like hallucinations, street kids from the projects racing their hammerheaded mounts, their inner-city polo ponies. I admire their simple audacity to actually keep and race old horses in the middle of town. I admire their snot-nosed get-up-and-go.

"Ah jeez, they t'ink they're cow-byes and Indians," says an older woman in cat's-eye glasses. She watches them ride down toward the perfumed canal.

I carry a tin of cold beer back (some crappy brand) to the semi-detached house and stare at the big colour telly with my aunts in Dublin. Their light is blue. I am watching TV with my uncle and aunt in north London, watching TV in a seaside cottage in Essex, on the 747 streaking home over Iceland and Hudson Bay, watching TV with my widowed spitfire mother in Canada, with my cousins in Philly and Jersey and Holland Park and Madrid, with my unborn students on the west coast and the east coast, with my children, with the mummified East German, with the nineteenth-century man from the stony fields who kills himself with drink. I am watching TV with dead people, with people I haven't met yet, every soul on the crowded blue planet gazing at TV. It's a good show, something about murder.

1998

Paradice

ELIOT WEINBERGER

SNÆFELLSNES PENINSULA. ICELAND
has created the most perfect society on earth, one from which the
rest of the world has nothing to learn. For its unlikely Utopia is the
happy accident of a history and a geography that cannot be dupli-
cated, or even emulated, elsewhere.

Outside of the South Pacific, no ethnic group so small has its
own entirely independent nation-state. There are only 268,000
Icelanders, of whom 150,000 live in and around Reykjavík, the capital. The second largest city, Akureyri, known for its arts scene and
nightlife—their Barcelona—has 14,000. In the rest of the country
there are few people, and the treeless wilderness of volcanoes,
waterfalls, strange rock formations, steaming lava fields, geysers, gla-
ciers, and icebergs seems like the ends of the earth, as though one
were crossing into Tibet and found the sea.

Nearly all the roads are sparsely travelled and unpaved, yet this
is a modern Scandinavian country where everything works, and
where the state protects its citizens from birth to death. There is no
unemployment, no poverty and no conspicuous wealth; education
is universal. Per capita book consumption and production is by far
the highest in the world. They live longer than almost anyone else.
There is no pollution: the entire country is geothermally heated.

It is non-violent: no army, no guns, little crime. Prisoners,
except the dangerous, go home for holidays; small children walk in

the city alone. For the last thousand years, Icelandic women have had rights that were long unimagined elsewhere, such as the ability to divorce and keep half the property. It was the first nation with a woman president, and is the only one with an all-women political party with seats in Parliament. The Icelanders invented the idea of a parliament.

Incredibly, it is a capitalist consumer society without excess. They have everything, but only one or two kinds of everything. They live without the bombarded frenzy of competing brands, the demands of consumer expertise, and the attendant dread that one has made the wrong choice. The traditional occupations of the major exports—fishing and sheepherding—are now performed by only a fraction of the population. The rest of the tiny workforce must fill all the roles of a modern society: ambassador, plumber, anesthesiologist, programmer, cellist, cop. There is one television station, one well-known film director, one Nobel Prize novelist, one international rock star. In Iceland, modern life is complete, but lived on the scale of the tribal.

Like a tribe, it is a society rooted in the archaic. They may be the only technological people on earth who could speak fluently with their ancestors from a thousand years ago: Icelandic has remained the same since it split from Old Norse, and its alphabet retains two runic letters that no one else uses. They are required by law to have traditional names, and follow the ancient system of first name plus father's or mother's name plus "son" or "daughter." The telephone book lists people by their first names, and they're all the same: Jóhann Magnússon, Magnús Jóhannsson, Gréta Jóhannsdóttir. They can differentiate one another because they *know* one another.

Islanders, they are self-absorbed. In the 13th century, they produced a vast body of literature, unlike anything in Europe, that was a meticulous description of themselves. These are the sagas: the tales, not of heroes or gods, but of ordinary people: the actual settlers who had come to the uninhabited land two hundred years before. There are scores of sagas, all interlocking: the same stories are told from different points of view; a person mentioned in passing in one becomes the protagonist of another. It is an enormous "human comedy" of love, greed, rage, lust, marriages and property settlements, travels, revenge, funerals and festivals, meetings, abductions, prophetic dreams and strange coincidences, fish and sheep. Nearly everyone in Iceland is descended from these people, and they know the stories, and the stories of what happened in the generations since.

One travels through Iceland with *The Visitor's Key,* an extraordinary guidebook that follows every road in the country step by step, as though one were walking with the Keeper of Memories. Iceland has few notable buildings, museums or monuments. What it has are hills and rivers and rocks, and each has a story the book recalls. Here was a stone bridge which collapsed behind an escaping convicted murderer, proving his innocence. Here lived a boy whose magical powers were such, he could wither grass. Here a man died of exposure in a snowstorm, not knowing he was a few yards from his house. It is said that two chests of silver are hidden somewhere on this hill. In this hot spring, a famous outlaw boiled his meat. A man was buried here because the horses carrying his body refused to take another step. Here a man who stole more sheep than he needed was slain by a twelve-year-old boy. This farm refused shelter to a travelling pregnant woman, and was buried in a landslide that night. Some people have seen a man walking by this cliff with his head under his arm. Here was the home of a clergyman who was honoured abroad for his development of medicinal cod liver oil, and was also known for having kidnapped his bride. Here lived a popular postman in the 18th century.

What other modern society so fully inhabits the landscape it lives in? Where else does the middle class still remember?

Sir Richard Burton, after the tropics and the deserts, was appalled by it. William Morris learned the language and translated some sagas, but preferred his reading to his two visits. Jules Verne never came, but placed the entrance to the centre of the earth at the

Snæfellsjökull volcano. Trollope came, late in life, and wrote a jolly account of huge meals and pretty women, but was shocked to find no bank. Here the young Auden, just before the war in Spain, wrote his strangest book.

They bake bread by putting it in the ground; they prefer their shark meat rotten. The use of pesticides is unknown among them. Nearly all the women have their first child before marriage. They allow no dogs in the capital. Their eyes are the exact pale blue shade of an iceberg. They believe in Hidden People. Their horses grow long coats in the winter, and sleep lying down. I have never seen so many kinds of moss.

1999

Biographies

R. Cheran is a poet and journalist based in Toronto. Born in Jaffna, Sri Lanka, Cheran was the deputy editor of the *Saturday Review,* the only independent English-language weekly in Sri Lanka between 1981 and 1987. Cheran's published anthologies include *The Second Sunrise, The Lord of Death, The Song of Mirage, The Procession of Skeletons,* and *At the Time of Burning.* Cheran was the editor of *We'll Live Amidst Death,* an anthology of Tamil resistance poetry published in 1985 and 1997 in Sri Lanka and India. Cheran's poetry has been translated into English, German, Sinhala, and Dutch. For the past ten years, Cheran has been an editor of *Sarinihar,* a Tamil-language biweekly newspaper dedicated to uncensored coverage of the ongoing civil war in Sri Lanka. Cheran can be reached at cheran@cheran.net.

Karen Connelly is the author of several books of poetry and non-fiction. She is the recipient of the Pat Lowther Memorial Award for poetry and the Governor General's Literary Award for non-fiction. She is currently working on a novel and a collection of essays about Burma. Connelly's most recent book of poetry is enti-tled *The Border Surrounds Us,* published by McClelland & Stewart. Connelly's other books include *Touch the Dragon, A Thai Journal* (Governor General's Literary Award winner for non-fiction in 1993 and national bestseller), as well as *The Small Words in My Body, This*

Brighter Prison, One Room in a Castle—Letters from Spain, France, and Greece, and *The Disorder of Love.* Her books are published in the UK, Australia, Germany, and Asia.

Kim Echlin is the author of *Elephant Winter,* nominated for the Chapters/Books in Canada First Novel Award. Her novel *Dagmar's Daughter* will be published by Viking/Penguin in 2001. Echlin is fiction editor at the *Ottawa Citizen* and is a freelance producer/writer, most recently for *Life & Times* at the CBC. Her non-fiction writing has appeared in *Best Canadian Writing.* She currently holds a McGeachy fellowship in support of her fiction.

Charles Foran has published five books. A sixth, the novel *House on Fire,* is forthcoming in spring 2001 from HarperCollins. He lives in Peterborough, Ontario.

Catherine Frazee has been involved in the equality rights movement for many years. As a writer, educator, and researcher, her primary focus is the rights, identity, experience, and well-being of persons with disabilities. Her work has been published in textbooks and academic journals as well as a variety of specialty magazines, including *Abilities, Entourage, ARCHtype, B'yadeinu,* and the *Womanist.* In 1998, Frazee's lecture about the untold harms of contemporary eugenic ideas was featured in Vision Television's Voices of Vision lecture series commemorating the fiftieth anniversary of the Universal Declaration of Human Rights. She is currently compiling a collection of essays, speeches, and lectures aimed toward deepening societal responses to the experience of disability.

A shorter version of "Still Life" is scheduled for publication in *Saturday Night.*

Don Gillmor has won six National Magazine Awards and three Author's Awards. He is a contributing editor at *Saturday Night* and a regular contributor to *Toronto Life* and the *Globe and Mail.* His work has appeared in *Rolling Stone, GQ,* and *Premiere.* His recent book, *The Desire of Every Living Thing,* was shortlisted for the Carol Shields City of Winnipeg Book Award. Gillmor has written five children's books, two of which were shortlisted for the Governor General's Literary Award. *The Fabulous Song* won the Mr. Christie's Book Award. Gillmor is currently working on the first volume of *Canada: A People's History,* to be published by McClelland & Stewart.

An abridged version of "Home Movie" appeared in *Saturday Night* in October 1998, with the title "The Last Picture Show."

Mark Anthony Jarman is a graduate of the Iowa Writers' Workshop and the author of *19 Knives.* Previous books include *New Orleans Is Sinking* (stories), *Salvage King Ya!* (a novel), *Killing the Swan* (poetry), and *Dancing Nightly in the Tavern* (stories). He also edited *Ounce of Cure,* an anthology of alcohol-related stories. He has been published in *Best Canadian Stories* and *The Journey Prize Anthology* and nominated in the United States for the Pushcart Prize and the O. Henry Award. Jarman has published recently in the *Georgia Review, Washington Square, Canadian Fiction Magazine,* the *Globe and Mail,* the *New Quarterly,* and *Mattoid* (Australia). A shorter version of "Wankers and Widows and Chancers and Saints" won *Event's* Creative Non-fiction contest in 1999, and another Irish piece won PRISM international's MacLean-Hunter Endowment Award for Literary Non-fiction in 2000. Both will be part of an Irish travel book published by House of Anansi Press in 2001. Jarman has taught at the University of Victoria and the University of New Brunswick.

A nationalist and lifelong journalist—most recently as senior editor and editor-at-large at *Saturday Night*—**Barbara Moon** is the author of hundreds of major articles in magazines such as *Maclean's* and *Saturday Night* and features in newspapers such as the *Globe and Mail.* She has also written dozens of television documentaries— among them several segments of the experimental CBC-TV *Images* *of Canada* series—and books, including *The Natural History of the Canadian Shield*. From 1992 to 1998, she was a senior editor for the Creative Non-fiction and Cultural Journalism Program (formerly Arts Journalism) at The Banff Centre for the Arts. She remains a contributing editor at *Saturday Night* and is a partner, with Wynne Thomas, in Editors-at-Large. Among relevant honours, Moon holds a Maclean-Hunter first prize for Editorial Achievement, the University of Western Ontario's President's Medal, and the National Magazine Foundation's Award for Outstanding Achievement.

Don Obe is a professor in the School of Journalism at Ryerson Polytechnic University. He is a former chairman of the school and founder of its acclaimed magazine, *Ryerson Review of Journalism*. His professional experience includes editor-in-chief of the *Canadian* magazine and *Toronto Life,* and associate editor of *Maclean's*. For ten years, he was a senior editor, and at times acting chair, of the Creative Non-fiction and Cultural Journalism Program at The Banff Centre for the Arts. Obe has won a gold medal for ethical writing in the National Magazine Awards and, in 1993, his industry's highest honour, the National Magazine Award for Outstanding Achievement.

Erna Paris is the winner of seven national and international writing awards, including a gold medal from the National Magazine Awards Foundation, a bronze medal from the White Award for local issues reporting (Canada–US) and four Media Club of Canada awards for feature writing and radio documentary. Paris is the author of six books of literary non-fiction, including *The End of Days: A Story of Tolerance, Tyranny and the Expulsion of the Jews from Spain,* which won the 1996 National Book Award for History.

An expanded version of *"If the Nail Sticks Out, Hammer It Down"* was published in Paris's book *Long Shadows: Truth, Lies and History,* published by Alfred A. Knopf Canada.

Patricia Pearson received a gold medal from the National Magazine Awards Foundation for a version of "My Violent Art" that appeared in *Saturday Night*. She is the author of *When She Was Bad,* which won the Arthur Ellis Award for best non-fiction crime book of 1997. Pearson is currently a columnist for the *National Post* and *USA Today* and a contributing editor to *Saturday Night*.

Larry Pratt is an Edmonton writer. He has a doctorate from the London School of Economics and is the author/co-author or editor of eight books of non-fiction, including *The Tar Sands, Prairie Capitalism,* and *The Last Great Forest*.

Alberto Ruy-Sánchez is a Mexican writer and editor and the author of thirteen books, seven of them non-fiction. He has his Ph.D. from Jussieu University in Paris, where he lived for eight years. His novel *Mogador,* published by City Lights in 1993, was awarded the Xavier Villaurrutia Prize, the most prestigious literary recognition in Mexico. The New Mexico State University awarded Ruy-Sánchez as Literary Essayist in 1991, and he was also a Fellow of the J. S. Guggenheim Foundation. Since 1988, Ruy-Sánchez has been the publisher and founding editor of Latin America's leading arts magazine, *Artes de Mexico*. In ten years, this magazine has received fifty-two national and international awards for its achievements in editorial, design, and printing.

Sandra Shields grew up in Calgary and studied political philosophy at Carleton University, graduating with an M.A. in 1990. She has worked as an editor and freelance writer, often collaborating with her husband, photographer David Campion. Their work has received honourable mention at the National Magazine Awards and a National Media Award from the Canadian Association for Community Living. With support from the International Centre for Human Rights and Democratic Development, they travelled to Namibia in 1996 to document the situation of the Himba tribe.

Shields currently lives in Vancouver and is at work on a book about consumer culture.

Dragan Todorovic is a writer and digital artist. He was born in Kragujevac, Serbia, and lived in Belgrade before moving to Canada in 1995. His previous titles include *A View through a Window of a Subway, Hurricane Called Bruce, Jockey Full of Bourbon,* and *A Shadow and a Dream.* Todorovic has spent several years as a radio/TV host and producer and has made two documentaries, *Darkness on the Edge of Town* and *The Sad Heart of the Joyful City.* His articles have been published in *Saturday Night,* the *Toronto Star, This Magazine, Now,* the *Ottawa Citizen,* and various publications around the world. Todorovic lives in Toronto and can be reached at dragant@gncom.com.

Eliot Weinberger's essays are collected in *Works on Paper, Outside Stories,* and *Karmic Traces,* all published by New Directions. He is the author of a study of Chinese poetry translation, *19 Ways of Looking at Wang Wei,* and the editor of the anthology *American Poetry Since 1950: Innovators & Outsiders.* His many translations of the work of Octavio Paz include *Collected Poems 1957–1987, In Light of India,* and *An Erotic Beyond: Sade.* Among his other translations are Vicente Huidobro's *Altazor,* Xavier Villaurrutia's *Nostalgia for Death,* Jorge Luis Borges' *Seven Nights,* and Bei Dao's *Unlock.*

Weinberger's edition of Jorge Luis Borges' *Selected Non-Fictions* recently received the National Book Critics Circle prize for criticism. In 1992, he was given the first PEN/Kolovakos Award for his work in promoting Hispanic literature in the United States, and in 2000 Weinberger was the first American literary writer to be awarded the Order of the Aztec Eagle by the government of Mexico.